MEN and Their RELIGION

MEN and their RELIGION

Honor, Hope, and Humor

DONALD CAPPS

TRINITY PRESS INTERNATIONAL
Harrisburg, Pennsylvania

Trinity Press International, P.O. Box 1321, Harrisburg, PA 17105

Trinity Press International is a division of The Morehouse Group.

Cover design: Brenda Klinger

Library of Congress Cataloging-in-Publication Data
Capps, Donald.
    Men and their religion : honor, hope, and humor / Donald Capps.
        p. cm.
Includes bibliographical references and index.
    ISBN 1-56338-383-7 (pbk. : alk. Paper)
    1. Men—Religious life. 2. Melancholy. I. Title.
    BL625.65 C37 2002
    200'.81—dc21
                                                                2002002855
Printed in the United States of America

02 03 04 05 06 07   10 9 8 7 6 5 4 3 2 1

To the memory of Holden Francis Capps
1904–1990

⌒

The good are befriended by weakness and defect. As no man had ever a point of pride that was not injurious to him, so no man had ever a defect that was not somewhere made useful to him. The stag in the fable admired his horns and blamed his feet, but when the hunter came, his feet saved him, and afterwards, caught in the thicket, his horns destroyed him. Every man in his lifetime needs to thank his faults.

—From "Compensation" by Ralph Waldo Emerson

Contents

∼

Acknowledgments

I want to express my deep appreciation to Henry L. Carrigan, Jr., editorial director at Trinity Press International, for his unflagging support; to Joan Blyth, who transformed my rough typewritten versions into a finished manuscript; to Don Parker-Burgard, whose copyediting skills contributed both stylistically and materially to the final draft; and to everyone at the Press who has had a hand in making this book come about.

As is perhaps all too predictable with books of this sort, mine too is dedicated to the memory of my father. During the times I knew my parents best, my mother believed that his religion was "not very deep." A friend of hers suggested he needed a "spiritual rebirth." I agree with my mother but not with her friend. His religion was not deep. Rather, it was an open book, self-evident, and there for anyone to see. At his funeral, the minister guessed that his religion was deeper than he allowed others to see. I rather doubt this. But there is no need to suppose something deeper unless one has been taught to be critical of what appears on the surface. As Reinhold Niebuhr once remarked, "The surface is not necessarily superficial." I am comforted by my belief that my mother in time embraced what she saw and was content to leave well enough alone.

This book is my attempt to explain how we men come by the religion my father exhibited, what this religion avails us, what it costs us, and why we cling to it as if our lives depended upon it; which, of course, they do.

Introduction

In *Reviving Ophelia: Saving the Selves of Adolescent Girls*, Mary Pipher discusses the problem of distant fathers whose only roles in the family seemed to be those of breadwinner and rule enforcer. Distant fathers, she notes, are generally perceived by adolescent girls to be more rigid than mothers, less understanding, and less willing to listen: "As one girl put it, 'If Dad moved out, we'd be poorer, but there'd be more peace around here'" (Pipher 1994, 118).

I'm guessing that when they read this girl's statement, many women (and not a few men) read it pretty much at face value. Dad brings in the money, but his presence creates tension and conflict in the home. When I first read it, I responded somewhat angrily, "The girl assumes that if anyone is going to leave home, it's Dad. It doesn't seem to occur to her that he might force anyone who doesn't agree with his rules to leave the house." I am not suggesting that this is what he *should* do. I am only observing that a man—*this* man, at any rate—may read a negative account of "distant fathers" rather differently, focusing on a less-than-obvious implication of a statement whose meaning seemed rather self-evident. But why the anger? This is one of the things this book seeks to explain.

A few years ago, I began teaching a course on the problems of contemporary men. I figured that by this point in my career, my belief in feminist viewpoints was evident to my colleagues and to students who knew me, and that a course on men taught by me would not be viewed as provocative. In addition, I had been using Daniel Levinson et al.'s *The Seasons of a Man's Life* (1978) in a course on the life cycle for two decades, so it wasn't as though I hadn't been teaching about men. However, the experience of actually teaching a course in which the class was overwhelmingly male (an average of three women will enroll in a class of some thirty-five each time I teach the course) has been a very enlightening experience.

The presence of women in the course has generally been well received, though there have been a few somewhat volatile incidents. One was when a male student got irritated with a woman who talked a lot in class the first couple of sessions. One morning he blurted out, "This is *our* class. I wish you would keep your views to yourself." While flattered that any student would speak of a course of mine with such a degree of ownership, I intervened, saying that it was her class too, and that she was addressing the assigned material. Later she informed me that the male student had apologized to her for his behavior. His apology is also what this book tries to explain.

Another time, a woman in the class expressed her view on several occasions that the problem with men is that they are not spiritual enough. I did not begin each class session with prayer—as some of my colleagues do— though I would usually select a poem or two related to the topic for the day to read at the beginning of class. This poetry reading time was intended to help the class shift into a more thoughtful mood after having to rush to an early morning class. One day, halfway through the class session, she got up to give a brief report on a couple of chapters on the assigned book for the day, Stephen Boyd's *The Men We Long to Be* (1995). She began by noting that the class had not begun with prayer, and, therefore, she would say a prayer before she gave her report. It was essentially a prayer about helping men to come to the Lord so that they would be better fathers, sons, and brothers. After she finished, she gave her report, which was an extremely superficial presentation of the chapters that elicited no response from the other class members. Upset that she had criticized my failure to begin the class with prayer, I was rather glad that they did not respond to her presentation. I was also disappointed, though, that these key chapters of Boyd's book were not discussed. These chapters specifically challenge the body-spirit distinction, which she appeared to espouse, on the grounds that it had been harmful to men.

I have learned several things about men from teaching this course that I would not have learned otherwise. One is the overwhelming longing of young adult males to connect with their fathers. Frank Pittman's term "father hunger," in *Man Enough* (1993), is precisely on target. Not only is this a common experience among young adult males but it is also one that they are able to share with one another in class discussion. For example, one of the men read a poignant poem he had written to his deceased father.

Another thing I have learned is that the subject of mothers is one that the same men seem very reluctant to talk about. I have tried many different approaches to encourage men to talk about their relations with their mothers and their feelings toward them, such as asking them to read Pittman's chapter on "mother love" and to frame a question or comment for class discussion, or presenting my own theory of the roots of male melancholia (see Capps 1997), or offering personal disclosures of difficulties in my own mother-son relationship. One or two of the male students may venture a comment, but in our class sessions on mothers, there is nothing like the open discussion of the father-son relationship. Occasionally, perhaps aware of the men's discomfort, a woman in the class will present her views on the mother-son relationship. While this keeps the discussion going, I suspect that the views women express on this issue are quite different from the attitudes and feelings of the men, which, however, go unexpressed.

Had I not been aware of the psychoanalytic concept of resistance, I might have thought that the men simply could not care less about their own mother-son relationship. Instead, I knew the resistance was meaningful, even, as James E. Dittes claims, "a sign of vitality" (Dittes 1967, 136–85). But this does not mean that I was successful in counteracting it. Nor is the existing literature on men, which is predominantly concerned with the father-son relationship, of much assistance in this regard.

Another thing I learned is that when a class consists primarily of men, and the subject, in effect, is themselves, there is a great deal of "male banter." While there are humorous moments in other courses I teach, the course on men is in a class by itself. Men kid and tease one another, they poke each other affectionately, and when there is an especially spirited class presentation, the class can become almost giddy with laughter. They will interrupt the speaker at will, throwing barbs his way, and then applaud wildly at the conclusion of his presentation. One student's presentation on the journey of the magi on the final day of class—a rare case of men asking directions instead of relying upon their inner compass, with fateful consequences (see Dittes 1996, 84ff.)—will remain in my own memory for a very long time. The "spirit" in the room that day was palpable.

Recently, a TV reporter, informed that *The Three Stooges* videos had become a hit in New York City, set out to find out why. She asked passersby what they thought of *The Three Stooges*. Not a single woman considered them to be funny, calling their routines "stupid," "inane," "weird," or "violent" ("They just beat up on each other"). Conversely, when the reporter asked men their opinion, they visibly brightened and warmed to the subject, saying that *The Three Stooges* is "funny," "great," "wonderful," and "hilarious." Then they would recount their favorite scenes, such as when one of the stooges whacked another on the top of his head with a brickbat, or threw a bucket of water in his face, or shoved a broom handle up one of his nostrils. Violent? Not to these men. The reporter concluded that this brand of slapstick comedy must be "a guy thing." While expressing her inability to comprehend why anyone would "consider this stuff funny," she herself laughed as she witnessed the men's obvious pleasure in recounting these scenes for her benefit.

I learned from this course the importance of humor in men's lives—much of it self-directed—and of the significant role that it plays in sustaining men's spirits. Humor is not the same thing as play. As the psychoanalyst Erik H. Erikson has noted, play to the child is what work is to the adult, and, in this sense, play is often very serious business. For Erikson, it is the growing child's primary means of working through his ambivalences, rages, and other inchoate feelings and impulses (see his discussions of play in 1963, 209–22; and 1977, 17–51). Humor is a very different thing. Especially in chapter 7, I will discuss its importance for the major theme of this book, the melancholy self.

These three discoveries—men's "father hunger," their reluctance to discuss their relationships with their mothers, and the liberating role of humor in their lives—have influenced the conception of this book in both direct and indirect ways. As indicated, other influences on the writing of this book include my emotional responses to the high school girl's statement that "If Dad moved out, we'd be poorer, but there'd be more peace around here," the male student's equally emotional reaction to the woman who talked too much in "our" class, and my (and, I believe, other men's) resentment toward the idea that men need to be prayed for by women so that they might become better fathers, sons, and brothers. What are these emotions about? What is going on here? My hope is that this book will provide compelling explanations for men's "father hunger," for their reluctance to talk about their mothers, for the liberating role that humor plays in men's lives, and for their emotional reactions to statements and behavior of women such as the ones indicated.

As the table of contents indicates, this is a book about "the melancholy self." I could have said "melancholy men," but the word "self" serves to make an important point, namely, that there is a melancholy self in every man—owing to certain circumstances relating to his early development—and that this "self" takes its place alongside the various other "selves" that comprise a man's personality. I assume that most—perhaps all—men experience themselves as complex. To view or represent men as simple is to reduce them to a caricature. But what does it mean to say that a man is complex? As the dictionary indicates, *complex* means "consisting of two or more related parts" or "not simple; involved or complicated." In its noun form, the primary meaning of complex is "a group of interrelated ideas, activities, etc., that form, or are viewed as forming, a single whole." A secondary meaning is "an assemblage of units such as buildings or roadways, that together form a single, comprehensive group." A third meaning is the psychoanalytic one. It means "an integration of impulses, ideas, and emotions related to a particular object, activity, etc., largely unconscious, but strongly influencing the individual's attitudes and behavior" (for example, the Oedipus complex, or a Messiah complex).

In comparing the word *complex* with related words such as *complicated*, *intricate*, and *involved*, the dictionary says that *complex* refers "to that which is made up of many elaborately interrelated or interconnected parts, so that much study or knowledge is needed to understand or operate it (e.g., a complex mechanism)." *Complicated* adds the idea that it is "highly complex" and therefore "very difficult to analyze, solve, or understand (e.g., a complicated problem)." *Intricate* suggests "a perplexingly elaborate interweaving of parts that is difficult to follow (e.g., an intricate maze)," and *involved* adds the implication that it is complicated "to the point of being, or seeming to be, disordered (e.g., an involved argument)." To say that a man is complex does not entail that we make the further assertion that he is complicated, intricate, or involved. Some men may be those things too, but the word *complex* applies to all men.

The first two meanings of *complex* are what I have in mind when I say that a man experiences himself as complex. The third, psychoanalytic, meaning is relevant, however, in the sense that for many men the melancholy self is largely unconscious, yet it plays a significant role in their lives. I hope, therefore, that this book will help men come to greater awareness of this feature of their personality in order that they might (as one of the men I study in depth later expresses it) know themselves "more honestly and completely."

In *Identity: Youth and Crisis*, Erikson notes that our "composite Self" is made up of "various selves":

> There are constant and often shocklike transitions between these selves: consider the nude body self in the dark or suddenly exposed to light; consider the clothed self among friends or in the company of higher-ups or lower-downs; consider the just awakened drowsy self or the one stepping refreshed out of the surf or the one overcome by retching and fainting; the body self in sexual excitement or in a rage; the competent self and the impotent one; the one on horseback, the one in the dentist's chair, and the one chained and tortured. (Erikson 1968, 217)

From this enumeration of the "various selves" and the "constant and shocklike transitions" to which they are subject in the real world, Erikson concludes, "It takes, indeed, a healthy personality for the 'I' to be able to speak out of all these conditions in such a way that at any given moment it can testify to a reasonably coherent Self" (217).

Erikson's view of the "composite Self" or "reasonably coherent Self" as being composed of "various selves" helps to clarify what it means to say that a man experiences himself as complex. He is complex because he is made up of various selves. To be "a healthy personality," he needs to be able to hold these various selves together. These "selves" may therefore be viewed as the "two or more related parts" of his experience of himself. As Erikson's illustrations suggest, a man may have several such selves, and different social conditions bring out different facets of each of these selves.

Thus, this is a book about "the melancholy self" and not a book about "melancholy men." "Melancholy men" seems to imply a particular subgroup of males; most likely, a small minority. A book on the melancholy self enables me to affirm that there are many "selves" that comprise a man's sense of "I" other than the melancholy one, and it also allows me to recognize that there are some men in whom the melancholy self seems to play a much larger role than in most other men, while also affirming that this melancholy self, because it is shared by all men, is one of the things that makes them brothers for life. I view this book, then, as an effort to shed some light on what James E. Dittes (1985) calls "the male predicament," for melancholia is something all men have in common.

This is also a book on religion and, specifically, the connections between melancholia as men experience it and the ways in which men are religious. In my view, the melancholy self plays a major role in determining how men are religious. I realize that many men do not think of themselves as religious. When asked to identify persons they consider religious, they often point to some of the women that they know or to priests, ministers, rabbis, monks, mullahs, shamans, gurus, and various other "holy men" who have dedicated their lives to a specifically religious vocation. They rarely point to themselves. Conversely, if women are asked to identify persons they consider "religious," they do not normally think of the men they know unless one of them happens to be unusually "devout."

One of the reasons I have written this book is that I want to challenge this way of thinking about men as nonreligious. This is not because I have an agenda, such as the one reflected in the woman student's desire to help men become "more spiritual" so that they would thereby become better fathers, sons, and brothers. Quite the contrary. My point is that men are already religious, but that their religiousness tends to be invisible even to themselves. This religiousness is directly related, as I have indicated, to their melancholy self, and is therefore a religiousness, as I will explain, formed in early childhood. It may or may not manifest itself in religious observances, commitment to spiritual disciplines, or religiously motivated participation in social causes or in acts of personal sacrifice. While it is not inimical to any of these, neither is it defined by them.

This, then, is a book about a man's "personal religion," the religion that informs everything he is and does. As noted, he may not be aware of the fact that he is religious in this sense, and if the characteristics and qualities that I will be identifying as comprising his religiousness were to be pointed out to him, he may say that he does not consider these to be religious per se. My concern is to persuade men—and, secondarily, women who may happen to read this book—that these are, in fact, evidence of men's religious natures, and that they therefore do themselves a personal disservice when they make disclaimers ("I am not especially religious") or believe that they need to make an extraordinary effort, such as committing themselves to a spiritual regimen, in order to become truly religious.

If this appears to make the claim to be religious too easy, a bit like declaring all the citizens of a country "Christians" on the basis of the king's conversion to the Christian faith, my emphasis on "the melancholy self" should allay any fears in this regard. I do not say, "Men are religious and this is good." Rather, I say that men are religious and that the way in which they are religious may not be good for them, but, in any case, there is no "cure" for the kind of religion that they have. The language of incurability may seem to imply that it would be more accurate to say, "Men are religious and this is bad." I do not take this view either. For one thing, some pathological conditions have many important secondary benefits. I have written, for example, about the positive uses of social phobias (Capps 1999) such that a person might reject a cure even if one were available. For another thing, no one can claim to be perfectly healthy, and religion—at least the form that is the subject of this book—may be a better way in which to manifest one's lack of perfect health than many other ones.

Thus, when I use a word such as *sick* or *pathological*, I do not automatically make a negative value judgment against it. Instead, I tend to subscribe to William James's view that the only way we can determine the worth of any particular religious form or expression is by its "fruits for life." Contending against the view that "the worth of a thing can be decided by its origin," he argues instead that "our spiritual judgment" or "opinion of the significance and value of a human being or condition, must be decided on empirical grounds exclusively" (James 1982, 237). Alluding specifically to religious conversion, he asserts, "If the fruits for life of the state of conversion are good, we ought to idealize and venerate it, even though it be a piece of natural psychology; if not, we ought to make short work with it, no matter what supernatural being may have infused it" (237). This, in my view, is how a man's religiousness, which arises from a melancholic condition, needs to be understood and evaluated.

Also, by saying that a religiousness having its basis in melancholia is "incurable," I mean to suggest that while we should not expect or promise a cure for the underlying condition itself, religion itself may offer remedies. As I will show, the search for remedies is the reason why a small boy, afflicted with melancholia, turns to religion in the first place. I believe that this initial intuition is right—one *should* turn to religion for remedy—but I also believe that some remedies may be more effective than others. As I will show, religion's support for men's sense of honor, hope, and humor is the basis of its remedial role for the male melancholy self. In a sense, I am claiming that religion is the best remedy for the pathology that it also reflects and represents.

As we know, this is the theory behind vaccinations—that one applies smaller doses of the pathology in order to help the host develop an immunity to its more virulent forms.

A brief word about the structure of this book. The first section focuses on the formation of the melancholy self. It employs psychoanalytic theory to explain how melancholy develops in boys, and to explain why melancholy has a direct connection to the ways in which boys become religious. The first two chapters focus especially on the role that a boy's mother plays in the formation of his melancholy self, while the third and fourth chapters center on how the father figures into its formation.

The second section of the book is devoted primarily to two case studies, both derived from Ana-Marie Rizzuto's *The Birth of the Living God* (1979). Her book, which is also informed by psychoanalytic theory, is concerned with how the child's experiences and relations with each parent influence his or her representations of God. Rizzuto is not oblivious to the fact that a child's representation of God may be influenced by other environmental factors—both within the family and through experiences in more formal religious settings. But her thesis is that parents play a key role in this respect, and that this can be shown by asking adults about their experiences and relations with their parents throughout childhood and adolescence, and about how they understand and relate to God, and then demonstrating correlations between these parental representations and their God representations. To show these relationships in depth, she provides four case studies, two women and two men, all drawn from her own psychiatric setting. While this focus on psychiatric patients may seem to load the deck toward viewing these God representations as inherently pathological, Rizzuto contends that a pilot study comprised of patients and nonpatients (hospital personnel) showed no appreciable differences.

In chapters 5 and 6, I use Rizzuto's two case studies of men to differentiate between the two ways in which the melancholy self becomes religious. One is the way of moral rectitude; the other is the way of questing. While I believe that most boys adopt both paths, these cases enable us to see each path in bold relief and to identify the psychodynamics—largely relating to the boy's experiences and relations with parents—behind them. Thus, these two cases represent my evidence in support of the theory developed in section I.

While I recognize that these may be somewhat extreme examples of the melancholy self, at least at the time the two men were being studied, William James makes what I consider to be a persuasive argument for his own decision to focus on the more extreme expressions of religious experience in *The Varieties of Religious Experience*. Drawing on his earlier professional experience as a physiology instructor at Harvard University, he notes, "It is a good rule in physiology, when we are studying the meaning of an organ, to ask after its most peculiar and characteristic sort of performance, and to seek its office in that one of its functions which no other organ can possibly exert. Surely the same maxim holds good in our present quest" (James 1982, 45). If the essence of religious experiences is "that element or quality in them which we can meet nowhere else," this quality will be "most prominent and easy to notice in those religious experiences which are most one-sided, exaggerated, and intense" (45). I suggest that the same maxim applies to the study of the melancholy self. As James makes clear, his reason for focusing on extreme cases of religious experiences is so that he may shed light on its less extreme, more ordinary manifestations.

A chapter on humor follows my discussion of these two cases. While it is brief, it is very important to the general argument of this book. For reasons that will be made clear, this chapter reflects my view that humor should never have been "defined out" of religion. Even James, whom I greatly admire, suggests that one of the essential features of a religious experience is that it be "solemn." To be sure, he has a particular meaning of "solemn" in mind: "There must be something solemn, serious, and tender about any attitude which we denominate religious. If glad, it must not grin or snicker; if sad, it must not scream or curse. It is precisely as being *solemn* experiences that I wish to interest you in religious experiences" (38). However, as Freud shows in an essay on humor that I discuss in some detail in chapter 7, humor is not necessarily solemn. In fact, it is more likely to express itself in mock solemnity.

If religion plays a major role in the formation of the melancholy self, humor is one of the primary ways—honor and hope being the others—in which religion provides a remedy for men's melancholia. Not a cure, mind you, but an effective remedy. Since the two men in Rizzuto's case studies are Jewish and Roman Catholic, I focus in this chapter on a Protestant—Martin Luther himself. This inclusion of the three major forces in the Judeo-Christian tradition makes the point that the melancholy self is pervasive in the West and is deeply implicated in its primary religious tradition.

I.
THE FORMATION OF
THE MELANCHOLY SELF

CHAPTER 1

The Origins of the Melancholy Self in Early Childhood

The dictionary defines melancholia as "a mental disorder, often psychotic, characterized by extreme depression of spirits, brooding, and anxiety." This suggests that it is a mental pathology, which is how it has often been understood. However, as Philip W. Jackson points out in his historical study of melancholia, it has meant various things over the past two millennia:

> At any particular time during these many centuries the term that was in common use might have denoted a disease, a troublesome condition of sufficient severity and duration to be conceived of as a clinical entity; or it might have referred to one of a cluster of symptoms that were thought to constitute a disease; or it might have been used to indicate a mood or an emotional state of some duration, perhaps troublesome, certainly unusual, and yet not pathological, not a disease; or it might have referred to a temperament or type of character involving a certain emotional tone and disposition and yet not pathological; or it might have meant merely a feeling state of relatively short duration, unhappy in tone but hardly a disease. Clearly the various conditions so denoted were unusual mental states, but they ranged over a far wider spectrum than that covered by the term *disease*. (Jackson 1986, 3)

Jackson suggests that as a mood or emotion, the experience of being melancholy has probably been "as well known to our species as any of the many other human feeling states" (3). The words used to describe it here, in fact, have "reflected matters at the very heart of being human: feeling down or blue or unhappy, being dispirited, discouraged, disappointed, dejected, despondent, melancholy, sad, depressed, or despairing—states that surely touch something in the experience of just about everyone" (3). He adds: "From discouragement or dejection over material and interpersonal disappointments to sadness or despondency over separation and loss, to be human is to know about such emotions. We recognize many aspects of such affective experiences as being within the normal range, however unusual or unhappy" (3).

Jackson explores the literature on melancholia from ancient Greece and Rome through the nineteenth and early twentieth centuries, and then considers the tendency for the mid-twentieth century to replace *melancholia* with *depression*. One effect of this change in nomenclature has been a general tendency to shift the focus from men (who were considered more susceptible than women to melancholia) to women (244–45). The *Diagnostic and Statistical Manual* (*DSM-IV*) published by the American Psychiatric Association (1994) states, "Studies show that depressive episodes occur twice as frequently in women as in men," and notes that a "significant proportion of women report a worsening of the symptoms of a Major Depressive Episode several days before the onset of menses" (325). *DSM-IV* also indicates that a "post-partum onset specifier" is applicable to a major depressive episode or disorder if it occurs or develops within four weeks after the delivery of a child (386). (In *DSM-IV* terminology, "specifiers" enable the diagnostician to fine-tune the diagnosis of a patient, and specific criteria are provided for determining whether a specifier is applicable or not.) While depression among males has received greater attention in recent years, the view that it is predominantly a women's disorder has not significantly changed.

I do not challenge this view concerning depression. Instead, what I will be contending in this chapter is that melancholy and depression are two different things, and that similarities between them are largely superficial (see Frost 1992). This is because melancholy has a different origin. Before I develop this argument, however, I want to take brief note of William Styron's recent advocacy for the restoration of the word *melancholia* in *Darkness Visible: A Memoir of Madness*. He notes that when he was first laid low by the disease, which was diagnosed as "clinical depression," he felt a need "to register a strong protest against the word 'depression,'" contending that melancholia "would still appear to be a far more apt and evocative word for the blacker forms of the disorder, but it was usurped by a noun with a bland tonality and lacking any magisterial presence, used indifferently to describe an economic decline or a rut in the ground, a true wimp of a word for such a major illness" (Styron 1990, 37). He suggests that the scientist generally held responsible for the currency of depression in modern times, the Swiss-born psychiatrist Adolf Meyer, whom Jackson calls the dominant figure in American psychiatry between 1895 and 1940 (Jackson 1986, 195), may have "had a tin ear for the finer rhythms of English and therefore was unaware of the semantic damage he had inflicted by offering 'depression' as a descriptive noun for such a dreadful and raging disease" (Styron 1990, 37).

While I endorse Styron's desire to restore the word *melancholy*, my reasons for this differ from his. My concern is not the semantic issue—the fact that melancholia is far more descriptive than depression—neither is it the issue of the severity of the disease. Instead, I believe its restoration would enable us to make a clearer differentiation between a condition to which few, if any, men are strangers, and clinical depression, a treatable pathology to which, as indicated, women are more susceptible than men. *Clinical depression* is a term that is now firmly embedded in the psychiatric and psychotherapeutic vocabulary, while *melancholy* remains only as a "specifier" that the diagnostician may add to the primary diagnosis of depression.[1] Among other benefits, the restoration of the word *melancholy* to its former preeminence would enable us to focus on what our predecessors understood, namely, that melancholy has no fundamental cure (though it has several remedies). In addition, precisely because it is a condition and not necessarily a pathology, it has been viewed historically as a "religious problem" (see, for example, Ferguson 1995), a point to which I will return later in this chapter.

In this book, I will be arguing that melancholia is primarily a condition that men experience, due primarily to the boy's separation from his mother. I recognize, however, that it may be a condition that women also experience, but, if so, the etiology is quite different. The psychoanalyst Julia Kristeva argues in *Black Sun: Depression and Melancholia* that a female form of melancholia is traceable to the two to three-year-old girl's need to begin adopting the dominant ("symbolic") language of her culture, which is male-oriented, and thus to leave the security of her mother's language world (which is "semiotic"). In support of this view, she cites studies that both girls and boys show signs of "depression" with the onset of language acquisition (Kristeva 1989, 41–42, 133). If so, it would follow that boys adapt more naturally to the symbolic language of patriarchal culture and are therefore less subject to lasting melancholia as a consequence of language acquisition. I believe this argument has considerable merit. In a course that I teach on poetry, several women have attested to resentment in their college years over the need to learn an abstract or technical language when they were more naturally disposed to poetic language. Kristeva's argument that melancholia may be traced to early childhood experiences, however, lends indirect support to my view, which will be set forth in detail, that male melancholia has roots in the emotional separation between mothers and their three or four-year-old sons. In any event, Kristeva uses *depression* and *melancholia* almost interchangeably and does not, therefore, make the decisive distinction between them that I consider essential.

Melancholia and the Lost Object

To understand the origins of melancholia, Sigmund Freud's essay "Mourning and Melancholia" is absolutely critical. Freud is concerned in this essay with pathological forms of melancholy. However, James's principle that we can learn much about more typical expressions of a phenomenon from its more exaggerated forms suggests that we may gain considerable insight into the melancholy self that men in general possess through Freud's understanding of its pathological expressions.

As Jackson points out, Freud in his early writings often used the terms *melancholia* and *depression* interchangeably (Jackson 1986, 223). In general, however, he used the word *depression* as a descriptive term for a person's dejected state of mind, whether pathological or not, and used the term *melancholia* as a diagnostic term. As early as 1890, Freud made brief allusions to connections between mourning and melancholia in writings simply termed "drafts," and, in a discussion on suicide in 1910, he suggested that it might be valuable to undertake a comparison between melancholia and the affect of mourning (223).

Freud's "Mourning and Melancholia," published in 1917, was written for the psychoanalytically trained reader, so it assumes a familiarity with psychoanalytic concepts with which the general reader may not be familiar. To follow his argument, it helps to keep in mind his view that we "internalize" (his word was "introject") persons who are important to us. Also relevant is his view that we "repress" those thoughts and emotions that we dare not acknowledge because we are ashamed or afraid of them. In his view, such repressed material continues to have an influence on what we say and do, but we are often unaware of this. The purpose of psychoanalysis is to enable us to bring it to consciousness.

Freud begins the essay by noting that even as dreams have "proven of service to us as the normal prototypes of narcissistic mental disorders," so it may be the case that "a comparison with the normal emotion of grief, and its expression in mourning" will "throw some light on the nature of melancholia" (Freud 1963c,164). He proceeds to explore the similarities and differences between the normal grieving process ("mourning") and the pathology known to the psychiatric community of his day as "melancholia." He warns that this exploration may not bear much fruit, in part because the psychiatric definition of melancholia is so uncertain. Yet he believes that a correlation of the two is justified because they have the same cause: Both are reactions to the loss of someone or something that was deeply loved. In the case of mourning we assume that the loss will be overcome in the normal course of time, whereas melancholia is a pathological condition that may require medical treatment. How to account for these very different outcomes?

In Freud's view, the distinguishing features of melancholia are a profoundly painful dejection, diminished interest in the outside world, loss of the capacity to love, inhibition of all activity, and a lowering of one's self-regarding feelings to such a degree that one engages in self-reproach and self-revilement, often culminating in a delusional expectation of punishment. Many of the same traits are found in grief: the same feelings of pain, the loss of interest in the outside world, the loss of a capacity to adopt any new object or objects of love, and a turning away from active effort that is not connected with thoughts of the dead person. In the mourning process, however, there is little of the self-reproach that is invariably present in melancholia, nor is there the anticipation of impending punishment. In mourning, the loss is deeply painful, yet it is experienced not as punishment but as integral to life itself.

Why this loss of self-esteem in melancholia? Why this self-abasement? Why this delusional belittling of self? Why this expectation of punishment and chastisement? That some of this self-criticism is justified cannot be doubted. After all, the patient is as lacking in interest and as incapable of love and of any achievement as he says he is. Moreover, in his self-criticisms, he has a keener eye for truth than those who are not melancholiacs, for others cling to views of themselves and human nature that are much too positive and sanguine.

The issue, however, is not whether the melancholiac's distressing self-abasement is justified in the opinion of others but whether he is in fact correctly describing both his experience of himself and the underlying reasons for it. If he has lost his self-respect, which seems to be the case, is there some good reason for this, as he seems to believe there is? This, and not others' objective assessment of him, is the issue, and the more he protests that he has lost his self-respect for good and unassailable reasons, the more hollow these protests seem.

Given his loss of self-esteem, it might seem as though melancholia is the very antithesis of grief, for grief involves the loss of an object in the external world, whereas melancholia involves the loss of self. But, says Freud, this difference is only apparent, and further probing reveals why. Like the griever, the melancholic has experienced the painful loss of a loved object. But while the griever mourns the loss of the loved object who has been taken from him, the melancholiac experiences the loss of the object with considerable ambivalence, as he feels that the loss he is now having to endure is the object's own fault, that the object has abandoned him. This, however, is not a feeling that he can openly acknowledge, because the feeling of abandonment is more painful than the feeling, in grief, of bereavement, where the loved one has been "taken away." So the reproachful feelings he has toward the lost object are turned against himself. The lost object is not relinquished and released, as in grief, but is internalized, becoming an aspect of the ego, so that the ego itself becomes the focus of reproach and delusions of future punishment.

Freud suggests that this is how conscience comes to be created. Reproaches against the external object are redirected against the self. Thus, "in the clinical picture of melancholia dissatisfaction with the self on moral grounds is far the most outstanding feature; the self-criticism much less frequently concerns itself with bodily infirmity, ugliness, weakness, social inferiority" (Freud 1963c, 169). A fundamental sense of being "bad" or "wrong" is characteristic of pathological forms of melancholia. This sense of badness or wrongness is, however, exaggerated, for at least some of this reproach is against the internalized other.

By viewing the self-reproach of a melancholiac as the reproach of the lost object turned against the self, Freud suggests that another puzzling feature of melancholia also becomes more comprehensible. This is the fact that the melancholiac exhibits little if any signs of "shame before others." We would expect that anyone who genuinely felt himself to be worthless would shrink from the gaze of others. But this is not the case with melancholiacs: "On the contrary, they give a great deal of trouble, perpetually taking offense and behaving as if they had been treated with great injustice. All this is possible only because the reactions expressed in their behavior still proceed from an attitude of revolt" (169–70).

If the melancholiac is in a state of revolt, this means that he has vengeful feelings toward the lost object. In Freud's view, his revenge is the pathology itself, as his illness is the means by which he torments the one who has forsaken him. Such tormenting of the other is possible because, unlike with mourning, where the other is dead, the "person who has occasioned the injury to the [melancholic] patient's feelings, and against whom his illness is aimed, is usually to be found among those in his near neighborhood" (172–73). Thus, the melancholiac's relationship to the lost object has a twofold fate: the internalization of the object, which takes the form of self-reproach, and the punishment inflicted on the actual object by means of the pathology itself.

As a therapist, Freud takes a great interest in the question of whether melancholia is curable. He notes that melancholia is more complicated than mourning because the lost object evokes such highly ambivalent feelings. In melancholia, there are "countless single conflicts in which love and hate wrestle together" (177). Also, unlike in mourning, where the object is finally relinquished, in melancholia the release of the object is greatly complicated because the object has become so self-identified, meaning that the melancholiac is unconscious of the causes of his pathology.

On the other hand, just as the work of grief enables the ego to give up the object in time, so in melancholia each single conflict or ambivalence, by disparaging and denigrating the object, loosens the fixation to it. Thus, it *is* possible for the process in the unconscious to come to an end, either because the fury has spent itself or because the object is abandoned as no longer having value. Which of these two possibilities is the regular or more usual one in bringing the melancholia to a merciful end is impossible to determine. What is indisputable, however, is that, unlike grief, the melancholia ends as the sufferer experiences "the satisfaction of acknowledging itself as the better of the two, as superior to the object" (179), indicating that reproach of the other is in some sense justified.

It should be emphasized that the object in this case is the internalized other, which bears only a partial resemblance to the other in real life. The struggle is an internalized one, in which the ego (or I) wrestles ambivalently, mixing both love and hate, with the internalized other. That the struggle is internal helps to explain why the melancholiac typically experiences symptoms both of mania and of depletion. The mania is usually associated with the sense of triumph over the internalized other, while the depletion is the sense that the ego is weak and unable to hold its own against the superior power of the internalized other. When the ego feels strong, it has the ability to "slay" the object, bringing the melancholia to an end. Therapeutically speaking, the goal is to strengthen the ego so that it may defeat the internalized object, thus achieving, in an admittedly violent manner, what grief accomplishes without the need for violence.

Thus, Freud argues in this essay that what is common to mourning and melancholia is that the individual has suffered a very significant loss. He has lost an "object" to whom he had a strong emotional attachment. The major difference in the two experiences of loss, however, is that in melancholia the lost object is still "in the neighborhood," causing the person who has suffered the loss to feel abandoned.

To identify the emotional difference between the two experiences, we may compare the dictionary definitions of the words *bereaved* and *abandoned*. *To bereave* means "to deprive, or dispossess" or "to leave in a sad or lonely state." *Abandon* (in the sense intended here) means "to leave, as in danger or out of necessity; forsake; desert." The dictionary compares it with several synonyms (desert, forsake, quit), noting that *abandon* "implies leaving a person or thing, either as a final, necessary measure (to *abandon* a drought area) or as a complete rejection of one's responsibilities, claims, etc. (she *abandoned* her child)." *Desert* implies "leaving in willful violation, as of one's obligation or oath (the soldier *deserted* his post)." *Forsake* "stresses renouncing a person or thing formerly dear to one (to *forsake* one's friends or ideals)." *Quit* implies "to leave or give up (she *quit* her job)." The antonym of *abandon* is *reclaim*.

One interesting thing about the word *abandon* is that it is open to two very different interpretations. Any instance in which abandonment occurs might be viewed either as enacted "out of necessity" or as a "conscious act of rejection." In contrast, there is little ambiguity associated with desertion (a willful violation), forsaking (an act of renunciation), or quitting. The only way this ambiguity can be resolved is by the act of reclaiming, which gives the abandoned one reason to believe the abandonment was done out of necessity and was not an act of rejection. In my theory of the origins of the melancholy self, the ambiguity in the word *abandonment* plays an important role.

Two Cases of Melancholia

In "Mourning and Melancholia," Freud assumes that his reader knows what a melancholic patient is like, and therefore does not provide any example drawn from his own clinical work. Since the term *melancholia* (like *hysteria*) has virtually disappeared from contemporary psychiatric texts, we need to turn to nineteenth- and early-twentieth-century texts for clinical examples of melancholia. One of the best portrayals of what pathological melancholia is like is provided by William James in his chapter "The Perception of Reality" in *The Principles of Psychology* (originally published in 1890). He writes here that in certain forms of "melancholic perversions of the sensibilities and reactive powers, nothing touches us intimately, rouses us, or wakens natural feeling. The consequence is the complaint so often heard from melancholic patients, that nothing is believed in by them as it used to be, and that all sense of reality is fled from life. They are sheathed in india-rubber; nothing penetrates to the quick or draws blood, as it were" (James 1950, 2:298).

James then quotes from one of the best-known manuals on mental disorders, Wilhelm Griesinger's *Mental Pathology and Therapeutics*: "'I see, I hear!,' such patients say, 'but the objects do not reach me, it is as if there were a wall between me and the outer world!'" (298). Griesinger adds:

> Outer things, whether living or inorganic, suddenly grow cold and foreign to us, and even our favorite objects of interest feel as if they belonged to us no more. Under these circumstances, receiving no longer from anything a lively impression, we cease to turn towards outer things, and the sense of inward loneliness grows upon us. . . . Where there is no strong intelligence to control this blasé condition, this psychic coldness and lack of interest, the issue of these states in which all seems so cold and hollow, the heart dried up, the world grown dead and empty, is often suicide or the deeper forms of insanity. (298)

James does not discuss melancholy any further in this chapter, but toward the end of the chapter he takes up the role played by imagination in making unreal things seem real: "Who does not 'realize' more the fact of a dead or distant friend's existence, at the moment when a portrait, letter, garment or other material reminder of him is found? The whole notion of him then grows pungent and speaks to us and shakes us, in a manner unknown at other times" (303). This illustration implies that melancholy concerns absence and loss, and the desire to regain the lost object in one form or another.

In his chapter "The Sick Soul" in *The Varieties of Religious Experience* (originally published in 1902), James makes a case that there is a form of melancholia that may be termed "religious." This is because some melancholiacs yield themselves, and in yielding, experience the support of divine presence. He provides illustrations of melancholia that do not make this religious turn, and ones that do. One of his illustrations of the former is that of a melancholic patient in a French asylum whose "misery keeps his mind from taking a religious direction," but, instead, "tends in fact towards irreligion" (James 1982, 149). This patient provides a detailed account of his misery in a letter to a friend, emphasizing the "fear, atrocious fear" that "presses me down, holds me without respite, never lets me go." Then he launches into a bitter tirade:

> Where is the justice in it all! What have I done to deserve this excess of severity? Under what form will this fear crush me? What would I now owe to any one who would rid me of my life! Eat, drink, lie awake all night, suffer without interruption—such is the fine legacy I have received from my mother! What I fail to understand is this abuse of power. There are limits to everything, there is a middle way. But God knows neither middle way nor limits. (148)

He reflects on his use of the name "God," asking himself why he says "God" when

> All I have known so far has been the devil. After all, I am afraid of God as much as of the devil, so I drift along, thinking of nothing but suicide, but with neither courage nor means here to execute the act. As you read this, it will easily prove to you my insanity. The style and the ideas are incoherent enough—I can see that myself. But I cannot keep myself from being either crazy or an idiot; and, as things are, from whom should I ask pity? I am defenseless against the invisible enemy who is tightening his coils around me. (148)

He refers to this angry epistle as "ravings," for what else can one call it when a person has "neither brain nor thoughts left" (149)? While this Job-like complaint emphasizes God's own "abuse of power," it is noteworthy that the patient also makes a sarcastic reference to "the fine legacy I have received from my mother." I will make a point about this in a moment.

For an example of melancholy that does take a religious turn, James cites a case of what he calls "the worst form of melancholy." It is the worst because it takes "the form of panic fear" (159–60). Like the previous illustration, he represents the sufferer as a Frenchman, and says that he is taking the liberty of "translating freely." It is well known, however, that the afflicted man in this case is James himself (see Lewis 1991, 202–4). The episode he recounts occurred when he was in his late twenties, but he apparently wrote his account of it some years later.

He begins this account by noting that he was in a "state of philosophic pessimism." (In the previous example, the French patient also mentions that he had "chewed the cud of bitterness with the pessimists" in his philosophy year in college, and adds, "how true and right I was," for "there is more pain in life than gladness.") In addition, James was experiencing a "general depression of spirits about my prospects." This is related to the fact that while he had a medical degree, he did not want to practice medicine but to do research, and no position had opened up for him. Furthermore, he had no marital prospects (he eventually married at age thirty-six).

The account then relates how he had gone into "a dressing room in the twilight to procure some article that was there, when suddenly there fell upon me without any warning, just as if it came out of the darkness, a horrible fear of my own existence" (James 1982, 160). Simultaneously, "the image of an epileptic patient" arose in his mind, a young man whom he had seen in an asylum during his medical studies. This patient was

> a black-haired youth with greenish skin, entirely idiotic, who used to sit all day on one of the benches, or rather shelves against the wall, with his knees drawn up against his chin, and the coarse gray undershirt, which was his only garment, drawn over them inclosing his entire figure. He sat there like a sort of sculptured Egyptian cat or Peruvian mummy, moving nothing but his black eyes and looking absolutely non-human. (160)

It should be noted that, in those days, epilepsy was considered a form of moral degeneration, as the term *epilepsy* was applied to men who urinated in public, made lewd gestures, and so forth. Masturbation (or "self-abuse") was also considered one of the causes of melancholy, and was itself viewed as a sign of moral degeneration.

James indicates that what happened next was that "this image and my fear" combined in his mind—the fusion of a mental image and an emotion—producing the horrible thought that, potentially, "that shape am I." He continues:

> Nothing that I possess can defend me against that fate, if the hour for it should strike for me as it struck for him. There was such a horror of him, and such a perception of my own merely momentary discrepancy from him, that it was as if something hitherto solid within my breast gave way entirely, and I became a mass of quivering fear. After this the universe was changed for me altogether. I awoke morning after morning with a horrible dread at the pit of my stomach, and with a sense of

the insecurity of life that I never knew before, and that I have never left since. (160)

He notes that the experience "was like a revelation" to him, and that while "the immediate feelings passed away, the experience has made me sympathetic with the morbid feelings of others ever since" (160–61). His feelings of panic "gradually faded," but he was unable to go out into the dark alone for several months, and he dreaded being left alone.

Interestingly, he too mentions his mother in this account. He recalls "wondering how other people could live, how I myself had ever lived, so unconscious of that pit of insecurity beneath the surface of life," and then cites his mother as an example: "My mother in particular, a very cheerful person, seemed to me a perfect paradox in her unconsciousness of danger, which you may well believe I was very careful not to disturb by revelations of my own state of mind" (161).

James presents this experience as illustrative of *religious* melancholy. In the account itself, he concludes by saying, "I have always thought that this experience of melancholia of mine had a religious bearing" (161). In his commentary on the case, James indicates that "this correspondent" was asked (presumably by James himself) "to explain more fully what he meant by these last words." His answer was this: "I mean that the fear was so invasive and powerful that if I had not clung to scripture-texts like 'the eternal God is my refuge,' etc., 'Come unto me, all ye that labor and are heavy-laden,' etc., 'I am the resurrection and the life,' etc., I think I should have grown really insane" (161). Thus, unlike the patient in the French asylum who really did go insane, James was spared this fate because he clung to scripture-texts that affirmed the supportive presence of God.

These two illustrations point to different outcomes. In both cases there is an overwhelming sense of fear, a fear for one's very existence. This is not primarily a fear of physical annihilation, but of the loss of one's sanity. The fear of the loss of self is therefore at the very core of the experience of melancholy. In the aftermath of this dreadful experience, James became afraid not only of the dark but also of being left alone. This suggests that he fears abandonment, knowing that he is incapable of being alone. The patient in the French asylum experiences himself as having been abandoned, left to face his misery alone. To him, God might just as well be the devil. The Scripture verses to which James clings, however, give assurance that God has not abandoned him, that God is his refuge, that Jesus invites him to come unto him and place his cares upon him, that through Jesus there is resurrection and life. These are the accounts of two critically endangered young men, but with very different outcomes owing to the fact that the one "clung to scripture-texts" he had presumably memorized as a child.

Mother as the Lost Object

If the threats that melancholia poses to these two young men are those of the loss of self and of abandonment, their references to their mothers in these accounts may be more than coincidental. The patient in the French asylum refers, sarcastically, to "the fine legacy I have received from my mother," and James observes that his mother "in particular" would have been unable to comprehend what he was going through. To appreciate and gain a better understanding of these references to their mothers, we need to return to Freud's essay on "Mourning and Melancholia," and ask whether there is an implied "lost object" in this essay.

To be sure, Freud indicates that any emotional loss—of a person or a thing—could precipitate melancholia. The fact that melancholia is such a severe, pathological reaction to the loss suggests, however, that the lost object is far more likely to be a person than a thing (for a thing is ordinarily replaceable by an exact replica or an equally valued substitute, while a person is unique and therefore irreplaceable). One would also assume that this person is very important to the melancholiac, for, as Freud noted in an early draft on melancholia, "in melancholia it must be a question of loss—a loss in *instinctual* life" (quoted in Jackson 1986, 221; Freud's emphasis). This means that the person who has been lost was one with whom the "abandoned" person had a deep emotional connection, for, to Freud, "instinctual" refers to fundamental emotions, especially ones related to basic sexual and aggressive drives or impulses.

I suggest that a man's most purely instinctual relationship is the one he had with his mother prior to birth (when he was literally a parasite, living off her own body) and during the months after the birth when he was sustained by milk from her body. The American poet William Stafford, whose work may be viewed as melancholic (but in the more "yielding" form of James than the acerbic form of the patient in the French asylum), wrote these lines regarding his mother shortly before his death: "All my life I've tapped out our kind of truth. For nine months I studied what your heart was saying" (Stafford 1998, 30).

In my view, the melancholic condition of the patient in the French asylum and James's own melancholic episode were related to their mothers. If so, the fear of abandonment expressed in these accounts is rooted in an experience of actual or perceived abandonment by their mothers when they were little boys. Their susceptibility to melancholia in their twenties is related to some earlier experience or experiences of actual or perceived abandonment in early childhood, and they recapitulate the trauma experienced—but not worked through—in their early years. I suggest that the trauma is most likely to have occurred as a result of the boy's emotional separation from his mother around the age of three or four.[2]

Before I develop this argument, however, I want to return to the ambiguity inherent in the word *abandoned*. I believe that this very ambiguity is itself rooted in the small boy's experience of his mother as "lost" to him. If the loss is not due to her physical death, the fact that she has been lost and yet remains "in the neighborhood" accounts for the ambiguity inherent in the boy's experience of abandonment. If she had died, he could say that she was "taken away" against her will. Because she remains physically present, he is confused as to whether his emotional abandonment was voluntary on her part or was forced upon her by circumstances beyond her control. (Confusion is an important element in the French patient's letter to his friend as he expresses extreme puzzlement that he has become insane. James, too, seems perplexed that such panic fear arose from the simple act of entering a dressing room to procure a piece of clothing.)

While adult men are able to resolve this ambiguity (through "rationalization" or "insight"), the little boy is left in a quandary, his worst fears being that the abandonment was voluntary, and his greatest hopes being that it was due to circumstances beyond her control. In the latter case, he can believe that she would "reclaim" him if she could, and that she may be in a position in the not-too-distant future to do so. He may, in fact, fantasize that he will be the one who overcomes these untoward circumstances.

It should also be noted, as Freud points out in "Mourning and Melancholia," and as James's illustration of the patient in the French asylum bears out, that melancholia may have an aggressive, even hostile aspect. While mourning may also have an element of anger toward the deceased (one complains that the dead person should have taken better care of herself), this is normally not the predominant emotion the mourner experiences. In fact, if it is, we would be justified in saying that his reaction is a melancholic one (he believes that her failure to take care of herself amounts to willful abandonment). Thus, an act of suicide is likely to evoke the ambivalent feelings characteristic of melancholia. The interesting thing here is that the patient in the French asylum is actually more successful than James in externalizing his anger. He makes sarcastic comments about his mother's legacy, hurls accusations against God, claims that a pessimistic view of the world is "true and right," and so forth. Thus, he makes himself "dead" to the world, as if to say, "If the world wants to abandon me, let it. I will respond by abandoning it." The problem with this is that it leads to insanity.

In contrast, James makes a relatively mild accusation against his mother— observing that she simply could not comprehend what he was going through—experiences God as a supportive presence, and, with effort, finds his way back into the world of the living. Since there is little expression of anger over his having been abandoned, one may assume either that his experience of abandonment as a boy was not as traumatic as that of the patient in the French asylum or that he has internalized his anger in the form of self-contempt to a much greater extent.

The account itself does not give us enough evidence to decide this issue, but the fact that he saw himself as hardly different from the epileptic, and that epilepsy was considered a form of moral degeneration, suggests that he may well have internalized his anger at his mother in the form of self-contempt. Citing James's reference to his "moral degradation" three weeks after this episode, one of his biographers speculates that this was an allusion to auto-eroticism (Lewis 1991, 201). If so, he may have considered this to be a physiological cause of his melancholic state and a basis for his comparison of himself with the epileptic patient, since epilepsy was commonly believed to be caused by autoerotic acts.

In *Whatever Became of Sin?*, a book that enjoyed considerable popularity in the 1970s, Karl Menninger cites several examples of nineteenth-century psychiatric texts that ascribe mental diseases to masturbation, including mania, dementia, and melancholia. He notes, "To an extent difficult for the present-day reader to grasp, this was *the major sin* for middle- and upper-class adolescents a century or less ago" (Menninger 1973, 35). He bids his reader to "consider the emotional conflict in a boy (or girl), instructed in the faith, that Jesus, the good man, the Son of God, died 'for your sins,' whose chief sexual preoccupation was his propensity for repeating this dreadful act. I have seen a large room of university men bowed on their knees in prayer for forgiveness and for strength to resist the temptation of (this) sin" (35). Menninger notes that Freud considered it "the primary addiction" and that he viewed his life-long compulsive addiction to smoking as a substitute for "the great sin," the original sin, of masturbation (34).

If James was engaging in masturbation, this could account in part for his belief that he was unworthy to marry a woman of good breeding, and for the fact that he married relatively late in life. His student and friend, John Boodin, relates an occasion in which several of James's students were discussing, in James's company, a sermon they had heard preached on immortality. The preacher had argued that the issue is not whether a man knows he will in fact be granted immortality when he dies but that he should make himself worthy of it. James listened to this discussion for a while and then intervened, saying, "Which is better, to be worthy of having a wife or to have a wife, in spite of one's unworthiness?" (Boodin 1996, 221). While designed to settle a theological debate, this statement may be self-revealing, and may point to the tendency of the melancholic to engage in self-reproach. This self-reproach may also be reflected in a letter James wrote to his mother from Germany prior to the melancholic episode, in which he informed her that he had fallen in love with an actress of Bohemian origin, an indication that he may have considered himself fit only for a relatively disreputable woman

(Lewis 1991, 187). The fact that he never referred to this love interest again suggests that this "revelation" (whether true or fictitious) was intended to disconcert his mother, who would never have approved of her son's marriage to a Bohemian actress. At any rate, in light of the prevailing view that autoerotic acts may cause melancholia, it is little wonder that James disguised his identity in his account of the so-called "French sufferer."

A comparison of these two accounts of melancholia suggests that the internalization of anger in the form of self-contempt may play the rather paradoxical role of saving a man from outright insanity, but at the price of a low sense of self-worth, a tendency to beat up on himself, and so forth. To all appearances, he may seem perfectly healthy—he is not the raving maniac in the French asylum—but he *is* the victim of an undeserved self-abuse, as he takes out his anger toward his mother, whom he perceives has abandoned him, against himself.

There are two very important implications of the view that emotional separation from his mother around the age of three or four is responsible for the boy's development of a melancholic predisposition. The first concerns the role of melancholia in the formation of conscience and the fear of punishment. The boy believes that he has done something to warrant the loss of his mother and that if he makes certain reparations and promises he might win her back. Because, for reasons of gender differentiation, the son's separation from his mother is more decisive than the daughter's, he is also more likely to form a false conscience, one more delusional as to his own personal culpability for the initial separation and the failure to restore the relationship.

Secondly, if the mother is the original lost object, all subsequent experiences of loss for reasons other than death (where grieving is possible) will be reminiscent of his mother and will evoke similar feelings of shame and rage, guilt and remorse. These subsequent losses may be other people (e.g., women with whom he falls in love) or desires that are symbolically linked to his mother (e.g., the desire to pursue a career in art, music, or caregiving). As we will see in the following chapter, the desire for a symbolic replacement of the relationship to his mother is also a prominent feature in men's religion.

I have suggested that the emergence of the melancholic self may be traced to the separation trauma in early childhood. Freud does not identify the mother as the "lost object" in his essay on mourning and melancholia, and he does not make any attempt to explain why an adult would be susceptible to melancholia. His concept of the Oedipus complex, however, gives a clear indication that the lost object is the mother (see also Radden 2000a, 214). As he notes in *The Ego and the Id* (originally published in 1923), the Oedipus complex—which is due to the boy's intense "sexual wishes in regard to his mother" and consequent "wish to get rid of his father" (Freud 1960a, 22)— must be "demolished," as this is an untenable situation. This demolition requires the giving up of the boy's extreme "object-cathexis" toward his mother, its place filled by one of two things: either an identification with his mother, where his desire to *have* her is replaced by the intention to be *like* her, or an intensification of his identification with his father. The latter outcome is the more normal, as it "permits the affectional relation to the mother to be in measure retained" while it also "consolidates the masculinity in a boy's character" (22).

If we relate Freud's essay on mourning and melancholia to his concept of the Oedipus complex and the "normal" form of its demolition, the fact that the lost object is the mother is inescapable. Melancholia results from the fact that the boy's desire to "have" his mother must be given up. Freud's concept of the Oedipus complex has itself contributed to—while also being based upon—the popular view that in order for a boy to develop a "masculine" character, there needs to be an emotional separation or independence from his mother. Thus, most developmental theorists believe that the son's separation from the mother is more decisive than the daughter's, and they have supported the common belief that this is how it should be, for otherwise, the boy will not successfully bond with his father and develop a masculine identity. (I will discuss an important recent challenge to this view in the following chapter.)

My wife, who is a preschool teacher, once related to me an episode that bears directly on this issue. A girl of about four years of age told my wife that she did not want to go on the field trip planned for the following day because "field trips are boring." My wife was about to respond that this one would be very exciting and to give reasons why this was so when a boy (also about four years old) who had overheard the girl's comment said to her, "Oh, you just miss your mama," which elicited this reassurance from another boy: "I missed my mama too, but I got over it, and you will too." Interestingly enough, it was the two boys in this little episode who offered a "psychoanalytic" interpretation of the girl's expressed boredom.

If these four-year-old boys felt that they had already experienced emotional separation from their mothers—and assuming that they are fairly typical—it seems reasonable to suggest that the boy's experience of his mother as the lost object occurs during or before the fourth year, perhaps in the third year, which, in Erik H. Erikson's developmental schema, is toward the end of the "autonomy vs. shame and doubt" stage and the beginning of the "initiative vs. guilt" stage (Erikson 1959, 65–82). When Erikson lists the various fears to which young children are susceptible, and which they carry into adulthood in the form of anxieties, he views girls as the ones who are most likely to develop a fear of "being left," and suggests that this fear "seems to be the most basic feminine fear, extending over the whole of a woman's existence" (Erikson 1963, 410). Consequently, women must "learn to understand their fear of being abandoned" (411). If it is true that the son's separation from his mother is more decisive than that of the daughter, Erikson's view that the "fear of being abandoned" is typical of women may indicate either that he, being male, wants to minimize the trauma that the small boy experiences in "being left" by his mother, or that he believes that the boy has come to terms with this experience—"gotten over it"—whereas the woman, not having experienced it as decisively in childhood, has a greater fear of abandonment in adulthood. In my own view, the original abandonment is, in fact, a traumatic one for the boy, and the persistence of mild to severe forms of melancholia in adult males testifies to the fact that they have not "gotten over it." Instead, they have learned, more or less, to live with it, which is to say that the trauma of separation from their mothers has either been repressed (and hence, not worked through) or sublimated (redirected), or both.

Experiences That Precipitate and Reinforce Emotional Separation

When books on child development discuss the emotional separation between the small boy and his mother, they rarely comment on the fact that it is inherently traumatic. They often refer to the boy's separation as a "developmental task," implying by this phrase that it is something that a boy simply needs to do as a sort of achievement. This language not only minimizes the traumatic nature of separation but also makes it less incumbent on the developmental theorist to identify or describe the episodes that occur between mother and son that precipitate the separation. Typically, the "developmental task" is represented as prompted solely by the boy's inherent need for independence.

In my view, the paradigmatic episode that facilitates the separation is physical punishment by the mother. A student once told me that it was far more devastating for him as a small boy to be beaten by his mother than by his father. He took his father's beatings for granted, apparently on the assumption that his father had never liked him. The first time his mother beat him, however, he had to come to terms with the fact that the parent whom he loved—and who loved him—could turn against him and show a side of herself he had never experienced before. In effect, his mother had become two very different persons, with two very different appearances (a loving face and an angry face). He became determined to avoid any behaviors that would evoke the angry face.

A pastoral psychotherapist informed me of a man with whom he was working in therapy whose mother was frustrated by the fact that as a boy he was unusually difficult to toilet train. Exasperated, she would place his own feces in a bowl and force him to eat them.

Beatings and similar acts of abuse are, of course, extreme examples of the sorts of episodes that facilitate the emotional separation between a boy and his mother. A less extreme illustration is a story my wife told me about a four-year-old boy who had a two-year-old brother. When he saw his mother and his brother together on the playground, he dropped whatever he was doing in the classroom, ran out to the playground, and threw his arms around his mother, who was bending over to help his younger brother manipulate a miniature digging machine in the sandbox. She pushed the older boy away, exclaiming, "I told you, I don't like that." When she noticed that my wife, the boy's teacher, had observed her, she explained, "He's such a mama's boy." The message she was communicating to her older son was that she expected him to distance himself from her. No doubt, he also felt that her affections for him had been transferred to his younger brother.

Another common way in which mothers encourage their sons to separate from them is by discouraging them from playing with dolls and kitchen utensils and from dressing up in women's clothes. Preschool teachers are far more likely to be questioned by parents of boys than of girls about their child's play preferences in this regard. If a mother learns that her three or four-year-old son engages in behaviors associated with little girls, she is likely to ask whether he is also interested in "boys' activities." She is far more concerned with the "mama's boy" than the "tomboy" issue. These concerns (shared by fathers) are raised in spite of the fact that three or four-year-old boys (and girls) reveal confusion over what makes a person a man or a woman. For example, a teacher who wears a dress but has short hair may be asked whether she is "a boy," "a girl," or both.

I realize, of course, that a small boy will have his own needs for independence from his mother, and that a boy will actively resist his mother's efforts to control him. In fact, men like to recall episodes in which they, as small boys, expressed their independence, especially ones in which they took risks or put themselves in danger (as when they broke free from their mother's hand and began to run across the street). What they do not freely talk about, perhaps because, being traumatic, they have repressed such episodes, are ones in which their mothers initiated or abetted the emotional separation. Will the boy who ran out of the classroom onto the playground in order to throw his arms around his mother's neck recall this episode years later? Because it did not have the desired outcome, but instead provoked a reprimand, I doubt it. It will be repressed along with any other reprimands relating to the fact that he is "such a mama's boy."

In *In a Different Voice*, Carol Gilligan took Erikson to task for having constructed a developmental schema that was male biased. In her initial chapter on "Woman's Place in Man's Life Cycle," she argues that his schema is gender neutral at the outset, since the first stage, termed "basic trust vs. basic mistrust," is equally applicable to girls and boys. However, with the second stage of "autonomy vs. shame and doubt," it begins to take on a male orientation, and this male bias becomes even more apparent in the third—the "initiative vs.

guilt" stage—"which represents a further move in the direction of autonomy," and the fourth—industry vs. inferiority" stage—which "is the time when children strive to learn and master the technology of their cultures, in order to recognize themselves and be recognized by others as capable of becoming adults" (Gilligan 1982, 12). Gilligan asks, "But about whom is Erikson talking? Once again it turns out to be the male child" (12).

Gilligan is critical of Erikson's developmental model because it, like many other developmental theories constructed by men, fails to take into consideration "the continuing importance of attachment in the human life cycle." It is as though "woman's place in man's life cycle is to protect this recognition [i.e., of the importance of attachment] while the developmental litany intones the celebration of separation, autonomy, individuation, and natural rights" (23). In the following chapter on "Images of Relationship," Gilligan provides an illustration of the responses of two eleven-year-olds ("Jake" and "Amy") to a hypothetical situation involving a moral dilemma. For Gilligan, this illustration reveals the contrast between "a self defined through separation" (Jake) and "a self delineated through connection" (Amy).

My purpose here is not to challenge Gilligan's contention that Erikson's life cycle model is male biased (see, however, Capps 1993, 134–35, for a criticism of her view of "autonomy" as separation and independence; more central to Erikson's view of autonomy is that it involves self-governance). Instead, what is significant for our purposes here is her assumption that his theory is male biased precisely because it appears to be a theory that extols separation, especially from the mother, as this is considered the means by which the boy will develop into an independent, self-motivated child. Thus, her complaint that Erikson's life cycle theory is male biased supports my view that the need for a boy to experience an emotional separation from his mother is taken for granted and that any traumatic effects of this separation are minimized or considered inconsequential.

If, however, every boy's emotional separation from his mother is traumatic, are there some separations that are more traumatic than others? Or, put another way, do some boys grow up more melancholic than others? In *Men, Religion, and Melancholia* (1997), I focused on the lives of four men—William James, Rudolf Otto, C. G. Jung, and Erik H. Erikson—and argued that the emotional separation from their mothers in early childhood was especially traumatic owing to the circumstances in which it occurred. Jung's mother was sent to a mental asylum for several months when he was three or four years old. Erikson's mother, who was a single parent the first three years of his life (he was conceived out of wedlock), married a man who was falsely represented to him as his natural father so that Erik "would feel thoroughly at home in *their* home" (Erikson 1975, 27, my emphasis). He adds, "My sense of being 'different' took refuge (as it is apt to do even in children without such acute life problems) in fantasies of how I, the son of much better parents, had been altogether a foundling" (27). Rudolf Otto was almost certainly beaten by his mother, who was the family disciplinarian due to his father's frequent absences. Otto's two attempted suicides, one in which he leaped off a tower, another in which he tried to throw himself in front of a train, suggest a violent attitude toward his own body that might be traced to these early beatings. While William James was the oldest child, his mother clearly favored his younger brother Henry, who was only fifteen months William's junior. His mother's younger sister (for whom his father had a special affection and who lived in the James household) became William's favorite companion. Other circumstances, which I cannot discuss in detail here, contributed to the trauma these four boys experienced in the separation process, but these examples are illustrative of the circumstances that may exacerbate the separation which was already destined to occur.

The Issue of Mother Blaming

By citing these examples of boys' mistreatment by their mothers, I may appear here to be engaging in "mother blaming," thus perpetuating the very practice for which feminist authors have criticized—and rightly so—an earlier generation of psychologists and psychotherapists (an example of which were writings in the 1950s and 1960s that attributed schizophrenia in children to the mother's ambiguous or "double-binding" manner of communicating with the child). While I will be discussing this issue again in chapter 2, I have three initial responses to this possible charge of mother blaming. First, the idea that boys need to be encouraged to separate from their mothers is deeply rooted in American culture. This being the case, we can hardly blame individual mothers if their role in the separation is due, in part, to their acceptance of this cultural belief; in fact, mothers are likely to be correspondingly aware that they will be subject to severe social condemnation and ridicule if they allow their sons to remain emotionally attached to them (there is also a misguided concern regarding homosexuality that helps to fuel this fear).

Second, as I noted in my study of James, Otto, Jung, and Erikson, these melancholia-prone boys grew up to become very accomplished adults. Therefore, "blaming," at least as far as the adult outcome is concerned, is hardly relevant. In fact, I would argue that a boy with a highly developed melancholy self is especially likely to become a productive adult. Some of the reasons for this will be explored in the following chapter, where I consider the links between melancholia and male ways of being religious. Basically, however, they have to do with a boy proving that he is worthy of his mother's love, which leads to moral rectitude and embarking on quests that propel many men into the frontiers of their professions.

Third, and perhaps most significant, the melancholy self that exists in every man, whether rightly or wrongly, *does* hold grievances against his mother, though this is rarely openly expressed. Instead, as Freud's analysis of melancholia indicates, these grievances are repressed and internalized as self-reproach. The ability to *un*repress these deeply buried feelings toward her in the form of "mother blaming" may be the very beginning of the partial healing of melancholia. If so, condemning "mother blaming" may have the ultimately negative effect of making it even more difficult to bring these feelings to the surface so that they may be worked through. It may be that those male psychologists and psychotherapists who are now being criticized for engaging in implicit "mother blaming" in their writings on child development were, in this way, working through their grievances toward their own mothers. In any event, the unrepression of these deeply buried feelings might eventually lead a man to a more genuine appreciation not only of the fact that his mother gave him life but also for the many ways in which she nurtured him and fostered his development.

As Gordon W. Allport points out in *The Individual and His Religion*, the son who is able to represent his parents in a balanced way—recognizing both positive and negative qualities—has a more mature perspective than the son who speaks or writes about his parents in idealized ways. Such idealization almost certainly indicates that the more negative feelings have been self censored or repressed. Allport cites examples from a series of articles by Vera V. French on "the structure of sentiments." One daughter wrote about her father: "Dad is a perfect father. He loves his family and his family loves him. . . . He is looked up to in all the town, highly admired. . . . He will help anyone. He is noted for his fairness and honesty. Fairness and honesty are Dad." Allport comments, "This encomium betrays an undifferentiated sentiment. The father is just perfect, everything about him is right. The student's devotion to him is marked by such abandon that we suspect she has never made a close and analytic inspection of his character, and even that her lavish praise may cover some repressed animosity. Detailed study of this case shows this suspicion to be justified. Deep inside the girl dislikes many things about her father, though she denies this dislike even to herself. The sentiment therefore emerges as an oversimplified disposition, not well integrated with the deeper life of the subject" (Allport 1960, 58–59).

Another daughter described her father in the following way: "He is somewhat unsocial, but dramatic enough to be pleasing in company; irritable, but not at all ill-natured; conscientious, hardworking, puritanical; timid in some things, dogged in others. His imagination is shown in his love of travel, but

is not much in evidence otherwise" (59). Allport observes, "This daughter likewise approves of her father. Yet, unlike the first, she is observant, critical, not
merely abandoned in her admiration. One suspects that the very *differentiation*
of the sentiment in the second case prevents repressed criticisms and hostility
from forming. Her view of her father, if more complex, is more realistic" (59).

I suggest that men have the same tendency as the first daughter to think
and talk about their *mothers* in the same undifferentiated way. In my experience, their comments about their fathers are more differentiated, and this, as
Allport suggests, inhibits "repressed criticisms and hostility from forming." As
Allport emphasizes, both daughters approve of their fathers. The issue then is
not whether a man approves or disapproves of his mother, but whether he is
able to view her in a differentiated way, in a way that recognizes her own complexity. To discourage an adult male from expressing the negative feelings and
attitudes he has toward his mother on the grounds that this is tantamount to
"mother blaming" is counterproductive as far as his melancholy self is concerned, and it can be positively harmful to the other women in his life if, years
later, he takes out on them his repressed negative emotions toward his mother.
These three responses to the possible complaint that I am engaging here in
mother blaming lead to the issue that I will explore in the following chapter,
namely, that in *Real Boys: Rescuing Our Sons from the Myths of Boyhood* (1998),
William Pollack has recently challenged the common assumption that boys
must separate from their mothers.

Conclusion

Throughout this chapter, I have been emphasizing that men develop a melancholy self owing to the emotional separation that occurs between the mother
and the son in early childhood. This does not mean, of course, that all men—
or even most men—become pathologically melancholic. It only means that
the "typical" male has a predisposition toward at least mild forms of melancholia and that this predisposition remains a continual factor, threatening a
man's emotional stability, throughout adulthood.

This predisposition may be masked, hidden beneath an exterior having
none of the earmarks of melancholia. As indicated in the introduction, the
melancholy self is one of several, perhaps many, selves of which an individual
man's identity is comprised, and these other selves may be far more visible
than his melancholy self. In addition, there are men who have learned to deal
with their melancholic predisposition in the course of life, who have found
ways to modulate or even take advantage of it. They have done so without
necessarily becoming aware of the fact that they are afflicted with an underlying melancholia.

Since the word itself has gone out of favor, however, the methods that our predecessors developed for addressing it are less known to us today. As one learns, for example, from James Boswell's biography of Samuel Johnson (originally published in 1791), men in earlier eras were very much aware of their susceptibility to melancholia, and shared their knowledge and insights with one another about effective remedies that they had learned from others or had discovered on their own. They knew that there was no "cure" for it (a fact that, in itself, supports my view that it is traceable to the boy's emotional separation from his mother), but that there were remedies for it. In addition, Robert Burton's *The Anatomy of Melancholy*, a large tome that first appeared in 1621, was a virtual Bible on the causes, symptoms, and treatment of melancholia. The fact that it went through several editions during his own lifetime and has remained in print ever since indicates the degree to which men have been aware of melancholia's capacity to disable them. It was not until Freud related melancholia to an instinctual loss, however, that it became possible to see that melancholia has its origins in the son's emotional separation from his mother. If mourning is the typical response to the loss of a loved one through physical death, melancholia is a no less typical response to the emotional loss of a loved one who is still in the neighborhood. This very fact prompts the boy to wonder if his abandonment was a conscious, volitional rejection, and, if so, if there is anything he might do to persuade her to reclaim him.

Notes

1. *DSM-IV* does not have a category identified simply as "Depression." Rather, several disorders are identified in the section headed "Mood Disorders," the most relevant being "Dysthymic Disorder" and "Major Depressive Episode." The primary characteristic of Dysthymic Disorder is a "depressed mood for most of the day, for more days than not, as indicated either by subjective account or observation of others, for at least two years." Its symptoms may include "poor appetite or overeating, insomnia or hypersomnia, low energy or fatigue, low self-esteem, poor concentration or difficulty making decisions, and feelings of hopelessness" (349). For a diagnosis of "Major Depressive Episode," at least five from a list of nine symptoms must have been present during a two-week period. These include the symptoms indicated for Dysthymic Disorder, plus markedly diminished interest or pleasure in activities; psychomotor agitation or retardation; feelings of worthlessness or inappropriate guilt; and recurrent thoughts of death and/or recurrent suicidal ideation or an actual suicide attempt (327).

The "Melancholic Features Specifier" may be applied to the Major Depressive Episode when either the loss of pleasure in activities or lack of reactivity to pleasurable stimuli are present, and when three or more of the following are also present: distinct quality of depressed mood (i.e., it is distinctly different from the kind of feeling experienced after the death of a loved one); the depressed mood is worse in the morning; one awakens at least two hours before the usual waking time; there is marked psychomotor retardation or agitation; significant anorexia weight loss; and excessive or inappropriate guilt (384). Some of these criteria overlap with Major Depressive Episode criteria, but the fact that the depressed mood is different from the feeling experienced after the death of a loved one, and that excessive or inappropriate guilt is specifically noted, supports, as will be seen later, Freud's effort to contrast "mourning" and "melancholia."

2. None of the major psychiatric writings on melancholia in the nineteenth century cited emotional separation from one's mother as a possible cause (see Radden 2000b, 203–79). The closest precursor to Freud in this regard was probably Wilhelm Griesinger, the German psychiatrist who, in his *Mental Pathology and Therapeutics* (1867), considered the possibility of external causes, such as grief or jealousy, that persist longer than normal. Freud most likely was aware of such earlier associations of melancholy to mourning. In any case, the view that the primary cause of melancholia is an ambivalent response reaction to the lost object was Freud's original contribution.

CHAPTER 2

∼

The Melancholy Self and Male Religiousness

I am convinced that there is a direct psychodynamic connection between the formation of the melancholy self and the ways in which men are religious. To show how this works, I will first consider William Pollack's *Real Boys* (1998), which challenges the idea that an emotional separation from the mother is necessary in order for a boy to connect with his father and develop a masculine identity. In addition, I want to consider Frank Pittman's view, presented in *Man Enough: Fathers, Sons, and the Search for Masculinity* (1993), that the mother, for men, is the primary object of guilt. These two views will enable us to trace the consequences of the boy's emotional separation from his mother into his adult life. This, in turn, will permit us to see how religion may serve the adult male as a compensation for the emotional loss sustained in early childhood.

The Enduring Consequences of the Original Separation

In *Real Boys,* William Pollack directly challenges the assumption that mothers must foster a separation between themselves and their small boys (Pollack 1998, 11–12, 26–29). The boy's need to separate from his mother is a strongly held cultural value, based not only on fear that he will become too attached to his mother and thus unable to develop his masculinity, but also on the assumption that a boy cannot attach to his father *unless* he separates from his mother. Pollack questions these assumptions. He also wonders: What would happen to girls if they were believed to need to separate emotionally from their mothers? Wouldn't we assume that this is traumatic for them? And wouldn't we want to be very certain that such separation was necessary, that it would have the desired outcome, and that girls could in fact "survive" this separation emotionally? With boys, however, we assume that it must happen and that boys should be able to handle the separation without

27

its becoming traumatic, that only the "mama's boy" will be unable to separate naturally and easily.

A related issue Pollack raises is that boys are assumed to require more severe parental restraint than girls and that their bodies can "take" more punishment than girls' bodies. Moreover, the physical punishment is understood to toughen boys up and thus to make them capable of withstanding physical hardships later in life. Pollack notes that girls are more likely to experience sexual abuse, while boys are more subject to physical abuse. In effect, adults break a girl's spirit through sexual molestation, while they propose to toughen a boy's spirit by assaulting his body with belts and other means of physical force.

Pollack suggests that males experience two separations, each of them traumatic (meaning that they leave painful residues and have various future consequences): (1) separation from mother and the maternal environment at age six (as indicated, I think it occurs at age three to four); and (2) separation from the parental environment in adolescence as a boy is expected to develop an identity and establish his independence. They may also experience a third traumatic separation when parents divorce (144–47; 364–69). I agree with Pollack's critique of the assumption that a boy cannot attach to his father *unless* he separates from his mother; even if this were true in principle, it isn't working, since men often lament the absence of a close relationship to their fathers. However, I believe that Pollack's list of separations that are reminiscent of the original separation from the mother needs to be modified and expanded. This revised list more adequately fits the theory of the melancholy self presented here by showing that the original separation from the mother casts a very long shadow over the span of life, encompassing adulthood as well.

1. *Separation from mother beginning at age three or four* and leading to the perception that the boy did something to cause or precipitate the separation (i.e., it was not, as an adult might view it, a "natural" part of his individuation). Thus, he begins to develop a false conscience, one that at least partially distorts reality.

2. *Separation from mother in adolescence,* reminiscent of the first separation, now taking the form of overt behavior reflecting the original ambivalence toward mother (which, earlier, was internalized and expressed itself as *self*-hatred). That repressed feelings are now being expressed toward the boy's mother is revealed in the fact that his rejective attitude and behavior toward her is disproportionate to her current provocations. His awareness of this fact often precipitates further feelings of self-hatred.

3. *Separation from his "first love,"* the girl or woman whom he idealized as the "answer" to all of his aspirations and dreams, the one for whom he would, if asked, make every conceivable sacrifice (family, career, etc.). These relationships are often terminated by the woman precisely because the male

becomes overly invested in them ("falls head over heels in love"), which "scares" her because she is not ready to "get serious," because she finds his adoration of her and/or his jealousy of other males "suffocating," or because she is frightened off by his excessive neediness and/or desperation. In turn, he is puzzled by her reluctance to commit herself to him, asking, "What more could she possibly want? After all, I'm prepared to give her everything. The sky's the limit." Or he may wonder why she cannot realize or understand that "we were made for each other," and, this being the case, how can she possibly say that she needs to remain unattached, or that she needs to have more life experiences before she makes a commitment? The desperation in his pursuit of her, his belief that there is no one but her (that, like his mother once was, she is "everything I ever wanted"), and the severity of the devastation and disillusionment that follows its termination suggest that it is reminiscent of the earlier separation. The same bitterness and internalized rage are likely to result from this new experience of perceived abandonment. This experience may also be the first clue to the fact that the melancholy self is a significant part of who he is. As the nineteenth-century poets were especially aware, a young man's melancholy self often surfaced as a reaction to a woman's rejection of his proposal of marriage, especially in cases where this rejection was voluntary (i.e., not because her father disapproved of the marriage).

4. *Separation from his family of origin at the time of his marriage*, which reactivates guilt feelings associated with his original separation from his mother. Because his wife tends to remain in more regular contact with her family, often through the mother-daughter relationship itself, he may feel a greater sense of being without a family, an "orphan," as it were. If the marriage produces children, and his wife serves as "gatekeeper" to the children (a common complaint of young husbands; see Vickers and Thomas 1996), he feels further isolated and alone, which, of course, adds fuel to the fire of a pre-existing melancholic temperament. The home that he thought was his becomes, as had the home of his childhood, a place where he is decidedly not "at home" (recall Pipher's example of the adolescent girl who assumes her father would be the one to move out). He may, of course, claim a certain part of the home, the basement or garage, as his domain, or insist that a particular chair belongs solely to him, but this merely testifies to the fact that he is a stranger in his own home.

5. *Separation from his mother on the occasion of her death*, which also reactivates ambivalent feelings (even if repressed) toward her, in addition to accumulated guilt if he has failed to live up to her actual or perceived expectations of him, or if he has neglected her, or both. He may feel more free and independent as a result of her death, but also uneasy about his longings for her, his nostalgia for what might have been, for what unfulfilled promises there were in their relationship.

6. *If he divorces*, his emotionality (or seeming lack thereof) is reminiscent of his emotionality in the original separation trauma. The two experiences are, in fact, remarkably similar, for in both cases—and unlike mourning the loss of a deceased person—the "lost object" is still "in the neighborhood." In this sense, divorce sheds important light on the earlier separation and should help to disabuse us of the assumption that the original separation is experienced by the boy as natural and nontraumatic. The divorced man may claim to celebrate his newfound independence, but he feels abandoned even if he was the one who initiated the divorce.

7. *The fatal illness and death of his wife* or life companion, which may reactivate the feelings of abandonment he felt as a small boy. Donald Hall captures these feelings with remarkable precision in a poem, "the Porcelain Couple" (Hall 1998, 10–14), written in the wake of the death of his wife, Jane Kenyon, from leukemia at the age of forty-eight. He recalls his need to "*do something*" for her "when there was exactly nothing to do," and attributes this anxiety to the fact that "Inside him, some four-year-old understood that if he was good—thoughtful, considerate, beyond reproach, *perfect*—she would not leave him" (13).

One could add additional separations, particularly from one's work due to job loss or retirement, as these relate to aspirations originally associated with his mother's actual or perceived expectations for him; and his anticipated death, which may be accompanied by premonitions of meeting his mother in the afterlife, or even of being summoned there by her. As Freud notes in his essay "The Theme of the Three Caskets" (originally published in 1913), she is "the silent goddess of Death," the Mother Earth who takes him into her arms at the end of life, effectively ending the old man's yearning "after the love of woman as once he had it from his mother" (Freud 1958b, 301).

While one or another of these separations may cause some men to develop clinical depression, I believe that all men develop a more chronic melancholia owing to having to become inured to separations at various life intervals reminiscent of the earliest one.

Pollack has an agenda, which is to rescue contemporary boys from the "code of honor" that gained widespread sociocultural support in the late nineteenth century and has lived on into the twenty-first century, and his discussion of emotional separation from the mother is directly related to this agenda, as he believes that this code of honor develops from the emotional separation itself (Pollack 1998, 23–25). This code of honor is also relevant to the argument that I will present in more detail later, that one form religion takes among males is the determination to be "good" or "moral," a person of honor, so that one may win back or continue to merit one's mother's love. In this regard, men tend to be less forgiving than women of other men's dishonorable actions. Witness, for example, the greater support that President

Clinton received from women than men during the impeachment trials, in spite of the fact that he took advantage of the power-differential between himself and women who worked in the White House (cf. Lebacqz and Barton 1991, 114–21, on power-differential and freedom of consent).

Mother as Object of Guilt

In *Man Enough*, Frank Pittman centers primarily on men's relations with other men, with particular attention given to father-son relationships and the importance of father-surrogacy among young males whose relations with their own fathers are negligible or nonexistent (according to Pittman, this comprises the overwhelming majority of boys in our society). However, he has a chapter on "Mother Love" (following a chapter on "Father Hunger") in which he argues that the son never forgets that he owes his life to his mother—not only its procreation but also its early maintenance—and that he therefore owes her a debt that he cannot conceivably repay but that she may call in at any time (Pittman 1993, 145).

He also notes that the strongest emotional pull on the male psyche is maternally induced guilt, which tends to pull the boy or adult male back to his mother, thus reversing the separation that she herself fostered (148). He adds that a depressed mother is the hardest for a son to leave, for he will desperately try to make her happy, and may throw everything else in his life overboard in the effort, ultimately hopeless, to cheer her up (151–52). Men know that the only way to confirm the self-confidence that their mothers nurtured in them is to cut the cord of dependency on their mothers, but sometimes mother will not let him go, while other times he cannot make himself go, with most men experiencing both (152–53). Leaving is easier if he can perform a "great deed" in her behalf, such as going to war (fighting for her and his motherland), succeeding in life, marrying a fine daughter-in-law (who does the things for her that he is not disposed to do himself), or providing grandchildren. A sign of a man's maturity is the realization that there is nothing he *can* do to repay her (which, not incidentally, sounds much like the theological language associated with Christ's atonement for our sins). If he comes to this realization, he won't have to run away from her, or feel guilty, or try to please her completely. He can be "nice to her" and allow her a place in his life (157).

Pittman also discusses what he calls "the war against mothers" and the specific issue of "mother bashing," suggesting that while patriarchy is the larger horizon against which these issues must be viewed, the more immediate cause is the perceived power of the mother over her son, since "she is always inside him ready to keep him from doing anything she wouldn't want him to do" (159). He suggests that "mother bashing" may also originate from his fear of her, especially if our mothers "have no life except us. We are able to forgive our mothers anything except loving us more than they love themselves" (161).

While Pittman does not say that all this is a prescription for the development of a melancholy self, he does discuss male depression, though not in the chapter on mother love. Rather, it occurs in a chapter on how men may become part of "the quiet, accepting company of men." While acknowledging that male depression may have various causes, including "chronic pain or daily alcohol use, or because of a devastating loss, or because of an inherited tendency toward it," the "most likely cause of a man's depression is his failure to be the man he thinks he should be, a situation that leaves him beating up on himself and distrusting the love" he receives from his wife or other female and male companions (218–19).

Notably, Pittman's list of the causes of male depression includes "a devastating loss" and a perceived personal failure leading to self-recrimination and the "distrusting" of the love he receives from others, most notably his wife. This combination of causes is reminiscent of the original loss of his mother and of the resulting conditions for the development of a melancholy self, especially his perception that *he* is the one who has failed. As we saw in the previous chapter, the young boy is unlikely to perceive that the separation has occurred because his mother believes that this is what needs to happen, or that his mother is simply being arbitrary or cruel. At least on the conscious level, he is more likely to hold himself to blame or find other plausible reasons for his mother's behavior, and any anger that he feels toward her for mistreating or abusing him is likely to be repressed. After all, in melancholia, his attack is against the internalized mother, not the "real mother" with whom he may continue to relate as if nothing has happened to mar their relationship. This itself suggests that his negative emotions toward her have been effectively repressed.

Why the Boy and the Man Need to Believe Their Mother Loves Them

One wonders, however, why the *adult* male continues to take personal responsibility or blame for a situation that is largely beyond his control? If this is understandable in the small boy, it becomes less understandable in the adult. Why, as Pittman puts it, does he "beat up on himself"? As we have seen, Freud believes that the melancholiac's self-reproaches are too excessive to be accepted at face value. The melancholic male wants to blame the "lost object" for his difficulties and problems, but he blames himself instead. Why is he so prone to beat up on *himself*? Could it be because ever since boyhood he has held to the belief or conviction that it would be worse—for one reason or another—to place the blame elsewhere? Were there secondary benefits to blaming himself that occurred between then and now, and does he continue to need these secondary benefits even in adulthood?

Neither Pollack nor Pittman addresses this issue. While Pollack explores the consequences of the emotional separation between the boy and his mother in the life of the adult male, he is very careful not to point an accusing finger at any mother—or mothers in general—for their role in effecting this emotional separation. While Pittman is not concerned with the original emotional separation itself, he does acknowledge the phenomenon of "mother bashing." He attributes this phenomenon, however, to the son's perception of his mother's power over him—as the internalized voice that prohibits him from "doing anything she wouldn't want him to do"—or his fear of her excessive love for him, which, as he says, is the one thing a son cannot forgive (because, in his view, she should love herself at least as much as she loves him). Neither Pollack nor Pittman considers the possibility that the boy's mother may harbor ill will toward her son, or that she would be capable of acting toward him with malice or hatred. Because they do not, neither do they consider the secondary benefits that the boy—and man—may realize from their acceptance of full responsibility for the emotional separation itself.

In Pollack's case, the reason he does not consider the possibility that a mother may harbor ill will—even have hateful feelings toward her son—seems to be that he thinks the mother's motivation for the emotional separation is solely because she is aware of the cultural belief that a boy needs to separate from his mother in order to develop a masculine identity, and that she implicitly endorses this belief. He wants to challenge this belief so he encourages mothers not to be so concerned to help their sons separate from them. As he puts it in his section on "Premature Separation—The Trauma of Boyhood":

In my clinical practice, I have found that deep in the psyche of older boys and men lies the formative experience of a little boy struggling to maintain an early independent masculine sense of self. That little boy is *not* fending off too close a tie to mother, but rather is forever longing to return to her, and to the "holding" connection she once provided him, a connection he now feels he can never regain. *If a boy had been allowed to separate at his own pace, that longing and sadness would not be there, or would be much less.* (Pollack 1998, 27, my emphasis)

By challenging the belief that there is a causal relationship between separating from mother and developing a relationship with the father and thereby realizing a masculine identity, Pollack gives mothers warrant for resisting this commonly held belief. While I agree with him on this point, I also believe that he minimizes the mother's own motivations for facilitating the separation, some of which are less pure and noble, less altruistic. Because he does so, Pollack does not provide the adult male any grounds for claiming the validity of his own anger toward his mother, and thus he closes one important means by which the adult male may begin to externalize his self-reproaches and thereby initiate some healing of his melancholy self.

Pittman's failure to recognize the mother's mistreatment of her son as a potential factor in the emotional separation has a different reason, one that enables us to identify the secondary benefits that accrue from the son's belief that he is solely responsible for the emotional separation. While Pittman recognizes that a man may resent his mother's continuing power over him as the internalized object who keeps him "from doing anything she wouldn't want him to do," he also suggests that a man's *fear* of his mother is especially rooted in the threat that her *love* poses for him, especially when she loves him more than she loves herself. Thus, Pittman does not entertain the possibility that a boy's or man's fear of his mother may be due to factors besides her excessive love for him. Fear of one's mother could be caused by any number of things besides the fact that her love might be excessive. For a man, these might be his mother's ability to sabotage his relationships with other women, her capacity to undermine his self-confidence, her ability to manipulate his feelings, and so forth. Pittman reflects a phenomenon that is very characteristic of men, which is that they cannot consider these other grounds for their fear of their mothers because they need to believe that their mothers' love toward them was total and unconditional. That their mothers may have had very different feelings toward them may undermine their compensating—and idealized—view of themselves as sons who were worthy of their mother's unflagging love. In this way, men gain an extremely important secondary benefit from blaming themselves for the original emotional separation from their mothers and from their tendency, even as adults, to view their mothers in highly idealized ways.

Among psychoanalytic thinkers—the group of psychologists who would be the most likely to probe more deeply for less altruistic motivations for parental actions—D. W. Winnicott has been perhaps the most willing to do such probing into mothers' behavior toward their little boys. He paints a more realistic, less idealistic picture of the mother's motivations toward her son. In his essay "Hate in the Countertransference," he makes the startling and certainly provocative observation that the mother not only loves but also "hates her infant from the word go. I believe Freud thought it possible that a mother may in certain circumstances have only love for her boy baby; but we may doubt this. We know about a mother's love and we appreciate its reality and power. [But] let me give some of the reasons why a mother hates her baby, even a boy" (Winnicott 1993, 22).

Eighteen reasons follow, two of which are especially relevant to the issue of the melancholy self. The first is that "if she fails him at the start, she knows he will pay her out for ever." The second is that "at first he does not know at all what she does or what she sacrifices for him. Especially he cannot allow for her hate" (22). Winnicott's conviction that the mother hates as well as loves her infant is arguably the basis for his well-known "good enough mother" concept, which is not (as many of his interpreters believe) so much about a mother's best efforts being good enough even if they fall somewhat short of the ideal, but more about the fact that a mother who hates her infant is "good enough" in spite of this (Winnicott 1971, 55).

If the first of these two reasons suggests that her hatred grows out of her perception that he will eventually make her pay for her real or perceived fail-ures with him, the second suggests that his own idealized self-perception requires that he believe she has only love and no corresponding hate for him. Thus, men have much to gain from *rejecting* Winnicott's view that their mothers also hated them. As Pittman notes, since the 1960s, mothers have mostly been blamed by their sons for the sons' failures in later life because "they loved their boys too much," and that their love was "toxic and crip-pling" (Pittman 1993, 158). The thought does not occur to men that their mothers may actually have resented, even hated, their little boys out of antici-pation that, when grown, their sons might one day attribute their own real or perceived failures in life to their mothers' real or perceived failures in raising them properly

On the other hand, mothers' hatred of their infants is not necessarily a negative thing. While she endorses Winnicott's view that mothers are ambiva-lent toward their children, believing that there is indeed an element of hatred (not merely the coldness and distance) in this ambivalence, Rozsika Parker contends in *Mother Love/Mother Hate: The Power of Maternal Ambivalence* that Winnicott vacillates between a cynical and a sentimentalized view of mothers, and this leads him to miss "the creative role of the mother's hatred in the development of maternal thinking. . . . The singing of sadistic lullabies illustrates not only a way of safely containing hatred, but also how the unbearable coexistence of love and hate for the baby continually pushes a mother into the creative act of seeking reparatory solutions" (Parker 1995, 63). Thus, when the baby projects his own hate onto the mother, "where it meets her own infantile hatred mobilized by adult frustrated needs and desires both to satisfy and be satisfied," at such times "a mother's love may be over-whelmed by persecutory anxiety, promoting an impulse to attack the perse-cuting baby, and stymying the reparatory process. It is at this point that, instead of acting on the impulse, the majority of mothers try to help by singing, rocking, soothing or feeding. The painful conflict of love and hate itself provokes the desire to know and answer the baby's needs" (63).

The question this raises, however, is whether the same "reparatory solu-tions" when her child is a baby seem as urgent or necessary when the separa-tion process itself is underway and the same societal sanctions against parental cruelty are relaxed precisely in order to foster the desired separation. I suggest that it is during the separation process (when the boy is three or four) that a mother may feel especially justified in treating her son in a cruel or malicious manner because she is able to rationalize that she is doing this for her son's own good. As we have seen, Pollack believes that boys are more subject than girls to physical assaults by both parents because they are believed to be "tough enough to take it." (Or, alternatively, they need to be "toughened up" so that they *will* be able "to take it." Thus, the beatings themselves have the very purpose of "toughening them up.") Physical assaults, however, are not the only way in which a mother may treat her small boy cruelly. Harsh words can be just as devastating when they are spoken by the boy's own mother. As Freud says, "Words and magic were in the beginning one and the same thing, and even today words retain much of their magical power. By words one of us can give to another the greatest happiness or bring about utter despair" (Freud 1952, 21–22). A mother's words have a special "magical" power to bless or to curse. So, too, her silence may be an inaudible curse.

Men as Unconventionally Religious

With this discussion of the traumatic effects of the original emotional separation as background, I now want to consider the relationship between the formation of the melancholy self and the ways in which men are religious. In my view, men's religiousness is directly related to, and largely explainable by, the theory of the origin of melancholia presented in the previous chapter and augmented in the foregoing discussion in this chapter.

   I am aware, of course, that, in comparison with women, men frequently claim that they are "not very religious." In fact, most women believe that females are more religious than males, and many clergypersons believe this too. Empirical research seems to bear them out. Michael Argyle and Benjamin Beit-Hallahmi surveyed the literature and concluded that "women are more religious on every criterion," including church membership and attendance and frequency of prayer (Argyle and Beit-Hallahmi 1975, 71). National polls inquiring into the church membership and/or attendance of men and women show that there are some ten million more women than men who are church members or who attend church in the United States. A recent survey by the Barna Research Group reported in *The Lutheran* (2000) indicates that 45 percent of women and 35 percent of men attend church once a week or more. While these are revealing statistics in their own right, they do not begin to measure the differences in the degree of personal investment in church-related activities and functions. Clergypersons attest that women are usually the "backbone" of their congregations, whereas men are either more indirectly supportive or nonexistent.

In her chapter "Ministers and Mothers" in *The Feminization of American Culture*, Ann Douglas argues that the church in the nineteenth century "was apparently a feminine preserve. There was a shared consensus among mid-nineteenth century clergymen, voiced most vehemently by the liberal ministry, that the Protestant congregations of America were becoming increasingly and preponderantly female" (Douglas 1988, 98). She notes, for example, that Sebastian Streeter, a Universalist minister, "could say with every evidence of stating a commonplace that 'Christian churches are composed of a great disproportion of females'—so much so that in certain quarters it had become a joke" (98). Henry Ward Beecher "seemed to find nothing depressing or unusual in the fact that his first church in Laurenceburg, Indiana, consisted of nineteen women and one man" (98). Writing for the *Andover Review* in 1890, Howard Allen Bridgeman, a liberal Congregationalist, asked, "Have we a religion for men?" and "after quipping that 'the women naturally gravitate to the prayer-meeting, and men as naturally to the penitentiary,' he expressed in a more serious vein his dismay that his gospel appeared 'limited by sex distinctions'" (98).

Citing evidence that the ratio of female to male church members in the eighteenth and seventeenth centuries also favored women (roughly 70–80 percent), Douglas concludes that

> we have reason to assume that the nineteenth-century liberal ministers moaning over their largely feminine flocks as a signal and new disaster are telling us as much about their own anxieties as about any actual statistical developments. What is clear is that they felt increasingly dominated by their women members who had in the proliferating [women's] "societies" new arenas of activity available to them in the church; the ministers also perhaps felt increasingly drawn to their feminine congregation, and an issue of power or of attraction which was decidedly present became confused with an issue of numerical change which may or may not have been valid. (99)

If women were so predominant in the churches, why were men attracted to the ministry? Douglas notes that a significant number of these ministers "had been delicate, even homebound little boys," and that "ministers often exalted the maternal impulse because it had been a large force in their own lives" (99). Theodore Cuyler, a New York Presbyterian clergyman, wrote in his autobiography that "there is a ministry that is older and deeper and more potent than ours. It is the ministry that presides over the crib and impresses the first gospel influence on the infant soul" (100). In innumerable cases, "contemporaries stressed that a given minister had not only been influenced by his mother, but had inherited almost exclusively her temperament and her looks; they almost imply that his father had no share in his conception or for-mation" (100). This perception may have been indirectly (subliminally?) influenced by the belief that Jesus was born of a virgin, and by nativity paint-ings depicting Joseph as a very shadowy figure in the background.

In *Secret Ritual and Manhood in Victorian America*, Mark C. Carnes points out that men's fraternal orders (Freemasons, Knights of Pythias, Good Templars, etc.) in the late nineteenth century were designed as an alternative to the churches. Their meetings were held on Wednesday evenings, which directly coincided—and conflicted—with the churches' midweek prayer meetings. Men were forbidden to inform their wives and sisters about what went on at lodge meetings. Carnes argues that the men were not primarily attracted to these lodges because they were a means of achieving higher social standing or developing business connections, as most social scientific analy-ses of the orders have contended. Rather, they were attracted by the rituals that were provided. This is evident from the fact that if an order or lodge experienced a loss of membership, it would immediately reevaluate its ritual and revise it in order to recapture its lapsed members. In addition, higher levels of what might be called spiritual attainment were added, enabling men to aspire to higher and higher levels of initiation (called "degrees") into the "mysteries" of the cult.

Carnes provides a vivid account of an initiation rite in which men were led blindfolded into the darkened meeting hall to a coffin with the skeletal remains of a human male. The blindfold was then lifted and the leader bid the men to "contemplate the scene! Should it not humble human pride? Should it not awake the soul to a just sense of its responsibility to its God—of duty to itself?" He then spoke of the need to purify one's heart—"the foun-tain of all wrong"—for otherwise hatred, crime, and war would continue to afflict mankind (Carnes 1989, 21). A torchbearer, dressed in white, then began to describe the rose which, beautiful in the morning, fades in the after-noon, "its loveliness vanished away." So it was with man, he noted, who rejoices in his youthful beauty and power only to have the breath of life even-tually wither away: "Death is in the world and all that is born must die" (21). Carnes's emphasis on the role played by ritual in men's fraternal orders at the very time clergymen were bemoaning the fact that their congregations were overwhelmingly female indicates that it is much too facile to use church membership and attendance as a gauge of male religiousness.

This also means, however, that the emotional separation from mother cre-ates a kind of religious disposition in men that even the men themselves may not recognize as being religious, for they are accustomed to thinking of "being religious" in terms of church membership and attendance (i.e., more the way that women view "being religious"). I do not dispute the fact that many men *are* religious in this more conventional way, but I believe that the primary religious reason for men turning to "church religion" is in order to find compensation or a substitute for the "lost object," the mother from whom they were emotionally separated in early childhood. The question is whether the religion that they officially endorse is able to help them come to terms with their melancholy self. An even more important question, however, is whether the ways in which men *are* religious—quite apart from their endorsement or nonendorsement of an official religion—contribute to the healing of their melancholic condition. In order to answer this question, we need first to identify the essential features of men's basic religiousness (i.e., the religiousness that evolves out of the emotional separation they experience from their mothers in early childhood). I suggest that there are three primary aspects of men's basic religiousness. To set the stage for discussion of them, I want to return to Freud's point that, in melancholia, it is the internalized object that has become the instigation for self-reproach. Two early essays by Erikson have particular bearing on this point.

Male Religion and the Internalized Mother

One response I frequently receive when I present my argument that male melancholia has its origins in a boy's experience of maternal abandonment is this: "All this might apply to other men, but it does not apply to me. My relationship with my mother has been wonderful. She has been overwhelmingly supportive of me. In fact, we are great personal friends." Many men have said this to me, and when they have done so, I have often encouraged them to express their gratitude to their mothers for this, for it is frequently the best mothers who have the greatest self-doubt about the way they raised their sons. These mothers may, in fact, be so preoccupied with the "mistakes" they may have made that they fail to appreciate how good they really were as mothers. Thus, I do not for a moment question that such mother-son relationships exist, and it is certainly not my purpose here to challenge the truth of these claims. In formulating his theory of melancholia, however, Freud assumed the "power of the unconscious." Therefore, the mother who is internalized and then attacked, leading to the excessive self-reproach that Freud witnessed in melancholic patients, has been relegated, as it were, to the boy's unconscious. This "mother" may be very different from the real-life mother. In effect, this internalized mother is the one the boy experienced before the emotional separation occurred. She was the mother who, in his mind, had nothing but loving feelings toward him. Having now been disabused of this belief, however, he experiences her instead as a kind of fallen angel, as no longer the purely loving mother he had originally believed her to be. His primary grievance is not against the real-life mother but the mother who has been internalized, the mother who has become a partial stranger to him, who, at best, plays "hide and seek" with him and, at worst,. is bent on his destruction.

C. G. Jung writes in his autobiography, *Memories, Dreams, Reflections,* that sometime prior to his going to school, "the nocturnal atmosphere [in his home] began to thicken. All sorts of things were happening at night, things incomprehensible and alarming" (Jung 1961, 18). He explains that his parents were sleeping apart and that he slept in his father's room: "From the door to my mother's room came frightening influences. At night Mother was strange and mysterious. One night I saw coming from her door a faintly luminous, indefinite figure whose head detached itself from the neck and floated along in front of it, in the air, like a little moon. Immediately another head was produced and again detached itself. This process was repeated six or seven times" (18). These hallucinations may have been prompted by anxieties relating to the fact that his mother had been away in a hospital in Basel, her illness presumably having "something to do with the difficulty in the marriage" (8). He notes that he "was deeply troubled by my mother's being away. From then on, I always felt mistrustful when the word 'love' was spoken. The feeling I associated with 'woman' was for a long time that of innate unreliability. 'Father,' on the other hand, meant reliability and—powerlessness. This was the handicap I started off with" (8). The handicap, we might say, of melancholia.

I cite this illustration here in support of the idea that the small boy has internalized a "mother" who certainly bears a resemblance to the real-life mother but who is also "strange and mysterious," a source of deep anxieties. A child's interest in stories involving witches and vicious stepmothers may be due to his having internalized this mother. The threat these witches and evil stepmothers pose and their eventual defeat enables him to work through some of the anxieties this internalized mother engenders in him. In *Toys and Reasons*, Erikson gives the title, "Play Age and the Dramatic: The Act and the Image," to his discussion of the third stage (age 3–5) of the life cycle. He notes that "the play themes of this age often prove to be dominated by the usurpation and ambitious impersonation of victorious self-images and the killing off of weak and evil 'others'" (Erikson 1977, 100). He adds that "there is always the interplay of the child's imagination with the ritualized fantasy world offered in picture books and in fairy tales, in myths and in parables, which counterpose the best and the worst in human images" (101).

On the basis of what we popularly know about Freud's Oedipus complex theory, we might assume that the small boy's desire to kill off these "weak and evil others" applies only to the father, toward whom he is supposed to feel deep hostility. We should not assume, however, the absence of such desires toward the mother, especially when she punishes, shuns, or otherwise fails to give him the attention he seeks from her. This being the case, there is the additional anxiety that she, in her omniscience, will discern these malevolent thoughts and retaliatory desires and avenge herself against the boy for harboring them.

In an early essay on "Psychoanalysis and the Future of Education" (originally published in 1930), Erikson notes that picture books and fairy tales, however useful they may be in helping the boy express and thereby externalize his hostile thoughts and feelings toward the internalized mother, will eventually fall short. Moreover, the psychoanalytic recommendation of "sexual enlightenment" as the best approach for teachers to take with children does not really solve anything, for then the enlightenment itself becomes "a fairy tale for the affects of the child, just as the story of the stork remains a fairy tale for his intellect" (Erikson 1987c, 23–24). Thus, modern teachers who

forsake the symbol-filled darkness of ancient tales which combined so attractively the uncanny and the familiar [have] no reason to be optimistic, for while replacing them with more logical interpretations expressing some facts more directly and clearly, they neglect to include even vaguely much that is more fundamentally important. *Neither fairy tale nor sexual enlightenment saves the child from the necessity of a distrustful and derisive attitude toward adults, since in both cases he is left alone with his conflict.* (23–24, my emphasis)

The boy's distrust is due, in part, to the fact that as far as his mother is concerned he can never feel safe or secure: "Only yesterday he forsook his mother's arms and his possessive share of her body. Today he has a respite in which to accustom himself to his loss, but tomorrow, so he feels, something quite new and different and dangerous will present itself" (23). As a psychoanalyst, Erikson is aware that this anxiety may be entirely unconscious. After all, a trauma as serious as the boy's emotional separation from his mother can only be coped with if many of the feelings associated with it are repressed, or denied from consciousness. A self-assured exterior, one in which the boy relates to his mother as though he has nothing to fear from her, masks the very different feelings he harbors toward her that, however, have been forced underground.

The fear of his mother is likely to be associated with experiences in which she was angry with him, and most small boys will therefore do what they can to avoid making their mothers angry (unless this is the only way they can get her to pay attention to them at all). The Swedish psychophysiologist Arne Öhman reports (1986) on a study that he and his associates conducted in which three groups of subjects were exposed to pictures of faces posing expressions of anger, happiness, and a neutral emotion. They found that the angry faces showed much more resistance to extinction—that is, they remained in the subject's mind much longer—than either the happy or the neutral expressions. If the picture depicted the person directing her anger away from the subject, the subject's response was similar to his response to the happy faces. It was only when the anger was directed toward the viewing subject that the angry face was more resistant to extinction. We may conclude from this that, while a boy's relationship to his mother may be a very positive one, he nonetheless internalizes an image of her as angry with him. To forestall the reemergence of this angry or threatening mother, he tries not to misbehave, not only in her actual company, but also elsewhere, as he believes in her omniscience and therefore deems risky, even futile, the effort to get away with even small misdemeanors.

In another early essay, "Children's Picture Books" (originally published in 1931), Erikson discusses "a number of highly diverse picture books" reviewed during the Montessori seminar in which he (a candidate for certification as a Montessori-approved teacher) participated. He suggests that children's picture books perform another function besides that of enabling children to express their "distrustful and derisive attitude toward adults." This is that some picture books, often deemed "sadistic" by teachers and parents, enable the small child to experience vicariously the punishment of the fictitious child in the story. He cites the Struwelpeter stories, which present "not only scenes in which a creature (or creature identifiable with the child reader) is tormented but also some in which a child is punished" (Erikson 1987a, 32). Assuming that the child identifies with the hero in the story, Erikson concludes that "the children reading this book feel punished when Struwelpeter is punished, and we know how lasting such an impact can be, and how unforgettable the perverse enjoyment. Even terrified children return to this book" (32).

Erikson asks, Why do children feel joy and comfort at seeing themselves depicted as being punished? He suggests that the very young infant "delights in himself and in the growing radius of [his] movements and impulses" (33). He is therefore "used to having the big people (the powerful adults on whose love he depends) applaud his behavior." This continues "until he reaches an age at which he can be educated. Now, when he comes out with his most genuine and favorite behavior, adults more and more often state emphatically, 'You mustn't do that. We won't love you when you're like that'" (33). Thus, the child learns that certain actions are not genuinely lovable, and "he has to find some way of maintaining his old self-love (which is necessary for human survival) while also keeping the love of adults, which he needs just as badly" (33).

The "solution" is that the "child condemns some of his impulses on his own; by some enigmatic mechanism, he internally develops an authority that appropriates and represents the prohibitions of adults" (33). The child "likes himself now insofar as he, like the adult, has learned to watch over his thoughts and deeds. Thus he develops an often puzzling mechanism deciding what is 'good, well-behaved,' and he enjoys picture books in which good children are rewarded and bad ones punished" (33). The advantage of this mechanism of "conscience formation" is that the child "catches up in a short time with thousands of years of upbringing" (34). The negative side is that it is achieved at the price of the child's "inner unity," as there is "a split in his mental makeup. Under the pressure of the alternative—forgoing love and protection—between remaining what *he* is or becoming like the adult in order to please *him*, the child undergoes a transformation in [his] psyche. An inner voice arises, taking over the prohibitions of the adult milieu and making sure that the child's instinctual energy is tamed and, wherever necessary, punished for unruliness" (34).

If adults accept this "solution" without further ado, saying, "A normal child doesn't suffer all that much from this process," Erikson disagrees, noting that this inner authority becomes so dictatorial that parents "find themselves unable to cope with their overconscientious child." They would gladly erase, modify, or revoke their earlier prohibitions in order to reawaken the child who delighted in himself, but "their earlier image in the child's mind is stronger than their living voice" (35). The image of mother that he has now internalized has become an integral part of the boy's conscience, or superego, and he experiences this image as stronger than the real life mother, who wishes that he would "lighten up," exhibit his former spontaneity, and not take life quite so seriously.

Erikson suggests that another dynamic also occurs at this time, which is that the "cruel and deadly hatred that the small infant once aimed at the overpowerful adults is internalized in the course of his capitulation, and since the child must despair of any resistance, his hatred is turned against his own flagging inner world" (35). Erikson calls this a "self-directed sadism of the soul" (35). This is the emotional basis for the satisfaction he derives from his vicarious experience of the punishment of the child in the picture books.

In short, Erikson's essay on children's picture books identifies two important processes relevant to our interest in the internalization of the boy's mother. One is that the internalized image, because it is associated with the development of his conscience, may be a much more punitive mother than his real-life mother. The real-life mother may counteract this internalized image with assurances of her love and protection, but such efforts can only be partially successful. In addition, as Parker makes clear, the boy's real-life mother is struggling with ambivalent feelings of her own. She may therefore resent the fact that such reassurances are necessary, or even, in angry moments, give her son further grounds for entertaining his internalized image of her. The other dynamic is that he turns against himself the hatred he once felt toward her, and this hatred "rages inwardly," continuing to "harm us in a thousand possibilities of obvious or concealed self-punishment and self-degradation, illness and inhibition" (Erikson 1987a, 35). Even if this is "not visible in flagrant symptoms, it is at least sensed in what Freud calls the 'discontent of civilization'; a malaise shared by us all" (35).

Erikson obviously believes that these two dynamics continue into adulthood. The very fact that these picture books are produced by adults indicates that they, as children, went through the processes represented by these two dynamics and then "forgot what had happened" (33). Then, years later, "the adult (impelled by some urgent memory) feels the desire to draw a picture book for the child" (34). By viewing the book as written and drawn for educational purposes, the adult is able to revisit that period in his life when he experienced "a split in his mental makeup" (34). While few of us adults write and draw books for children, Erikson's view that these adults "forgot what had happened" applies to us all, and a healthy relationship with one's mother in later childhood, adolescence, and adulthood may actually contribute to this forgetting. As a result, such a man, who is to all appearances a well-adjusted person, may have greater difficulty recognizing the melancholic condition that flows, like an underground stream, throughout the course of his life. The foregoing discussions of Erikson's two essays have particular bearing on the first two forms of male religiousness.

The Formation of a Boy's Conscience: Toward a Religion of Honor

The first aspect of men's basic religiousness is the important role that melancholy plays in the formation of a boy's conscience. To the extent that he believes the separation from his mother is his fault—due to something that he said or did—he will believe that the way to regain the "lost object" is to be "a good boy," or "a better boy." The separation has taught him that his mother's love is a conditional one, and he will therefore try to win it—and her—back by being a good boy, one in whom she may take pride, one who, for example, is kind to his brothers and sisters, treats adults with respect, does not lie or cheat, and so on. The fact that men are more likely than women to have a moral—if not moralistic—view of what it means to be religious may be traced to this response to the emotional separation. When asked what it means to be religious, men are much more likely than women to emphasize keeping the Ten Commandments, obeying the law, and doing what's right. Women, on the other hand, are more likely to emphasize the "graceful," "meditational," "spiritual," and "empowering" aspects and themes of religion. The boy's—and man's—religion and code of honor are sometimes so closely related as to be indistinguishable from one another.

The boy's efforts to be "good" are likely to confirm the mother's belief that the emotional separation is having its desired effect. The fact that he is becoming good also supports her view that he was ready to become more independent of her, that he is able to be good on his own initiative. What she may not comprehend, however, is that this reverses cause and effect. He has become good not only or even primarily because he wants to prove that his independence is warranted, but in order to win her back. The paradox in this is that his efforts are therefore counterproductive. It is the "bad" boy who is more likely to receive her attention, and this may help to explain why some little boys persist in the same misbehaviors (and why punishment does *not* have its desired effect), as this is a way, admittedly a rather perverse one, for the boy to remain connected with his mother.

Thus, the religiousness of men is manifest in moral rectitude for which one is inadequately compensated. Resentment of less morally responsible men may result. If this resentment is inadequately understood and not worked through, it may even provoke a man to engage in immoral behavior that others judge to be out of character for him and reprehensible for a man of his professional and/or social standing.

Religion as Personal Quest: Toward a Religion of Hope

The second aspect of men's basic religiousness is that if men are more likely than women to view religion in moral terms, they are also much more likely to consider religion as a personal quest. This is because they may seek in religion a substitute or compensation for the "lost object," their mother. The psychologist of religion C. Daniel Batson has criticized Gordon W. Allport's view that there are essentially two ways in which individuals are religious: *extrinsic* (where religion serves instrumental goals) and *intrinsic* (where religion is an end in itself). Batson argues for a third religious orientation, which he calls religion as *quest*, and suggests that its primary characteristics are tentativeness, doubt, and complexity. In support of his view that there is a third way of being religious, he draws on Allport's own claim in *The Individual and His Religion* that "the mature religious sentiment is ordinarily fashioned in the workshop of doubt" (Allport 1950, 73). In *The Religious Experience*, he and his coauthor, W. Larry Ventis, quote Walter Houston Clark's summary of Allport's concept of mature religion: "Maturity requires an admixture of humility and makes it possible for the true believer to absorb new points of view into his truth system and so to make his religious progress a genuine quest" (Batson and Ventis 1982, 149). They also cite Peter Bertocci's view of religion as "creative insecurity," and his observation that "to flee from insecurity is to miss the whole point of being human, the whole point of religion" (150).

While Batson has not, to my knowledge, tested to see whether men are more likely than women to be "questers," the theory of the melancholy self that I am presenting here suggests that men do have greater reason to be questers. Having experienced the emotional loss of their mothers in early childhood, they are more likely than women to feel that there is something that they have lost. If they do not seek the lost mother herself, they quest after someone or something that will take her place. For Don Quixote, this becomes a quest for Dulcinea, the ideal woman who is the one who inspires his heroic exploits; when he actually meets "her"—in the guise of a peasant woman who eats garlic—he is so disillusioned that he returns home, repents of his sins, and dies. Another example is the cult of the Virgin Mary. In his book on the subject, Michael P. Carroll argues, "Fervent devotion to the Mary cult on the part of males is a practice that allows males characterized by a strong but strongly repressed sexual desire for the mother to dissipate in an acceptable manner the excess sexual energy that is built up as a result of this desire." In his view, "The distinctive features of the Mary cult over the centuries have been shaped primarily by the son's strong but strongly repressed desire for his mother" (Carroll 1986, 56).

We might assume that Protestantism, with its tendency to diminish the significance of the Virgin Mary, emphasizing instead the sole mediatorship of Jesus Christ, provides no outlet for this "strongly repressed desire for the mother." However, in *Young Man Luther*, Erikson argues that, while Luther had extremely negative—even vitriolic—things to say about the Virgin Mary, the Scriptures became for him a symbolic mother. In his discussion of Luther's view that rebirth occurs through prayer and that rebirth by prayer is passive, Erikson notes that this passivity "means surrender to God the Father; but it also means to be reborn *ex matrice scripturae noti*, out of the matrix of the scriptures" (Erikson 1958, 208). Erikson adds:

> "Matrix" is as close as such a man's man will come to saying "mater." But he cannot remember and will not acknowledge that long before he had developed those wilful modes which were specifically suppressed and paradoxically aggravated by a challenging father, a mother had taught him to touch the world with his searching mouth and his probing senses. What to a man's man, in the course of his development, seems like a passivity hard to acquire, is only a regained ability to be active with his oldest and most neglected modes. Is it coincidence that Luther, now that he was explicitly teaching passivity, should come to the conclusion that a lecturer should feed his audience as a mother suckles her child? Intrinsic to the kind of passivity we speak of is not only the memory of having been given, but also the identification with the maternal giver: "the glory of a good thing is that it flows out to others." (208)

Erikson concludes that "in the Bible Luther at last found a mother whom he could acknowledge: he could attribute to the Bible a generosity to which he could open himself, and which he could pass on to others, at last a mother's son" (208). Thus, the quest for the "lost object" in religion was no less a concern for Luther than for those men who embraced the cult of the Virgin Mary. In fact, one might argue that it was even more intense, in that his promotion of the doctrine of *sola scriptura* emerged out of his disillusionment with the Virgin Mary and other maternal saints.

As these examples show, a man may find in religion itself compensations for the original lost object. Alternatively, his investment in objects in the real (i.e., not "spiritual" or "symbolic") world may take the form of a quasi-religious devotion. He may, for example, idealize (even idolize) a particular woman—"worshiping the ground on which she walks"—or something else that substitutes or compensates for the lost mother. A representation of his mother—such as a picture or other physical object reminiscent of her—may serve as a quasi-religious icon.

In his biography of Erikson, Lawrence J. Friedman tells about his own efforts to discover the true identity of Erikson's natural father. After an extended visit with Erikson's relatives in Copenhagen, Friedman returned to the United States with a detailed family tree extending from the eighteenth century, a photograph of Erikson's mother as a young woman, and information on two potential fathers (both Danish photographers). To Friedman's dismay, however, "the detailed family tree was of little interest [to the ninety-year-old Erikson]. Likewise, the identities of two prospective fathers (both named Erik) meant little to this Erik, who, as a young man, had changed his last name to Erikson. At this point, I realized that his lifelong quest to discover the identity of his father would remain unfulfilled" (Friedman 1999, 19).

Although disappointed that Erikson exhibited little interest in the information he provided on the two potential fathers, Friedman was heartened by the interest Erikson took in the photograph of his mother: "But all was not lost. Erikson picked up the photograph of his young mother, Karla Abrahamsen, and gazed at her for many minutes. 'What a beauty,' he remarked. Although he was very frail and nearly immobile, his eyes had come alive. A smile crossed his face. Erikson was enjoying himself amid the flow of memories of his Danish mother" (19).

Note that Friedman uses the language of "quest" to describe Erikson's desire to learn the identity of his natural father. Yet what clearly held deep, emotional appeal for him was the photograph of his mother. Studying her picture, his eyes came alive, a smile crossed his face, and, most notably of all, he was "enjoying *himself*." By viewing *her* picture, *he* came alive. He invested her picture with a virtually religious devotion that made the question of the identity of his father seem almost mundane, an interesting puzzle, perhaps, but not nearly as emotionally charged as the photograph of his mother.

By viewing "quest religion" as an expression of the melancholy self, we are able to account for its basic characteristics while also challenging the idea that it is a "mature" form of religion. As Batson notes, the primary characteristics of quest religion are tentativeness, doubt, and complexity. We may ask why anyone would prefer to be religious in this particular way. Would we not expect, in fact, that where religion especially is concerned, one would prefer a faith that is not tentative but certain, not oriented toward doubt but belief, and not complicated but simple and straightforward? After all, tentativeness, doubtfulness, and complexity are the very qualities that, in other areas of life, a man is likely to be criticized for, since this usually leads him to be indecisive, and an indecisive man is considered weak, unreliable, and even cowardly. Why, in the area of religion, would a man (like Batson himself) extol these qualities as virtues? The fact that a man's religiousness is rooted in his melancholy self provides an answer. The boy's experience of separation from his mother leaves him in a quandary. Why has she turned against me? Was it because I misbehaved? If so, why doesn't my sister's misbehavior have the same effect? Why is my younger brother allowed to say and do the same things that I have said and done and, instead of being punished for this, he is viewed as clever or entertaining? If, in order to be reclaimed by his mother, the boy resolves to be good and demonstrates his goodness, why does the emotional separation remain? The situation as he experiences it creates a climate in which tentativeness, doubt, and complexity are especially likely to manifest themselves.

Of course, I do not assume that the small boy has the cognitive structure necessary to articulate this quandary as specifically as I have represented here. The point, however, is that the emotional separation from his mother *does* leave him in a quandary. Thus, we should not be surprised that his religion— having been formed out of this emotional separation—assumes a questlike quality, even if in other areas of his life he becomes decisive, sure of himself, and fully capable of boiling complicated issues down to their essentials. This may also help to explain why men do not trust their feelings, and why they tend to hold psychology—the study of the human psyche—at arm's length, often considering it to be "a woman's profession."

Given its roots in early childhood, there is something rather incongruous about Batson's claim, following Allport, that quest religion reflects a higher level of maturity. This very claim enables the claimant to ignore the immature roots of quest religion (i.e., in the emotional separation from the mother in early childhood). Bertocci's view of religion as "creative insecurity" captures its immature roots, but his intention is clearly to claim that acceptance of this insecurity is also a mark of maturity. These claims indicate how profoundly the emotional separation from one's mother has influenced men's views of religion, of how religion needs to be understood. Few women talk this way when they describe what religion is—or means—to them. Few women would suggest that the most mature form of religion is one that manifests itself in tentativeness and doubt. They would speak, instead, about certitude and belief (or "knowing"), and would likely extol "commitment" over "complexity."

In focusing on men's religion as quest, however, I am especially interested in the fact that religion offers an alternative (i.e., symbolic) means of expressing and entertaining desires that were formerly invested in the boy's mother, and these desires are reflected in men's tendency, as James E. Dittes puts it, to be "driven by hope," the title of his 1996 book on men and their search for meaning. In a personal conversation, he told me that his working title, considered too negative by his editors, was "afflicted by hope," which makes the point ever stronger. If, however, the religion of hope provides a means of expressing repressed desires, the religion of honor should provide a means to express hostility and rage to counter the "self-directed sadism of the soul."

Christianity has traditionally offered the mother of Jesus as such a symbolic alternative. In her idealized form, the Virgin Mary provides compensation for the mother the boy knew before the emotional separation. This image does not, however, afford the boy or man the opportunity to work through his sense of having been abandoned by his mother, nor does it counter the internalization of this abandoning mother whom he then attacks in the form of excessive self-reproach. If religion is to serve as compensation and consolation for the loss he has experienced—if it is to be truly reparative—it needs to do more than assuage his longings and yearnings. It needs also to enable him to project his internalized self-hatred onto a symbolically ambivalent mother, against whom he is given license to hurl the kinds of curses and invectives that primitive religions manifest but Christianity (in its claim to be a "higher" religion) disallows. Put another way, the Western Christian male has nothing comparable to the Hindu goddess Kali—that bloodthirsty goddess who hates her children—onto whom he can externalize his anger and rage for having been abandoned by his natural mother. He has only a highly idealized Virgin Mother who is without sin and harbors no evil thoughts (see Kristeva 1987a, 42–43; and 1987b, 234–63).[1]

In *Psychology of Religion: Classic and Contemporary*, David M. Wulff discusses the figure of Kali in his chapter on "The Mother in Religious Faith and Tradition" under the heading of "The Terrible Mother." Here is how he describes her:

A dark, naked, and full-breasted figure with flowing, disheveled hair, a garland of human heads around her neck, and a girdle of severed hands about her waist, Kali is depicted dancing victoriously on the body of Shiva, her consort, who lies prostrate in the middle of the cremation grounds. In one hand she bears a bloody sword and in another, the

freshly severed head of a man; with still another hand, in startling contrast, she offers an expression of assurance, and with a fourth the gesture
of benediction or the bestowing of boons. Blood courses down her
cheeks, framing an open, smiling mouth with protruding tongue and
powerful, fanglike teeth. In some representations she wears as earrings
yet another set of heads—or the corpses of dead infants. Today young
male goats are still sacrificed daily, by decapitation, before this terrify-
ing image. Earlier she was thought to require human victims, a conviction not unknown even in our own day. (Wulff 1997, 326)

Wulff views Kali as an especially terrible manifestation of a variety of
mother-goddesses found throughout the world who are portrayed as highly
ambivalent figures, for "the being who gives birth and lovingly sustains life
also proves to be the one who devours and destroys" (326). He discusses various psychoanalytic theories regarding this "terrible mother," noting, for
example, that in the representations of Kali, the father is eradicated:

The mother herself kills him, sometimes by beheading. Her malevolent arms, it would thus seem, are reserved for the father, whom she
strikes down in dramatic fulfillment of the son's wishes or in agreement
with the young boy's apprehension of cruelty in the act of intercourse.
In contrast, with her benign arms she invites her adoring but horrified
son to approach her, promising him blissful fulfillment of his deepest
wishes. (327)

In this sense, she may be viewed as the son's ally against the threat that his
father poses.
    Wulff also presents a brief biographical sketch of Ramakrishna, the Bengali
mystic, whose experience of Kali was more benign than Wulff's portrayal of her.
Yet, throughout his life Ramakrishna experienced her as one who played "the
game of hide-and-seek" with him, thus "intensifying both his suffering and his
joy" (235). Wulff also mentions the psychoanalytic view that Kali "might be
interpreted as a complex and ambivalent condensation of the wishes, fears, and
defensive maneuvers associated with the castration complex" (327).
    As Wulff shows, Kali lends herself to various Oedipal and pre-Oedipal
interpretations. The important point for our purposes here, however, is that
she enables her male devotee to externalize his anger or rage toward his own
mother for her abandonment of him in early childhood. The Western male
does not have a similar symbolic representation of "the Terrible Mother." The
only Divine Mother, the Virgin Mary, is portrayed as all-loving, all-beneficient,
as the giver of life but not the agent of death. Thus, the Christian religion, while
certainly less "primitive" than Hinduism's Kali cult, lacks a symbolic outlet for

the rage that is also—alongside the sorrow and need for consolation—a central feature of the male melancholy self.

There are, of course, consequences here for Christian women as well, as I hardly need to point out. As Freud suggests in his essay on mourning and melancholia, one way that melancholia comes to an end is when a man, typically in a manic act, "triumphs" over the internalized lost object. He also points out in "The Theme of the Three Caskets" that a man's beloved is often chosen "after the mother's pattern" (Freud 1958b, 75). To what extent, then, is the battered woman the victim of the convergence of these two phenomena? The unsuspecting wife or lover may not realize until it is too late that her man means to settle a score against his internalized lost object. If Rozsika Parker finds that singing "sadistic lullabies" enables the mother to resist the impulse to attack her persecuting baby, would some Christian equivalent to the goddess Kali enable men to engage in symbolic "mother bashing" so that they may exorcise their own self-hatred and view their beloved with eyes of unalloyed longing? A religion that helps to soothe men's melancholy longing, but turns a deaf ear to their melancholy rage, seems to offer only half a loaf.

Is half a loaf better than none? While the answer to this question might appear to be yes, this very question ironically recalls and recapitulates the original trauma of separation. So it should not surprise us if there are men who answer it with a sad but honorable no. If, as Ann Douglas argues, nineteenth-century ministers offered a gospel that was viewed as analogous to maternal care, could it be that men, even then, experienced this gospel as a half truth in that it failed to take account of their internalized rage against their mothers?

This gospel also minimizes what Parker calls "the power of maternal ambivalence" in mother-child relationships. As she points out, "The deepest roots of maternal guilt feelings lie in the experience and handling of ambivalence—in the way we both love and hate our children" (Parker 1995, 4). Yet when she, as a psychotherapist, interprets "a mother's feelings of hatred towards her child," she finds that the typical mother responds defensively or uncomprehendingly: "She more often than not will feel criticized or simply perplexed. Consciously she does not hate her child. And, indeed, both love and hate are rooted in the unconscious, but love has, so to speak, greater access to the light" (5). Parker suggests that the unacceptability of hatred and acknowledgment that one is capable of it has led to the misuse of the word *ambivalence* itself. To suggest that it merely has to do with "mixed feelings" distorts "the concept developed by psychoanalysis according to which quite contradictory impulses and emotions towards the same person co-exist. The positive and negative components sit side by side and remain in opposition" (5–6).

Parker's book was written for women, and her use of psychoanalytic ideas was intended, in part, to show that, due to the power of the unconscious, psychoanalysis helps us to see "how limited our control is over the impact we have on our children." Instead of a potential source of reproach for mother, psychoanalysis may therefore provide "a possible release from the omnipotent burden of getting it right" (xi–xii).

The Importance of Humor: Toward a Third Way of Being Religious

In the essay on children's picture books discussed earlier, Erikson comments briefly on another genre of picture books discussed in the Montessori seminar, one in which humor was the dominant feature. While these were picture books, Erikson notes that they were not aimed exclusively at children, for "their mature humor addresses any receptive human being" (31). He cites a character named Adamson and centers specifically on a picture "the appeal of which to children is well known to you all" (36). Adamson wants to smoke his cigar, but his better self (identifiable by its angel wings), who is standing behind him, takes the cigar from his mouth and throws it out the window: "For a moment the Adamson self is stunned, but then it races downstairs and catches the cigar before it has reached the ground. Rebellion has acted faster than conscience and the force of gravity. Immoral? Yet the most conscientious person laughs" (36).

Erikson quotes Freud's essay on humor (originally published in 1928, two years before Erikson gave his paper at the House of Children in Vienna) to explain what has happened here. Freud notes, "The wonderful thing [about humor] is obviously the victoriously defended invulnerability of the ego. The ego refuses to be offended and forced to suffer by any provocation in reality. It insists on not letting the traumas of the outer world get too close for comfort; indeed, it shows that they are merely an occasion for pleasure" (quoted in Erikson 1987a, 36).

While the Adamson character is an adult, he is "a childlike figure; he has a big hat, like a child acting grownup; he is always alone; he has no manly adventures. And his adversaries, human beings ('the big man'), are all taller than he is to the same degree that an adult is taller than a child" (36). Erikson asks, "How does humor speak through the depiction of this sly, struggling ego? It confronts the nasty superego with a kindly laugh which says [quoting Freud again], 'Just look, this is what the world is like, even though it appears dangerous. Child's play, just good enough to be joked about'" (36). Erikson concludes, "We now can look through what is so liberating about these books: For an instant they relieve the ego of the pressure of the superego." Humor smiles at the excessively severe, even sadistic conscience, "and we smile too. We like ourselves a bit more and perform some tiny detail better than we would have managed without that bright moment" (36).

Humor, then, is what the psychoanalytic tradition identifies as the counteractive force to the two dynamics that Erikson has identified, namely, the internalization of the mother (the parent who most concerns us here) and transformation of her into an object of fear and distrust, and the redirection of one's cruel and deadly hatred, previously aimed at overpowerful adults, against oneself. Against these dynamic processes, humor may seem to be a rather hapless combatant. By noting that small children find it liberating, however, Erikson indicates his belief that humor may succeed where parents' efforts to counter these dynamics are destined to fail. Moreover, the liberating power of humor is an experience that children and adults share, even to the extent that, as the Adamson character indicates, they may find the very same material amusing and oddly comforting.

Given the close association of religion and morality in Christian tradition, it is hardly surprising that humor has not enjoyed a central position in the Christian faith. By and large, the church has come down on the side of conscience, endorsing what Erikson calls the advantages of "the mechanism of conscience formation," i.e., that the child catches up in a short time with thousands of years of upbringing; and shares the general consensus of adults that a normal child doesn't suffer all that much from this process. Many men of my acquaintance view the severe punishment they received as children as a kind of "badge of honor," claiming that it has made them "better men," and one that they often want to bestow upon their own sons in the form of vigorous if not abusive disciplinary methods. The psychoanalytic argument that humor is liberating, however, suggests that humor may itself be a form of religiousness, that it may even be a more "advanced" form of male religiousness than those of honor and hope.[2]

Conclusion

This chapter on the melancholy self and male religiousness is an attempt to answer why it is that the men in my classes on men have been so reticent to talk about their mothers. While Frank Pittman puts his finger on one reason for such reticence—the man's feelings of guilt for not having lived up to what he perceives to have been his mother's expectations of him and/or for not having treated her as "nicely" as he ought to have—there are, in my view, deeper reasons for this, and these are reasons of which he is largely unconscious. These include the fact of her own ambivalent feelings toward him, which, were he to acknowledge them, would challenge his self-perception of himself as a boy whom, if anything, his mother loved too much; and the fact that, because his internalized image of her was associated with the formation of his conscience, he continues even into adulthood to fear her power over him and to distrust her motives toward him. Her most concerted efforts to disabuse him of this image are destined to fail. This is simply "the way it is." Neither mother nor son are to be blamed for this, but neither should we minimize its enduring force, for to do so will also cause us to fail to recognize that every man carries within himself a melancholy self. To the extent that he does, he is also religious, though his religion is largely based on a false conscience and an elusive quest.[3] In the second part of this book, we will explore in depth two men who are religious in these two ways, and we will see that these religious predispositions are not very effective in alleviating what Erikson calls the "self-directed sadism of the soul," that is, the melancholic condition itself.

Notes

1. I am aware that, in the history of Christianity, the Virgin Mary has not always been portrayed as the perfect mother. Her severity ("tough love") has certainly been a prominent theme. However, the historical development of her image has been toward her idealization and, indeed, her deification. Moreover, at no time has the Church attributed to her the "terrible" qualities ascribed to Kali.

2. Because my approach in this book is psychoanalytic, I do not discuss other psychological theories of humor. However, a series of empirical studies by Belgian psychologist Vassilis Saroglou deserve particular mention. In a recent study (2001), Saroglou and his coauthor, Jean-Marie Jaspard, hypothesized a negative effect of religion on spontaneous humor creation. Subjects were exposed to either a humorous or a religious video prior to being asked to imagine how they might react to a variety of frustrating everyday occurrences as depicted on twenty-four pictures with explanatory texts. Subjects exposed to the humorous video were far more likely to give spontaneous humorous responses than were subjects exposed to the religious video. If, for example, the situation depicted a woman returning to a shop and protesting that, for the third time, the clock she had purchased a week earlier stopped once she arrived home, a nonhumorous response by the shopkeeper might be, "That's odd, I'll need to examine it," or "Then we will replace it with another clock." A humorous response would be, "You're lucky, time stands still in your house," or "All my clocks suffer from separation problems, but I've never had one as unhappy to leave my store as this one."

The authors found that in both the religious exposure and the humor exposure groups, there was "a tendency for higher scores on humor creation among men than among women," and that the men's "score on human creation after exposure to the humor video was particularly high." As for why religion inhibits spontaneous humor production, the authors offer three not necessarily incompatible explanations. First, if other studies have shown that religious persons have a need for the reduction of uncertainty, they may be intolerant of the incongruity and ambiguity that are essential to the humor process. Second, the seriousness of religion may predispose a person to lower humor production. Third, religious people who are as able as nonreligious persons to perceive and enjoy such incongruity may inhibit their emotional expression and communication of humor.

3. Readers familiar with recent psychoanalytic writings on religion may wonder why I do not focus in this study on religious sentiments that emerge much earlier than age three or four. A commonly cited view is Erikson's emphasis, in *Toys and Reasons*, on the interaction between mother and her newborn child as "the first and dimmest affirmation," "the sense of a *hallowed presence*," and the original source, therefore, of humankind's awareness of "the numinous" (Erikson 1977, 85–92, his emphasis). In his earlier essay on "The Ontogeny of Ritualization in Man" (originally published in 1966), he specifically cites the "greeting ritual" that occurs between mother and infant in the morning as one that prefigures all subsequent experiences of the numinous (Erikson 1987b, 576–79). This ritual is the ontogenetic source of "a *mutuality of recognition*, by face and by name," that religions recapitulate in rituals in which the human supplicant receives and responds to the gaze of the deity, is lifted up, and called by name (Erikson 1977, 91, his emphasis).

That this encounter between mother and infant awakens and fosters the religious sentiment is compelling. Significantly, however, Erikson himself makes a strong case in *Young Man Luther* for the view that religion *as an orientation to life* has its developmental roots in melancholia. He draws a connection between the infant's "avaricious and sadistic orality," owing to his "*devouring* will to live," and "the disposition of melancholia." He suggests that this aggressive orality, which occurs in the "teething stage" and is directed against the mother (the giver and sustainer of life itself), marks "the prestages of what later becomes 'biting' human conscience" (Erikson 1958, 121). It introduces "very early" the "basic division of good and bad," which is portrayed in religion as the awareness of the loss of "a paradise of innocence" (121). To be sure, Erikson locates this experience toward the end of the "oral stage," thus after the "greeting ritual" but well before the third or fourth year (the focus of my study). Yet, he too seems to agree with Freud's argument in *Civilization and Its Discontents* (originally published in 1930) that the formation of a discernible religious *orientation to life* (as opposed to a nascent religious *sentiment*) is coterminous with the emergence of conscience (Freud 1961, 70–79, 83–84). Thus, Erikson links this "disposition of melancholia" to the child's awareness, in religious terms, of "the basic division of good and bad" and suggests that the two "infantile sources" of religious affect and imagery are "primary peace" and "secondary appeasement" (Erikson 1958, 121). As it is concerned with the relationship between the emergence of the melancholy self and religion, my study focuses on the "secondary appeasement" that emerges when the "primary peace," reflected in the mutual recognition of mother and infant, is disrupted or broken.

CHAPTER 3

∾

Identification versus Bonding with Father

In the preceding chapters, I have emphasized the importance of the emotional separation from his mother in early childhood in the development of a boy's melancholic self. Following Freud, I have viewed this development as due less to sadness over his loss and more to anger that has taken the form of self-reproach. I have also indicated my agreement with Pollack's argument that the traditional rationale for this emotional separation from one's mother—to enable her son to form a bond with his father and thereby develop a masculine character or identity—is a fallacious one, for there is no compelling reason why a boy cannot continue to be emotionally connected to his mother *and* form a bond with his father. No such assumption is made in the case of girls. Even if this rationale were not based on a false premise, it is not working anyway. As Samuel Osherson points out in *Finding Our Fathers: How a Man's Life Is Shaped by His Relationship with His Father*, "Both parts of the separation-individuation process in childhood are problematic for boys," these parts being (1) psychological separation from their mothers, and (2) identification and bonding with their fathers (Osherson 1986, 8).

In this chapter, I want to explore the son's failure to bond with his father, and to focus on the reasons for this. While this issue may appear to be tangential to the development of the melancholy self (the boy's mother being the "lost object"), it has relevance for this issue, as it helps to explain why the father typically fails to help his son cope with his sense of abandonment by his mother. It will also enable us to see how traditional Christianity contributes to and even endorses this failure. To make this argument, I will discuss Freud's concept of the Oedipus complex, a concept that has been much criticized but that, in my view, has great explanatory value for why sons and their fathers fail to bond with one another, and why this failure is not the fault of either one of them.

The Emotional Distance between Father and Son

As I indicated in the introduction, the men in my classes on men find it much easier to talk about their fathers than about their mothers. When they do so, however, there is often a note of wistfulness in how they talk about their relations with their fathers. They wish they had spent more time with them when they were growing up, that their relationship with their fathers had been more expressive, that they could have shared their feelings and problems with their fathers more easily, and that their fathers, in turn, could have been more self-revealing. They feel that they have learned much of what they know about their fathers—their fathers' family origins, coming of age, early years of marriage, vocational struggles—from their mothers. They also feel that they do not know very much about how their fathers spend their days, how they feel about their work, or what their fathers really want out of life (assuming that they know this themselves). Unlike their mothers, their fathers are something of an enigma to them.

I recall my older brother once saying to his three younger brothers, "I wonder what is going on in Dad's mind? He doesn't say very much." Inclined in those days to speak irreverently—and to feel guilty about it later—I ventured, "Maybe there's nothing going on in his mind. That's why he doesn't have much to say." The men in my classes do not believe this, and neither did I. They want to understand their fathers, in part because they believe that this will enable them to understand themselves better. They tend to believe, as Samuel Osherson's subtitle to *Finding Our Fathers* suggests, that a man's life is significantly, even profoundly, "shaped by his relationship with his father," and yet they feel that they cannot know how it has been shaped by him unless they know and understand him better. As Osherson notes, at one point in his own life he tried to "fill in the void" that existed between himself and his father by means of surrogate fathers. In time, however, he realized that this was neither the answer nor the issue, because "I recognized that my image of him was inside me. I was carrying along a sad, mournful, judgmental version of my father," and, at times, "I acted the same way: rigid, judgmental, remote" (Osherson 1986, 25). When he came to this realization, he found himself searching psychology texts for a good definition of the idea of *introjection*, "a psychological process whereby we take in conflictual figures, swallowing them whole in a distorted way, rather than identifying with parts of them in a more personally satisfying way" (25).

Why had he not been able to learn of his father's inner life when he was growing up? In his view, the problem was that "he and I were locked into the family pattern of *protective denial*, whereby children and mother collude with father to 'protect' him from emotionally challenging family subjects, denying too that the family has isolated and infantilized Dad. Instead you turn to mother for information and explanation, confirming the 'feminine' work of being the emotional switchboard in the family" (25–26).

Osherson suggests that men carry an image of their fathers inside of them that is highly distorted, as it is a composite of fantasy and reality that is itself owing, in large part, to the fact of the fathers' absence (relative to mothers). C. G. Jung's nocturnal images of his mother owing to her hospitalization indicates the extent to which a parent's absence may contribute to this distortion. As Osherson explains, "When a person is absent, either physically or psychologically, you need to explain why that person is not there. Father absence provides fertile ground for a son's mistaken imaginings about his father. The son's understanding of his father's absence is crucial. That is where sons start to idealize or degrade their fathers, misidentifying with them, and struggling with shame and guilt themselves" (29). Thus, there is "a cartoon quality to father images, suggesting a view of father built up by watching this person from a distance" (30).

A research psychologist, Osherson was struck by the fact that for many of the men he studied, "the fathers in these cartoons are angry or disappointed with us. They are often the images that a young boy might construct around a large, intimidating, puzzling older figure." There often seems a time when the relationship became stuck or frozen, with puberty, adolescence, and early childhood being the "key stress points," and the cartoon image reflects this (30). A psychotherapist gave the following account: "'Big Al? Do you want Big Al to come in?' a man might ask me after going over the struggles he's had with his father. There's often fear and awe in his voice. Then Big Al arrives for our appointment and turns out to be a tiny, eighty-five-year old man, short and gentle. But the father of childhood lives on in these men's minds" (31).

Osherson believes that the "fundamental male vulnerability rooted in the experience of father lies in our fantasies and myths to explain why father isn't there." For example:

> The son may experience his father's preoccupation with work or emotional unavailability at home as *his own* fault. It's because of something the son has done that father doesn't pay attention to him. The son may feel not good enough as a man in the face of this powerful, successful father, who hasn't enough time for him. Or the son may perceive a secret weakness in his father—feeling he is less than a man—and become determined to avoid the same fate. (29)

In contrast to the sense of abandonment that a boy experiences from the emotional separation from his mother, what he experiences in relation to his father is betrayal: "Many men I have interviewed carry around a feeling of both having betrayed their father and having been betrayed by him" (29).

Osherson's portrayal of his father's relationship to *his* father indicates that this is precisely how his father felt, that he had betrayed his own father because he reluctantly acceded to his wife's and children's desire to be released from kosher obligations and eventually abandoned the family business. This is also precisely how Osherson felt as *his* father became for him, in adolescence, "a pain in the neck, ridiculous and heroic and demanding at the same time" (27).

The sense of mutual betrayal is also due, in his view, to the experience of father as emotionally absent. This "emotional disconnection" between fathers and sons makes it difficult for them to "untangle these misunderstandings" (29). But why are fathers experienced as emotionally absent? Osherson notes,

> Numerous studies indicate that fathers spent relatively little time in close, leisurely interaction with their children. The family researchers Rebelsky and Hanks have suggested that fathers spend an average of thirty-seven seconds a day interacting with infants in the first three months of their life. Pedersen and Robson found an average of about an hour a day of direct play between fathers and nine-months-old infants, including time spent together on weekends. The pattern continues as children age. (29)

This suggests that the emotional distance between father and son begins extremely early in life, and that the father is primarily responsible. After all, an infant is too young to initiate the relationship, and as the boy matures, the pattern of emotional distance is already set. Osherson notes that many of the fathers he has talked with did not like this emotional distance but felt powerless to do anything about it: "Many of them were secretly angry and depressed, feeling considerable rage and depression at the traditional bargain they had made with their wives, exiled from their families, consigned to the world of work" (42). Having entered into this bargain, "which seemed entirely natural and which they were powerless to change," they felt entrapped. One man told Osherson that "he could either cultivate the role of lover or the role of provider," and that, in his case, he "never knew he had a choice. I was brought up to be responsible, to be the provider" (42). In consequence, he "never knew his children except as objects: 'I'd look at my kids as somebody to be examined to make sure the kid's not sick. You make sure the kid's not doing anything dangerous. . . . The kids always tell me there was an insurmountable wall. I felt that they were first of all a responsibility'" (42). Thus, for many of the men, the primary reason for their emotional distance from their sons is what another man called "the deal all men make," choosing, as it were, between being the provider or being emotionally available.

In *Man Enough*, Frank Pittman underscores the degree to which "the provider role" defines a man's perception of himself as father. He cites John

Demos's study of patriarchy in eighteenth-century America, which includes the following list of things that were expected of fathers: pedagogue, benefactor, controller, moral overseer, psychologist, example, progenitor, companion, and caregiver. After the Industrial Revolution in the nineteenth century, however, "masculinity ceased to be defined in terms of domestic involvement, skills at fathering and husbanding, but began to be defined in terms of making money. Men had to leave home to work. They stopped doing all the things they used to do. Instead they became primarily, in Demos's phrase, Father the *Provider*, bringing things home to the family rather than living and working at home within the family" (Pittman 1993, 122–23).

Pittman suggests that fathers gradually found other roles to fulfill "when they visited home after working somewhere else." These were the *disciplinarian* ("Wait till your father comes home") and the *audience* ("Tell Daddy what you did today"). As it became clear that mothers and children could manage without a grown man around the house, father assumed other roles, including the *intruder*, disrupting the rhythm of the household; the *abdicator*, the man who got away and provided no child support; the *anachronism*, embarrassingly representing old-fashioned values; and the *incompetent*, out of place in the business of the home, serving no useful domestic function, just getting in the way and looking foolish (123).

The *provider* role, however, continued to be primary, and this inevitably led to husbands and fathers being assessed, relative to other men, as successful or failing, depending on how well or poorly they provided for their own families. Conversely, mothers were evaluated for their success or failure in the raising of children. Pittman cites the comment by a man whom he saw in therapy about the problems of his son. He said, "I don't know what Betty could have done wrong in raising that boy. I know it wasn't anything I did, since I was busy working and left it all up to her. I barely saw the kid so I wouldn't have done anything wrong" (128).

Thus, like Osherson, Pittman emphasizes the emotional distance between fathers and sons, focusing on the father's understanding of himself as the family provider as the primary reason for this distance. Pittman believes that this emotional distance creates in boys and men a "father hunger." He notes, "Life for most boys and for many grown men is a frustrating search for the lost father who has not yet offered protection, provision, nurturing, modeling, or, especially, anointment" (129). Anointment, an important theme for Pittman, refers to the adolescent boy's need to be treated "as good enough to be considered a man" (130).

Osherson notes that "many men today who are trying to spend more time at home are responding to a sense that their fathers missed out on a valuable experience of intimacy and nurturing" (Osherson 1986, 43). On the other hand, their efforts to be more intimate and nurturing are not always successful because of the version of fathers that they themselves have introjected. Fathers' efforts to involve themselves in the family often provoke new conflicts, as they have a "fear of becoming the angry father they carry around in their heads, like the father who said that whenever he disciplined his kids he heard the angry voice of authority screaming 'No!' at them" (43). This fear is entirely realistic. In *Lost Boys: Why Our Sons Turn Violent and How We Can Save Them*, James Garbarino cites the case of a fifteen-year-old boy who killed a convenience store clerk who dared to oppose him when he demanded all the money in the cash register. The boy's response to the clerk before he shot him—"Don't you ever talk to me like that"—echoed his father's words to him before his father beat him. He was "surprised, even stunned" when the parallel was pointed out to him (Garbarino 1999, 45–46).

Thus, efforts by contemporary fathers to be more available to their sons are unlikely to be effective unless fathers are able to recognize the introjected image of their own fathers and to find ways to counter its potential for damaging the very relationship that the father wants to foster. As with the issue of "mother blaming" discussed in the preceding chapter, we need to avoid any facile blaming of the individual father for the emotional distance between fathers and sons. As Pittman's brief discussion of the history of patriarchy in the United States makes clear, there were very strong socioeconomic pressures involved in the diminishment of the father's role to that of provider. The father who challenged these pressures was subject to severe social censure, even if he could justifiably claim that he was, nonetheless, "a good father." A father, for example, who barely provided for his children's needs yet was emotionally available to them would not have been viewed as a good father. This view may be changing, but the vast majority of men continue to define themselves in provider terms, and therefore experience the demand that they also be emotionally nurturing as an added burden, especially when the expectations placed on the "provider" have tended to escalate. As the father told Osherson, "It has to be one or the other," and "I was brought up to be responsible, to be the provider" (Osherson 1986, 42). The societal expectation that he will be the provider, even if this is all that he is, is reflected in the fact that divorced men who are living apart from their families are expected to continue to provide for them; otherwise, they carry the social opprobrium of the "abdicator."

The Son's Emotional Ambivalence toward the Father

By focusing on the father's provider role, both Osherson and Pittman identify an important reason for the emotional distance between father and son. But this, in Osherson's view, is a partial explanation, and does not get at the deeper psychological reasons for this distance. In his view, the issue is more complex than this, for the father's emotional distance has a deeper psychodynamic cause. This is that the father has deeply ambivalent feelings toward his son. He notes, "Our fathers perhaps secretly feared us too. The ambivalent love between fathers and sons is underestimated. It is the dark side of the high value boys are given in our society. Since so much of male identity is based on performance, sons will someday outdistance Dad" (Osherson 1986, 43). As a result, "We become ambivalent objects, loved and feared by our fathers" (43). It is interesting that Osherson chooses the word *feared* over the word *hated*, in spite of the fact, as Rozsika Parker points out, that *ambivalence* means the existence of simultaneous conflicting feelings toward another person. (The dictionary actually uses *love* and *hate* to illustrate the meaning of the word *ambivalent*.)

In any event, Osherson notes that as researchers have learned more about fathers and sons, they have proposed the "Laius complex" to refer to "the father's feeling of threat from the son and need to put him down. King Laius in the Oedipus drama haughtily refused to move aside in the road for his son, precipitating the fateful slaying" (44).

Osherson recognizes that the son also bears ambivalent feelings toward the father, noting that "some men may have fears of hurting their fathers with their aggression," and that "two themes are acted out over and over again in the adult life of men: the search for and rejection of our fathers. We want redemption and want to destroy them" (44). He emphasizes, however, the father's ambivalence toward his son, citing Donald Hall's poem "My Son the Executioner" to illustrate the father's ambivalence toward his son because his son represents "a father's mortality in very uncomfortable ways. As the son becomes a man, the father must recognize his own aging" (44).

Interestingly enough, however, Osherson's representation of the son as a young man is not true to the poem itself. The poem was written when Hall's first son was born (Hall 1990, 19):

My Son, My Executioner

My son, my executioner,
    I take you in my arms,
Quiet and small and just astir
    And whom my body warms.

Sweet death, small son, our instrument
    Of immortality,
Your cries and hungers document
    Our bodily decay.

We twenty-five and twenty-two,
    Who seemed to live forever,

Observe enduring life in you
  And start to die together.

It is true that the infant is his father's executioner, but he is not the young man who causes the father to feel that his time is past, for the father is only twenty-five years old. *He* is the young man. Rather, it is the vulnerability of the baby—its cries and hungers—that "document" the father's own "bodily decay."

In a conversation with Bill Moyers (Moyers 1995), Hall pointed out that this poem was "written when my first child was born, my son Andrew. I may have felt my decay more at twenty-five than I do approaching sixty-five! But when he was born I was shocked by this feeling, which came over me very strongly, that my replacement had arrived. I worried about what my son would think of this particular poem when he grew up. When he was about fourteen he said to me, 'That wasn't really about you and me. It was about you and your father.' I think it was. My father was still healthy—he had not contracted cancer—but he died just a year and a half later. He was not a vigorous man. He was an old fifty when my son was born, and perhaps I was worried about replacing him myself. A poem is so often, obviously and correctly, pointing south while at the same time something under it is going north" (150–51).

If the poem has an association with the story of Oedipus and Laius, this is not the encounter at the crossroads of life when the father haughtily refuses to move aside in the road for his son, but in the sense that the infant is an oracle of things to come, when the father will meet his death and his son, while executioner, will become his "instrument of immortality." The very fact that Hall's poem is about a baby brings us to Freud's view that sons' ambivalent feelings toward their fathers have roots in early childhood.

As Freud asserts in *A General Introduction to Psychoanalysis* (originally published in 1920):

> Well, it is easy to see that the little man wants his mother all to himself, finds his father in the way, becomes restive when the latter takes upon himself to caress her, and shows his satisfaction when the father goes away or is absent. He often expresses his feelings directly in words and promises his mother to marry her; this may not seem much in comparison with the deeds of Oedipus, but it is enough in fact; the kernel of each is the same. (Freud 1964, 341)

In this scenario, the "absent father" so much lamented in recent literature about fathers and sons is actually the fulfillment of the son's most fervent dreams! What is puzzling about this, in Freud's view, is that "the same child on other occasions at this period will display great affection for the father" and "such contrasting—or, better, *ambivalent*—states of feeling, which in adults would lead to conflicts, can be tolerated alongside one another in the child for a long time, just as later on they dwell together permanently in the unconscious" (341–42).

The Myth of Oedipus: What Does It Mean?

In my view, we need to take a closer look than Osherson affords at the small boy's ambivalence toward his father as an important factor in the emotional distancing of father and son. The purpose of this exploration is not to shift the blame for this distance from father to son, but rather to enable us to recognize the complexities that are involved in this distancing between them. Freud's Oedipus complex concept helps us to see how the son's ambivalence—love *and* hate—toward his father contributes to this distancing, and also enables us to see that the Judeo-Christian religious tradition plays a very significant role in this distancing. In the remaining pages of this chapter, I will focus on the emotional distancing itself. I will take up in the following chapter the issue of how religion, in its Judeo-Christian form, is largely responsible for it.

Before we move into this discussion of the Oedipus complex, there is a preliminary issue that needs to be addressed. This is the fact that, in the original Oedipus story by Sophocles, the oracle that Oedipus would kill his father and marry his mother led to his abandonment. That he was saved was fortuitous in the short run but in the long run this created the circumstances whereby the oracle was in fact fulfilled. Freud's Oedipus complex theory has therefore been criticized for its failure to recognize that Oedipus was the victim of abandonment and deception. In his discussion of the "infanticidal impulse" in *Disease, Pain, and Sacrifice*, David Bakan acknowledges that

> Freud's notion of the Oedipus complex certainly recognized the psychological significance of the identifications and conflicts in the father-son relationship. . . . [But] Freud did not carry this sufficiently far to recognize that the Oedipus complex might itself be a reaction of the child to the infanticidal impulse in the father—Laius leaving Oedipus to die as a child—and a defensive response of the child against aggression. (Bakan 1968, 104)

James E. Dittes has more recently advanced a similar argument in *Driven by Hope: Men and Meaning*, though he develops it more fully. For him, Freud has made the tragic Greek figure of Oedipus

> the emblem and epitome of the male experience, the prototypical man in his canon, as Adam is in the biblical canon. The "Oedipus complex" becomes, for Freud and for many of us, the kernel of male identity. But

if we accept Freud's intuition that we understand our maleness more clearly when we see ourselves as Oedipus, we should take care to know Oedipus more completely, more honestly, than what Freud chose to describe. . . . There is much more to the Oedipus story and to our story than Freud told us—or, more accurately, more than he *consciously* told us. [There is ample reason to suppose] that Freud was drawn to this tragic figure and identified with him, as he asked us each to identify with him, precisely for what is portrayed in that part of the story he did *not* tell us. After all, if we are to believe Freud's own principles, the part of a story not told is the most important part, the most revealing. A fixation as strong as that which Freud lodged on Oedipus most likely suggests intense unconscious energies. (Dittes 1996, 34)

Dittes' own telling of the story emphasizes that Oedipus was the victim of abandonment and deception. He suggests that Laius, on learning of the oracle that he was destined to be killed by his son, "took the preemptive precaution of ordering the newborn abandoned on a mountainside" (34). When the adult Oedipus heard the same oracle, "he took the honorable precaution of leaving home" (35). What Freud did was to pluck "from this story the fact that Oedipus killed his father and married his mother, as though this were done knowingly rather than out of the best of intentions and ignorance, and he assigned Oedipus's name to a boy's deliberate but unconscious desires to do the same" (35).

Dittes believes that Freud's "one sided portrayal of Oedipus" overlooks the fact that Oedipus was "the victim of abandonment and abuse" (35). Freud tells us "nothing about the wrongs inflicted on the child Oedipus," about "Oedipus abandoned and helplessly vulnerable" (36). Nor does he tell us about Oedipus "the intrepid pilgrim in earnest and conscientious pursuit of his own destiny" (35). Instead, Freud tells us only "about the wrongs the adult Oedipus inflicted" (36). Thus, "How perverse for Freud to make Oedipus the symbol for *wanting* to murder one's father. That's the one thing Oedipus did not want to do. Oedipus wanted much, above all else a father who would deal honestly and responsibly with him. But Oedipus decidedly did *not* want to kill his father" (37).

Far from wanting to murder his father, Oedipus did everything he could to avoid it. Far from wanting to murder his father, his father wanted to murder him. Far from wanting to murder his foster father, he only needed for the man to tell him the truth. Far from intending to transgress the taboo against incest, he was the victim of a taboo against truth and full disclosure. Far from being guilty of immorality, he was too duped by betrayal and deception to be capable of responsible moral choice. (37)

For Dittes, Freud's one-sided reading of the Oedipus story has contributed to a "disparaging portrayal of men" in our time. In this portrayal, "the Oedipus within each man is said to name the villainous part of him, a sober warning of just how far 'macho' can go if left untethered, competitive to the point of killing even one's father, exploitative of women to the point of claiming even one's mother" (35). The Oedipus that Dittes seeks to rehabilitate is a man who tried to act with honor, who wanted to be a man of high moral rectitude, and whose personal quest was only to find his own destiny, not to avenge wrongs committed against him by his self-serving father. Thus, in Dittes' reconstruction, Oedipus is the "religious" man whose tragic end was not the consequence of the fact that his best intentions were not good enough, but of the fact that he was the victim of abandonment, deception, and abuse.

Freud's Oedipus Complex: The Public Version

Dittes' (and Bakan's) criticisms of Freud's one-sided portrayal of Oedipus are ones with which I am in agreement—up to a point. Freud's interpretation of Sophocles' drama *is* one-sided, as it does not deal with the issue of the abandonment of Oedipus or the issue of his foster father's failure to inform him that he was another man's son. As noted earlier, Erikson's stepfather and his mother attempted a similar deception. Unlike the infant Oedipus, however, Erikson was three years old when this occurred. He was therefore skeptical of this deception, though he "played along" with it.

On the other hand, we should be careful not to misread the original story nor to misrepresent what Freud *does* say about the Oedipus complex. As for misreadings, or, at the least, important omissions, both Bakan and Dittes indicate that it was the father, Laius, who abandoned his son. This suggestion, however, is based on a statement by Jocasta, the mother, early in the play, a statement whose veracity may be doubted. When she is interrogated about the oracle, she says that Laius received the prophecy that he was fated to die by his son's hand, so "three days after his birth Laius fastened his ankles together and had him cast away on the pathless mountains" (Sophocles 1959, 50). She tells this story to support her contention that one should not pay any attention to the prophecies of other humans: "If God seeks or needs anything, he will easily make it clear to us himself" (50).

Much later in the play, however, a shepherd discloses that Jocasta herself brought the child to him because she wanted him to "destroy it." When Oedipus asks, "Her own child?" the shepherd responds, "She was afraid of dreadful prophecies" (88). When Oedipus asks what they were, the shepherd replies, "the child would kill its parents, that was the story" (88). This shepherd, feeling pity for the infant, gave it to another shepherd whom he thinks will take it to the foreign country from which he came, and the child's life was thereby spared.

In effect, both Bakan and Dittes accept the veracity of the story that Jocasta tells, and the fact that Oedipus's foot was permanently injured by the metal pin (hence, the name "swollen foot") seems to give credence to her account. The translator, Bernard Knox, also accepts her version. In his introduction, he says that Laius "drove a metal pin through the infant's ankles and gave it to a shepherd, with instructions to leave it to die of exposure on the nearby mountain" (x1). But the shepherd's account indicates that it was the infant's mother who gave it to the shepherd and asked him to destroy it, and that the explanation she gave him was that dreadful prophecies had foretold that he would kill his parents. This suggests that she herself believed the prophecies but also misrepresented them. The prophecy of incest was omitted from her story and was replaced by the suggestion that Oedipus would kill *both* parents. Thus, whatever Laius's involvement may have been—we have only Jocasta's word for this—the story is one of maternal abandonment, an interpretation that neither Bakan nor Dittes (and not even the translator) consider. Is this misreading similar, in its way, to Pittman's need to believe that a mother has only love for her boy from the word go?

My present concern, however, is with their critique of Freud. If they believe that Freud's interpretation of the story of Oedipus is onesided, I believe that they perpetuate a onesided protrayal of the Oedipus Complex concept itself. In what follows, I will argue that Freud's concept of the Oedipus complex has considerable relevance to the problem of the failure of fathers and sons to develop an emotional bond, thus contributing to the fact that, as Osherson puts it, the two phases of the boy's "separation-individuation process"—emotional separation from mother and identification and bonding with father—prove problematic. Freud's concept of the Oedipus complex enables us to see that "identification and bonding" with one's father is inherently problematic, as these two ways of relating to one's father are mutually exclusive.

In his public lectures that were published as *A General Introduction to Psychoanalysis*, Freud does not discuss the Oedipus complex until the twenty-first of twenty-eight lectures. Even in this lecture, entitled "Development of the Libido and Sexual Organizations," he makes an effort to prepare his audience for what he will say by anticipating their negative reaction. He tells about a staunch adherent of psychoanalysis who was stationed in his medical capacity on the German front in Poland during World War I. When he achieved unexpected results with some of the fighting men, his medical colleagues were intrigued, and he was invited to give talks on the subject to his colleagues and superiors. For a while all went well, but when he introduced his audience to the Oedipus complex a superior officer "rose and announced he did not believe this" and that "it was the behavior of a cad for the lecturer to relate such

things to brave men, fathers of families, who were fighting for their country."
He "forbade the continuation of the lectures" (Freud 1964, 339).

Having related this story, Freud remarks, "Now you will be impatiently
wanting to hear what the terrible Oedipus complex comprises. The name tells
you" (339). He reminds his audience of the Greek myth (which "you all
know") of King Oedipus, "whose destiny it was to slay his father and to wed
his mother, who did all in his power to avoid the fate prophesied by the oracle, and who in self-punishment blinded himself when he discovered that in
ignorance he had committed both these crimes. I trust that many of you have
yourselves experienced the profound effect of the tragic drama fashioned by
Sophocles from this story" (339–40).

He compares the dramatist's work, which "portrays the gradual discovery
of the deed of Oedipus, long since accomplished, and brings it slowly to light
by skillfully prolonged enquiry, constantly fed by new evidence," to the
course of a psychoanalysis. He notes in this connection that "the deluded
mother-wife Jocasta" resists the continuation of the enquiry by pointing out
that "many people in their dreams have mated with their mothers, but that
dreams are of no account" (340). (It was just such a dream that caused
Oedipus to begin to suspect what had happened.) Freud notes that dreams
are very important to psychoanalysis, and that Jocasta's very denial of the significance of the dream reveals that it is "related to the shocking and terrible
story of the myth" (340).

Next, Freud expresses surprise that audiences do not respond indignantly
to Sophocles' tragedy, noting that such a response would be "much better justified" in this case than it was in the case of the "blunt army doctor." Why?
Because "at bottom it is an immoral play; it sets aside the individual's responsibility to social law, and displays divine forces ordaining the crime and ren-
dering powerless the moral instincts of the human being which would guard
him against the crime" (340). He suggests that audiences are dissuaded from
reacting in this way because Sophocles has engaged in a pious subtlety "which
declares it the highest morality to bow to the will of the gods, even when they
order a crime" (340).

For his own part, Freud does not consider this moral to be one of the
play's virtues, but neither "does it detract from its effect; it leaves the hearer
indifferent; he does not react to this, but to the secret meaning and content
of the myth itself" (340). That is, the reader "reacts as though by self-analysis
he had detected the Oedipus complex in himself, and had recognized the will
of the gods and the oracle as glorified disguises of his own unconscious; as
though he remembered in himself the wish to do away with his father and in
his place to wed his mother, and must abhor the thought" (340–41).

Thus, the listener experiences himself as culpable even though he has not
done these things. The dramatist's word seems to him to mean, "In vain do

you deny that you are accountable, in vain do you proclaim how you have striven against these evil designs. You are guilty, nevertheless; for you could not stifle them; they still survive unconsciously in you" (341). If the listener's conscious mind can say of Oedipus, "Thank God, I haven't done these heinous acts," his unconscious mind objects. As Freud explains, "Psychological truth is contained in this; even though man has repressed his evil desires into his Unconscious and would then gladly say to himself that he is no longer answerable for them, he is yet compelled to feel his responsibility in the form of a sense of guilt for which he can discern no foundation" (341).

What the Oedipus complex is intended to explain, at least in part, is why a man feels guilty even though he has done nothing wrong. As far as he can discern, there is no foundation for this sense of guilt: "There is no possible doubt that one of the most important sources of the sense of guilt which so often torments neurotic people is to be found in the Oedipus complex" (341). Freud briefly alludes at this point to his *Totem and Taboo* (originally published in 1913), as it expresses a "suspicion that the sense of guilt of humankind as a whole, and which is the ultimate source of religion and morality, was acquired in the beginnings of history through the Oedipus complex" (Freud 1950, 241). He chooses not to go into this subject, however, because it would necessarily involve an extended discussion, and his concern in the lecture is with "individual psychology."

It is at this point in the lecture that he introduces the subject of young children and applies the Oedipus myth to them. He asks, "Now what does direct observation of children, at the period of object-choice before the latency period, show us in regard to the Oedipus complex?" (Freud 1964, 341). Because the subject of this lecture is the development of the libido and sexual organizations, Freud is especially interested here in the boy's erotic feelings toward his mother (and less with the boy's designs against his father), noting that the little boy expresses "sexual curiosity about his mother, wants to sleep with her at night, insists on being in the room while she is dressing, or even attempts physical acts of seduction, as the mother so often observes and laughingly relates" (342). This cannot be accounted for solely on the grounds that the boy's egoistic interests are involved. It is true that his mother looks after his needs and therefore "it is to the child's interest that she should trouble herself about no one else" (342). But we should not forget that the mother "looks after a little daughter's needs in the same way without producing this effect," and "that often enough a father eagerly vies with her" troubling himself for the boy "without succeeding in winning the same importance in his eyes as the mother" (342).

From a purely egoistic point of view, a boy would be foolish "if he did not tolerate two people in his service rather than only one of them" (342). Instead, the boy expresses a clear preference for his mother, and "wants his mother all to himself, finds his father in the way, becomes restive when the latter takes it upon himself to caress her, and shows his satisfaction when the father goes away or is absent" (341). The most direct expression of his feelings toward his mother, and corollary feelings toward his father, is his promise to marry her.

The lecture continues with a discussion of the reverse form of the Oedipus complex in little girls, the expansion of the Oedipus complex into a "family complex" when other children appear (with the hatred now being focused, and much more openly expressed, on the new arrivals), the possible transfer of the boy's affections from his "faithless mother" to his sister, the hostile rivalry between brothers to win the favor of a little sister, a brief reference to the importance of birth order, a commentary on prohibitions in law and custom against incest, and an allusion to Theodor Reik's work on puberty rites among primitive peoples that show that the meaning of these rites "which represent re-birth is the loosening of the boy's incestuous attachment to the mother and his reconciliation with the father" (344).

The final paragraphs of the lecture focus on adults who have become neurotic and the practical value of the Oedipus complex concept for treating these adults. Here Freud observes that, in the case of neurotic patients, "the analytic picture of the Oedipus complex is an enlarged and accentuated edition of the infantile sketch; the hatred of the father and the death-wishes against him are no longer vague hints" and "the affection for the mother declares itself with the aim of possessing her as a woman" (345). This "enlarged and accentuated edition" of "the infantile sketch" introduces the problem of "retrogressive phantasy-making," that is, the unintentional importation into the infantile period of intermediate and present feelings, thereby falsifying the past. There can be no doubt that "the hatred against the father has been strengthened by a number of motives arising in later periods and other relationships in life, and that the sexual desires towards the mother have been moulded into forms which would have been as yet foreign to the child" (345). But, Freud contends, the whole of the Oedipus complex cannot be explained by such retrogressive fantasies and motives originating later in life. How do we know this? Because the "infantile nucleus" of the Oedipus complex is "confirmed by direct observation of children" (345).

In concluding the lecture, Freud notes that the practical value of the concept is that it enables the therapist to explain the neuroses that doctors often encounter in their patients. Specifically, it explains what ought to have happened in puberty but failed to occur in persons who are neurotic. In puberty, the "infantile object-choice" of the mother, which was "but a feeble venture in play," comes into force, with a "very intense flow of feeling. This flow of feeling comes into direct conflict with the need for a man to devote himself, from puberty, "to the great task of *freeing himself from the parents*" (345,

Freud's emphasis). Only after "this detachment is accomplished can he cease to be a child and so become a member of the social community" (345–46). For the son, "the task consists in releasing his libidinal desires from his mother, in order to employ them in the quest of an external love-object in reality; and in reconciling himself with his father if he has remained antagonistic to him, or in freeing himself from his domination if, in the reaction to the infantile revolt, he has lapsed into subservience to him" (346).

These tasks are "laid down for every man," yet "it is noteworthy how seldom they are carried through ideally." Even if they are carried out in a "socially satisfactory" way, they are seldom solved "psychologically" (346). In neurotics, however, "this detachment from the parents is not accomplished at all; the son remains all his life in subjection to his father, and incapable of transferring his libido to a new sexual object" (346). For the daughter, it happens in reverse. Freud concludes: "In this sense the Oedipus complex is justifiably regarded as the kernel of the neuroses" (346).

I have presented this lecture in which Freud discusses his Oedipus complex concept in some detail because it sheds light on why the "separation-individuation" process in early childhood, as presented by Osherson, is so problematic. Freud's comments about the "infantile nucleus" of the complex are especially valuable in this regard. Several things he says about the small boy's feelings and behavior toward his father are noteworthy. One is his claim that the small boy is truly ambivalent. He "shows his satisfaction when the father goes away or is absent," yet "the same child on other occasions at this period will display great affection for the father." These ambivalent feelings would lead to conflicts in adults, but these ambivalent feelings "can be tolerated alongside one another in the child for a long time, just as later on they dwell together permanently in the unconscious" (341–42). Thus, the small boy is not torn apart by these contrasting feelings, and is certainly not distressed by the inconstancy of his feelings toward his father. After all, his object-choice of his mother, while certainly real, is also "but a feeble venture in play" (345).

Second, this object-choice of his mother becomes so absolute that there is nothing the father can do, by way of "looking after" his son, that would enable him to win "the same importance in his eyes as the mother." This, of course, does not mean that all fathers do in fact "look after" their small sons, but it *does* suggest that whatever they do, it will not carry nearly as much weight with the boy himself as the care that his mother bestows on him.

Third, the really serious Oedipal problems do not arise in early childhood, but with the onset of puberty. This is when the boy's object-choice of his mother comes back in full force (after a period when it was more latent than manifest) and clashes with the "great task of freeing himself from the parents." Freud's comments on the son-father side of this "great task" are especially noteworthy, as they suggest that this is the time when a boy may undo the interpersonal effects of the infantile nucleus of the Oedipus complex (augmented by intermediate experiences that have made it more problematic). For the boy who has remained antagonistic to his father throughout childhood, there can be a reconciliation, and this reconciliation enables him to free himself psychologically from his father. For the boy who reacted to his "infantile revolt" by lapsing into subservience to his father, he can achieve liberation from his father's domination and free himself from his father in this fashion.

However, freeing himself from his father—whether through reconciliation or liberation from a domination/subservience relationship—depends, at least to some extent, on his ability to release his libidinal desires from his mother in order to employ them in the quest of an "external love-object in reality." This, Freud implies, is the most difficult of the two tasks, for this is also when "the sexual instinct first asserts its demands in full strength" (345). In contrast to the object-choice of the mother in puberty, the infantile object-choice of her seems rather like child's play. In fact, the small boy's real ambivalence toward his father exerts a certain constraint on the degree to which the boy actually wants to have his mother all to himself.

This summary of Freud's main points in his public lecture regarding the son-father relationship suggests that representations of his Oedipus theory emphasizing the little boy's hostility toward his father are vastly overdrawn. These portrayals conflate the infantile nucleus of the Oedipus complex and the elaborations that have developed later. In addition, they ascribe to this infantile nucleus various neurotic manifestations of the complex that arise in the puberty and postpuberty periods. They even present a false picture of the normal resolution of the Oedipus complex in the postpuberty period. As this synopsis of the lecture shows, Freud's primary concern was to explain the neuroses, and he used what we can directly observe about small children to provide such an explanation. Popular conceptions of his Oedipus complex concept have reversed this process, using his views on the Oedipal nucleus of neuroses to portray the infantile nucleus of the Oedipus complex.

Like William James, who uses extreme, even pathological, forms of melancholia in adults to illumine its more mundane expressions, Freud suggests a similar comparison between neurotic and normal adults, noting that normal adults effect the necessary detachment from their parents (though few accomplish it ideally), while neurotic adults do not accomplish it. Such comparisons help us to understand why even normal (i.e., nonpathological) adult sons have unresolved conflicts with their fathers, as the required reconciliation or liberation has not been "carried through ideally." What Freud's discussion here does not allow, however, is the conflating of adult neurotics' attitudes toward their fathers (which tend to be overwhelmingly antagonistic or servile) and those of little boys, who are able to tolerate their ambivalent feelings toward their fathers. The nucleus of the adult neuroses is found in the small boy's object-choice of his mother and his satisfaction when his father is absent. Freud insists on this point. But the attitudes toward their fathers that are held by adolescent boys and older men, and are accentuated in adult neurotics, represent a *strengthening* of the hatred against the father "by a number of motives arising in later periods and other relationships in life" (345).

I now want to take a closer look at Freud's views on the infantile nucleus itself. This will enable us to see that, from Freud's own perspective, the son-father side of the "separation-individuation process" is inherently problematic. As we will see, the problem is in the fact that the boy's identification with his father and his emotional bonding with his father are mutually exclusive. Where Osherson seems to assume that they are compatible and the problem is to identify the reasons why emotional bonding does not occur, Freud's analysis of the infantile nucleus of the Oedipus complex indicates that they are inherently contradictory. If one occurs, the other cannot, and this is simply the way it is.

The Two Forms of the Oedipus Complex

In *The Ego and the Id* (originally published in 1923), Freud discusses the Oedipus complex in a much more theoretical fashion than in the public lectures on psychoanalysis. In the preface, he indicates that this book is "a fuller development of some trains of thought" presented in his *Beyond the Pleasure Principle*, published a year earlier. In contrast to the former book, however, "it is more in the nature of a synthesis than of a speculation and seems to have . . . an ambitious aim in view" (Freud 1960a, 1). His discussion of the Oedipus complex occurs in his chapter on "The Ego and the Super-Ego (Ego Ideal)," and the general thrust of the chapter is that the superego replaces the Oedipus complex in the small child. In effect, the formation of the superego requires the "demolition" of the Oedipus complex.

As Freud sees it, an exploration of the demolition of the Oedipus complex (so that the superego may take form in its place) is complicated by two factors: the triangular character of the Oedipus situation and the constitutional bisexuality of each individual (21). To show just how complicated it is, he identifies two forms of the Oedipus complex as it occurs in little boys. The one he calls *positive*, the other *negative*. The positive form is the one with which we are most familiar. He describes it as follows: "At a very early age the little boy develops an object-cathexis for his mother," and he "deals with his father by identifying with him" (21). For a time, "these two relationships proceed side by side, until the boy's sexual wishes in regard to his mother become more intense and his father is perceived as an obstacle to them; from this the Oedipus complex originates" (21–22). The boy's "identification with his father then takes on a hostile coloring and changes into a wish to get rid of his father in order to take his place with his mother," and, from this time forth, "his relation to his father is ambivalent; it seems as if the ambivalence inherent in the identification from the beginning had become manifest. An ambivalent attitude to his father and an object relation of a solely affectionate kind to his mother make up the content of the simple positive Oedipus complex in a boy" (22). Thus, the boy's primarily loving attitude toward his father has taken on a new hostile coloring. The ambivalence occurs because hatred of his father has become manifest, which means that previous to the intensification of his sexual wishes toward his mother, his love for his father was predominant.

While Freud calls this the positive form of the Oedipus complex, it nonetheless creates an untenable situation, because the boy's previous identification with his father is now based on a wish to get rid of his father. Thus, the complex needs to be "demolished." How is this accomplished? Essentially, "the boy's object-cathexis of his mother must be given up," and its place is filled by one of two things: either an identification with his mother, where his desire to *have* her is replaced by the intention to be *like* her; or an intensification of his identification with his father. The latter outcome is the more normal, as it "permits the affectionate relation to the mother to be in a measure retained," and, because the identification with his father is intensified, "the dissolution of the Oedipus complex . . . consolidates the masculinity in a boy's character" (22).

Two things are noteworthy about the way this form of the Oedipus complex is demolished. One is that the boy's identification with his father (i.e., the intention to be like him) does not begin with the complex itself, but precedes it. Thus, what the demolition of the Oedipus complex achieves is the *intensification* of this identification as compensation for the reduction of the object-cathexis with the mother (which is not completely given up but is "in a measure retained"). The second is that object-choice (or cathexis) and identification are two distinct ways of relating. Object-choice implies affection for the object itself (the desire to *have* the object), whereas identification implies that he puts himself in the other's place (intending to be *like* the object) and develops characteristics and behaviors similar to those of the object. Thus, one possible outcome of the Oedipus complex is that the boy would relinquish his object-choice of his mother entirely and identify with her instead. This is a conceivable outcome, since it was the boy's object-choice of her that was responsible for his relationship to his father, which previously was based on affection, now assuming a hostile coloring. As indicated, however, Freud believes that the more normal outcome is the intensification of the boy's identification with his father. As a result of this intensification, his object-cathexis with his mother is diminished but not given up, an identification with her does not occur, and he is now on his way toward the consolidation of his masculinity.

Thus, in this process, the boy's identification with his father has gone through three stages: first, an original identification in which he related positively to his father; next, a negative identification in which he wants to get rid of his father; and, finally, an intensified desire to be like his father. This intensification of his identification with his father may occur in spite of his continued object-choice of his mother, since he can actually think of himself as progressing, as it were, from a "little boy" to a "little man," one who does many of the things that his father does and which are, presumably, the basis for his father's appeal to his mother. What he can no longer entertain, however, are the desires that usurp his father's primary prerogatives. The attempts to "seduce" his mother (which, as Freud noted in his lecture, are quite amusing to mothers) are among these proscribed behaviors. This does not mean, however, that he must abandon his mother as his object-choice (e.g., by choosing his father instead). As Freud noted in his earlier lecture, there may be some transfer of this object-choice to his sister. Nonetheless, if his object-choice of his mother had been completely abandoned, there would be no occasion for problems to arise in puberty, when feelings associated with this object-choice are intensified.

Freud indicates that focusing on this "simple positive" version of the Oedipus complex may be sufficient. This has certainly been the case with subsequent discussion of his views on the Oedipus complex by others. The demolition of the Oedipus complex is rarely, however, as uncomplicated as this version implies. For, in addition to this positive form of the Oedipus complex, there is a negative form, which has its origins in the fact that children are bisexual. Thus, "a boy has not merely an ambivalent attitude toward his father and an affectionate object-choice towards his mother, but at the same time he also behaves like a girl and displays an affectionate feminine attitude to his father and a corresponding jealousy and hostility towards his mother" (23). It is this "complicating element introduced by bisexuality that makes it so difficult to obtain a clear view of the facts in connection with the earliest object-choices and identifications, and still more difficult to describe them intelligently" (33). Psychoanalytic experience, however, suggests that the two forms may best be viewed as on a continuum, "so that the result is a series with the normal positive Oedipus complex at one end and the inverted negative one at the other, while its intermediate members exhibit the complete form with one of its two components preponderating. . . . The relative intensity of the two identifications in any individual will reflect the preponderance in him of one or other of the two sexual dispositions" (23–24).

This negative form of the Oedipus complex—the inversion of the positive form—is rarely discussed in the secondary literature describing Freud's theory. Nor, as we have seen, did Freud present it in his public lectures on the subject. His suggestion that the boy "displays an affectionate feminine attitude to his father and a corresponding jealousy and hostility towards his mother" is a feature of the Oedipus complex that we hear very little about, perhaps because we so emphasize the boy's identification with his father that we overlook the fact that his father may also be the object of desire. To the extent that he relates to his father as an affectionate object-choice, the jealousy and hostility we normally attribute to his attitudes toward his father are instead felt toward his mother. *She* is viewed as the impediment to his affectionate relationship with his *father*.

Assuming that the Oedipus complex rarely, if ever, appears in its simple positive form, the existence of its negative form not only complicates the observer's task of understanding what is going on in the Oedipal situation—the shifting dynamics of its triangular character—but it also complicates the process of its demolition in the mind or psyche of the small boy. Therefore, says Freud, "it is advisable in general, and quite especially where neurotics are concerned, to assume the existence of the complete Oedipus complex [i.e., both of its forms]. Analytic experience then shows that in a number of cases one or the other constituent disappears, except for barely distinguishable traces" (23). He suggests that mild forms of homosexuality in men confirm that the boy's identification with his father is "a substitute for an affectionate object-choice" (27).

Freud's proposal that there are two forms of the Oedipus complex enables us to see why the second step of the "separation-individuation" process outlined by Osherson—identifying *and* bonding with one's father—is inherently problematic. This is because the boy's "object-choice" of his father (what Osherson calls "bonding with" the father) and "identification" with his father are two different forms of relating. If the boy's original desire is to bond with his father, this form of the Oedipus complex is demolished in order that he will instead make his mother his object-choice. The demolition of this earlier form of the Oedipus complex allows his identification with his father to persist; in fact, this identification takes the form of the fantasy that he, his father's rival, may replace his father in his mother's affections. This intermediate form of the Oedipus complex, however, also needs to be demolished, and this is accomplished by the diminution of his object-cathexis of his mother and the intensification of his identification with his father. This intensified version of his identification with his father involves a determination to become more like his father together with an acceptance of the fact that his father has prerogatives (sexual) with regard to his mother. The fantasy that he will replace his father in his mother's affections needs to be relinquished (repressed) as he intensifies his efforts to emulate his father in other respects. Also, as Freud suggests in his public lecture on the subject, the boy may transfer some of his object-choice of his mother to his sister.

As far as his relationship to his father is concerned, however, the demolition of both forms of the Oedipus complex means that relinquishing his object-choice of his father is one of the prices to be paid for the intensification of his identification with his father, and the relinquishing of *this* object-choice is more absolute than is the case with his object-choice of his mother. Thus, as identification with his father increases, his object-choice of his father decreases to the point of extinction. This explains why the dual task of identification and bonding with his father is inherently contradictory. It helps to account for the fact that men who have achieved the desired masculine identification (i.e., have developed a masculine character or identity) feel the absence of a loving relationship with their fathers. Moreover, the fact that they once had this loving relationship—when their fathers *were* their primary object-choice—remains in their unconscious and informs them of what they once had but have since given up. That is, they know from their own earlier experience what an emotional bond with their fathers is like. It is no mere figment of their imaginations. Then, however, their object-choice of their mothers emerged, and with this, their ambivalent feelings toward their fathers also became manifest, as their fathers became the object of jealousy and hostility.

Conclusion

While Freud's concept of the Oedipus Complex has been the subject of much criticism, even ridicule, it provides an explanation for why the second step of the "separation-individuation" process—that of identifying *and* bonding with one's father—is inherently problematic. If, in the preceding chapters, we saw how the emotional separation from the mother—the first of the two steps in the separation-individuation process—is also problematic, we have seen in this chapter that the second step is also doomed to at least partial failure. In the next chapter, we will see why identification must prevail over object-choice of (or bonding with) one's father, and we will see that, for Freud, religion plays a decisive role in ensuring that this occurs. As we will also see, the effects of religion in this regard happened in early childhood, long before the boy was ever conscious of "being religious."

CHAPTER 4

~

The Father of Personal Prehistory

In the preceding chapter, we saw that the small boy's desire to relate to his father in an affectionate way is undermined by his choice of his mother as his primary object of desire. This makes it possible for an intensification of his identification with his father to emerge. The question that I want to take up in this chapter is what prompted the boy to relinquish his father as his object-choice, and what ensures that he will not regress back to this object-choice later but will instead continue on the course that has been laid out for him? This question introduces Freud's view that religion, especially in its Judeo-Christian form, plays a decisive role in this regard. This means that, as far as relations between fathers and sons are concerned, religion is profoundly implicated in what James E. Dittes calls "the male predicament" (1985). Religion ensures that emotional bonding with one's father cannot occur, and that intensification of identification occurs instead.

One very important implication of this argument is that more "enlightened" approaches to child rearing—those in which the father has a greater role in the process—will not succeed in bridging the emotional distance between father and son. Another implication, however, is that individual fathers and sons ought not blame themselves for this failure, for they are confronting a very long and very powerful tradition. That any degree of emotional attachment between a father and a son is achieved may be counted as something of a miracle, and it ought to be celebrated as such.

What Happens to a Boy's Longing for His Father?

In the preceding chapter, we saw that the normal way in which the Oedipus complex is demolished is through an intensification of the boy's identification with his father. This raises the obvious question: What happens to his affectionate object-choice of his father? In his discussion of the Oedipus complex in *The Ego and the Id*, Freud suggests that this object-choice is repressed, such repression being one of the functions of the superego, which is the heir of the Oedipus complex. Thus, the superego is "not simply a residue of the earliest object-choices of the id; it also represents an energetic reaction-formation against those choices" (Freud 1960a, 34). In this way, a boy is set on a path in which, as Freud puts it, his "higher nature" will predominate over his "lower nature." Central to the development of his higher nature is his identification with his father, including the capacity to discriminate between the ways in which he may and may not identify with his father; that is, some of his father's activities and characteristics are ones that a small boy may not emulate. Thus, the superego (or ego-ideal) "answers to everything that is expected of the higher nature of man" (37). Furthermore, it is "a substitute for a longing for the father," and, therefore, "it contains the germ from which all religions have evolved. The self-judgment which declares that the ego falls short of its ideal produces the religious sense of humility to which the believer appeals in his longing" (37).

Thus, Freud introduces religion as a pale substitute for the boy's object-choice of his father, and therefore as assisting, albeit indirectly, in the achievement of the intensification of the boy's identification with his father. Hence, religion offers a compromise: In exchange for its demand that the boy give up much of his object-choice of his mother and intensify his identification with his father, religion provides means by which a boy may continue to give expression to his longing for—his object-choice of—his father, but only if he does this within the framework of self judgment. In effect, he adopts a "feminine attitude" toward his father in this act of humility, and in this way he is able to recognize—though not openly express—his affectionate desire for his father. Religion is a pale reminiscence of this object-choice, and his confession is a compromise-formation. By "confessing," he is able to express the forbidden desire in a disguised form. The act of confessing and seeking forgiveness is the vehicle by means of which he keeps his object-choice for his father alive, though in a much diminished—and redirected—form.

It makes sense to ask why the boy is confessing in the first place. Of what is he guilty? To be sure, his guilt is partly associated with the fact that his mother is the object of his desire. Thus, he anticipates that by humbly confessing this desire for his mother to his father—adopting an attitude of humble supplication and repentance—he will placate his father and avoid his father's punishment. This explains, in part, why, as Freud suggested in his public lectures on the Oedipus complex, some boys become "subservient" to their fathers. They are doing penance, as it were, for having made their mothers their object-choice. This is confession as the positive form of the Oedipus complex would represent it. The boy may also, however, feel guilty for his object-choice of his father, for this object-choice is a remnant of his "lower nature." This is confession as the negative form of the Oedipus complex would understand it. For reasons which I will set forth in a moment, guilt over the object-choice of his father is likely to be much stronger than guilt over the object-choice of his mother.

To summarize Freud's argument thus far, Freud views religion as the locus in which a boy may continue to express his affectionate desire for his father, but indirectly. In effect, religion enables him to act toward his father as his object-choice, but in such a disguised form that he does not make himself vulnerable to social censure. His "confession," after all, is not addressed to his real father but to his heavenly Father. Thus, what Freud calls his "feminine attitude" toward the father is given expression only in the circumscribed arena of religious devotion. Outside of religion, the consolidation of his masculinity continues according to the requirements of the demolition of his positive Oedipus complex. By circumscribing the negative form of the Oedipus complex, religion thus serves the larger objective of the resolution of the positive form of the Oedipus complex. Also, by confessing to his heavenly Father, not his actual father, he does not evoke any of the anxieties his father might otherwise have regarding the meaning that the boy's object-choice may have for his own (i.e., the father's) masculinity. Religion is an outlet, a safety valve, a place where the "feminine attitude" of the boy toward the father can be humbly—and guiltily—expressed.

If this were the whole story, we would be justified in concluding that religion is a relatively benign factor in the development of a boy toward manhood, as it is the locus in which he may safely express, even indulge, his desire to have the father for himself. No doubt, there are many men who have found religion to be benign in just this sense. What, after all, is wrong with affirming one's "feminine attitude," especially if this occurs within the carefully circumscribed limits that religious devotion affords? Surely this is preferable to assuming a subservient attitude toward his own father, which may threaten or even undermine his identification with his father's masculine character. And what is wrong with adopting an attitude of humility—of humble submission to his heavenly Father—even if this is the only form in which he may legitimately give expression to his object-choice of the father?

There is a more ominous side to this compromise-formation, however, which arises from the fact that the boy's object-choice of his father must be sacrificed in favor of the intensification of his identification with his father. We are so accustomed to viewing the sacrifice required by the demolition of the Oedipus complex in terms of the boy's need to temper, if not totally relinquish, his *mother* as his object-choice that we are virtually oblivious to the sacrifice of his object-choice of his father, which, as Freud points out, is a more absolute sacrifice. To explore this sacrifice further, we need to consider its homophobic implications. In my view, this is the dark side of the demolition of the Oedipus complex in both of its forms.

Homophobia: The Dark Side of the Demolition

It may have occurred to some readers that Freud's discussion of the father as the boy's object-choice may provide an explanation for why some boys become homosexual. That is, they are unable to relinquish this object-choice and are thus disposed toward same-sex relationships. As we have seen, Freud believed that some "mild cases" of homosexuality provide evidence for his view that fathers are a more original object-choice than mothers for boys in early childhood. But he does not make the claim that homosexuality is "caused" by the failure to relinquish this object-choice. In fact, he does not believe that any boys do in fact fail to relinquish it. The "cause" or "causes" of homosexuality need to be sought elsewhere.

His discussion of this issue in *Group Psychology and the Analysis of the Ego* (originally published in 1921) indicates that he has a very different explanation for male homosexuality. In his chapter on identification, he presents an earlier version of his analysis of the two forms of the Oedipus complex that he expands upon in *The Ego and the Id*. Here he makes a distinction "between an identification with the father and the choice of the father as an object. In the first case one's father is what one would like to *be*, and in the second he is what one would like to *have*" (Freud 1960b, 106). Instead of arguing that the boy's object-choice of his father is the genesis of male homosexuality, however, he suggests that, in a large number of cases, its genesis follows this trajectory: "A young man has been unusually long and intensely fixated upon his mother in the sense of the Oedipus complex. But at last, after the end of puberty, the time comes for exchanging his mother for some other sexual object" (50).

But what if the adolescent boy does not exchange his mother for another sexual object? Supposing that "things take a sudden turn: the young man does not abandon his mother, but identifies himself with her; he transforms himself into her, and now looks about for objects which can replace his ego for him, and on which he can bestow such love and care as he had experienced from his mother" (50). In effect, the boy's object-choice of his mother has been replaced by intensified identification with her. Freud believes that this is how a boy, at the end of puberty, takes a homosexual turn. Thus, for him, homosexuality does not have its origin in the object-choice of his father. Rather, it has largely to do with a boy's object-choice of his mother being transformed into an intensified identification with her, which leads him to search for objects to whom he may relate as a kind of surrogate mother. This shift from object-choice to intensified identification with his mother (the very pattern he followed in relation to his father in the demolition of the negative form of the Oedipus complex) inhibits an "exchange" of his mother for a female sexual object. Freud seems to assume here that a man can "mother" another man more naturally than he could "mother" a woman.

While this view of how homosexuality may develop might appear to lend support to the view that an emotional separation between a small boy and his mother needs to occur (for, otherwise, he will become a homosexual when he reaches adulthood), this seems to me to be a serious misunderstanding of what the demolition of the Oedipus complex in early childhood is principally about. As we have seen, Freud does not contend that the small boy's object-choice of his mother needs to be wholly given up. In fact, not only is this an unrealistic expectation, but this would also create the opposite danger that the boy would revert back to his object-choice of his father, which in turn would inhibit the intensification of his identification with his father, which is the primary goal of the demolition of the Oedipus complex.

This means that Freud does not endorse an emotional separation initiated by the small boy's mother in early childhood. Fear that her small son will become a homosexual adult if she does not distance herself from him—the "mama's boy" phenomenon—is an unfounded anxiety. Also, Freud takes for granted that the young man "has been unusually long and intensely fixated upon his mother" during puberty, and he does not imply that the man who becomes a homo-sexual adult is unique in this regard. The difference occurs at the *end* of puberty, when a young man needs to exchange his mother for another sexual object. The homosexual youth does this, but the difference in the way he does it is that he exchanges his object-choice of his mother for an intensified identification with her. This directly influences his new object-choice.

There may well be problems with Freud's argument in *Group Psychology and the Analysis of the Ego* as to how some young men become homosexually oriented. Certainly this brief synopsis leaves many unanswered questions. But for our purposes, the argument as presented here makes clear that, for Freud, the boy's object-choice of his father in early childhood has little if anything to do with the genesis of male homosexuality. It may, however, be profoundly implicated in male homophobia. Christopher Lane makes this point in *The Burdens of Intimacy: Psychoanalysis and Victorian Masculinity*. Citing Freud's essay, "Dostoevsky and Parricide," published in 1928, Lane notes Freud's argument that the demolition of the Oedipus complex in early childhood does not completely resolve "the boy's 'feminine attitude' toward the father. Instead, the ego—striving for internal harmony at any price—reproduces this attitude in a modified form and adopts a passive relation to the superego, which is 'a substitute for a longing for the father'" (Lane 1999, 115). In other words, "the ego's submission to the superego is not only an indication of femininity, but implicitly a punishment for it: the superego administers threats and judgments that respond to the boy's residual sexual interest in his father" (115). Thus, "Freud gives us the basis of a complex psychoanalytic account of homophobia here, in which the boy's renunciation of effeminacy ('the feminine attitude') is an effect of psychic and, to a lesser extent, cultural pressure" (115).

Homophobia, therefore, originates in the repression of the boy's object-choice of his father. To express love for his father—the desire to *have* his father as his own—is to generate homophobic fears, that is, fears rooted in the expectation of being punished for his "feminine" object-choice of his father. Lane points out that this fear is more the effect of psychic than cultural pressures. I would add that it is also more the effect of internal physic pressures than of the actual behavior of the boy's father toward him. The superego, after all, is an internal reality, and it may not bear much relation, if any, to the actual attitudes of the boy's father toward his son's expressions of longing for him. As Freud's lecture on the Oedipus complex indicates, a father may actually try to win his son over by his benevolent concern for him, only to be rebuffed because the boy's mother is his new object-choice.

In short, guilt over the desire to relate to his father in terms of object-choice underlies homophobia, and deeply implicated in this homophobia is the boy's psychic reaction against behaving like a girl toward his father. It is only in religion, when a boy (or man) adopts the posture of humble confession, that he is able to express his longing for the father in a way that does not evoke a homophobic reaction. Thus, homophobia is the price we pay   as individuals and as a society—for the demolition of the positive Oedipus complex in the way Freud describes it. If the demolition of the Oedipus complex solves the problem of incest involving mother and son, it creates the problem of homophobia. The guilt and punishment from a cruel superego that a boy experiences regarding his object-choice of his father may thus be deeper and more traumatic than the guilt and fear of superego punishment he feels for his object-choice of his mother. After all, there is a sense in which the object-choice of his mother serves an important psychic purpose, namely, that of preparing the boy to make an "appropriate" object-choice when he reaches manhood. The object-choice of his father serves no comparable use, for it only stands in the way of the further development and consolidation of his identification with his father. In this sense, the boy's object-choice of his father has an indirect, but very tenuous, connection to homosexuality via the role of this object-choice in the genesis of homophobia. The roots of this homophobia are not, however, due to same-sex desire as such but to the psychic perception that desire for the father is feminine, and thus a threat to the boy's consolidation of his masculinity.

Why Object-Choice of the Father Is Not a Factor in the Development of a Melancholy Self

We have seen that the boy's object-choice of his father is not, for Freud, the direct cause of homosexuality. But is it a factor in the boy's development of a melancholy self? This question arises because, in his chapter on identification in *Group Psychology and the Analysis of the Ego*, Freud follows his discussion of how homosexuality develops with a consideration of melancholia. He alludes here to his earlier essay on "Mourning and Melancholia," and suggests that melancholia occurs when an object-choice is insufficiently compensated by the intensification of identification. When such compensation does not occur, the emotional loss of a loved object results in "a cruel self-depreciation of the ego combined with relentless self-criticism and bitter self-reproaches. Analyses have shown that this disparagement and these reproaches apply at bottom to the object and represent the ego's revenge upon it. The shadow of the object has fallen upon the ego" (Freud 1960b, 51). Thus, melancholia occurs when a boy's identification, because it is not intensified, does not compensate for the repression of his affectionate desire. Without such intensification of identification, he is uncompensated for his loss, and he turns against the lost loved object which, now internalized, is an aspect of his own ego. As in the case of homophobia, Freud refers here to an internal, psychic process. With melancholia, the ego is divided, "fallen apart into two pieces, one of which rages against the second. The second piece is the one which has been altered by introjection and which contains the lost object" (52). The first piece is the superego, which behaves "cruelly" toward the second piece in the form of self-depreciation and reproach. What melancholia masks is the fact that the real object of reproach is the lost, loved object who has been given up as a viable love-object.

By relating our earlier discussion of confession to Freud's consideration of the church in *Group Psychology and the Analysis of the Ego*, we can see that religion (at least in its Judeo-Christian form) *inhibits* the development of a father-related melancholia in the young boy. As we have seen, the religious sense of humility (the "feminine attitude") reflected in confession enables the boy to reveal his longing for his father in a socially acceptable way. Confession is a means by which the boy "informs" the object of his confession (his heavenly Father) that, while he occasionally lapses into the desire to have his own father as his own, he is in fact dedicated to the intensification of his identification with his father. Confession, then, may be viewed as an antidote against a melancholic reaction to the loss of his object-choice of his father. This is because confession—the adoption of a feminine attitude toward his heavenly Father—provides an alternative response to the loss of his father as a loved object to that of internalized rage and melancholic self-reproach. Through the adoption of an attitude of feminine humility and submission, confession does its reparative work by precluding the development of a deeper, more patho-logical self-reproach, and by inhibiting the impulse to avenge his loss by replacing this impulse with an appeal for forgiveness for desiring the object and for any resentment felt over having to relinquish the object This analy-sis helps us to understand why confession—usually to a father figure (priest) who represents the heavenly Father—assumed such great importance in the history of Christianity. By institutionalizing confession, Christianity reduced the likelihood of the development of melancholia in relation to the earthly father. It provided an outlet for the indirect expression of longing for one's father, and by providing this release, it inhibited a revengeful attitude toward one's father and assisted in the consolidation of masculinity through the intensification of identification with father and father's world.

Freud's discussion of the church in his chapter "Two Artificial Groups: The Church and the Army," in *Group Psychology and the Analysis of the Ego*, provides another, complementary explanation for how Christianity inhibits the development of melancholy over the loss of one's father as object-choice. Here Freud complains that recent analyses of groups by social scientists have failed to take adequate account of the role of the leader in keeping social groups from disintegrating. To illustrate his point, he suggests that the church and the army are two groups that are not held together by fear but by love, especially the illusion that the head of the church (Christ) and the head of the army (commander-in-chief) love "all the individuals in the group with an equal love" (33). It is this illusion that enables the group to remain intact even in cases where fear of external threats would cause other social groupings (e.g., mass audiences) to panic: "Everything depends upon this illusion; if it were to be dropped, then both Church and army would dissolve, so far as the external force permitted them to" (94). As far as the church specifically is con-cerned, "This equal love was expressly enunciated by Christ: 'Inasmuch as ye have done it unto one of the least of these my brethren, ye have done it unto me'" (94). This means that "he stands to the individual members of the group of believers in the relation of a kind elder brother; he is their substitute father. All the demands that are made upon the individual are derived from this love of Christ's. A democratic strain runs through the Church, for the very reason that before Christ everyone is equal, and that everyone has an equal share in his love" (33).

Freud views Christ as both "a kind elder brother" and "substitute father." What the Church offers the boy who has relinquished his father as his love-object is Christ, the "substitute father." Christ is the one to whom the boy (and man) may relate in terms of love—male object-choice—as long as he relinquishes the desire for an exclusive love between himself and Christ. Christ is shared with others. As Freud indicated in his public lecture, the

Oedipus complex gets transformed into a family complex, with, for example, the object-choice of the mother being partially transferred to the sister. His analysis of the Church, with his suggestion that Christ becomes the "elder brother" who also serves as "substitute father," is consistent with this suggestion.

There may also be an autobiographical element in his view that Christ may be both substitute father *and* kind elder brother. In *The Psychopathology of Everyday Life* (originally published in 1901), he relates that his relationship "with my father was changed by a visit to England, which resulted in my getting to know my half-brother, the child of my father's first marriage, who lived there. My brother's eldest son is the same age as I am" (Freud 1989, 282). However, "the relations between our ages were no hindrance to my phantasies of how different things would have been if I had been born the son not of my father but of my brother" (282). Thus, his much older half-brother also doubled in his phantasy life as a substitute father. Conceivably, this older half-brother is the model for his representation of Christ as the head of the Church.

Freud's analysis of the Church suggests that Christ, its leader, is a deterrant to the development of melancholia relating to the loss of the father as object-choice. As the kindly elder brother, Christ takes the father's place. He endorses and reciprocates the transfer of the boy's object-choice from his earthly father to Christ (who is one with the Father) as long as he does not expect that Christ's love for him will be exclusive. There is, however, ample love to go around. An inclusive love of Christ for his church ensures too that the group will not disintegrate due to jealousy. Within the compensatory structure of love for Christ, the deep self-reproach and the revenge against the lost love-object characteristic of melancholia do not occur, and because they do not, the intensification of identification with the boy's earthly father proceeds without serious impediment.

If a melancholic reaction to the loss of his object-choice of his father is averted by the religious means indicated, the object-choice itself is nonetheless denigrated as the price to be paid for the intensification of his identification with his father and his father's world. His ambivalence toward his father, reflected in his continuing (if sharply reduced) desire to have—not merely be like—his father is denigrated as a vestige of his "feminine attitude," that is, of his failure to fully consolidate his masculinity, and this is something for which he feels especially guilty and ashamed. Our earlier discussion of homophobia among men indicates how deep this guilt and shame becomes. As we have seen, Christianity allows for the acknowledgment of these desires for the father, but only in the context of confession and via the ideal of being "brothers in Christ." Immediate and direct love for his father is proscribed. While this also means that loving relationships among men are allowed to the extent that they are "spiritualized" (i.e., reflective of their "higher natures"), I am principally concerned here with the father-son relationship, and with the fact that emotional bonding with one's own father is disallowed.

The question is whether religion is merely a consequence of this proscription—that is, merely compensatory for it—or is also its cause. Does religion contribute to a psychological predisposition for boys to be afraid of relating to their fathers as object-choices, and to assume that the only way they may safely relate to their fathers is by identification with them? And does it contribute to the boy's belief that he is wrong to feel jealousy toward his mother for her prior and more successful claim on his father as object-choice?

The Religion of the Father of Personal Prehistory

In his discussion of the Oedipus complex in *The Ego and the Id*, Freud indicates that religion is much more than a compensation for the proscription of love for the father, that religion is deeply implicated in the very origins of this proscription. This suggestion occurs in his discussion of the need for the boy, and subsequently the man, to develop the "capacity for resisting the influences of abandoned object-cathexes" (Freud 1960a, 31). He recognizes that whatever successes a boy or man may have in this regard, "the effects of the first identification made in earliest childhood will be general and lasting" (31). This, he points out, leads us back "to the origin of the ego ideal [or superego]; for behind it there lies hidden an individual's first and most important identification, his *identification with the father in his own personal prehistory*" (31, my emphasis). Freud notes that this original identification "is apparently not in the first instance the consequence or outcome of an object-cathexis." Rather, "it is a direct and immediate identification and takes place earlier than any object-cathexis. But the object-choices belonging to the first sexual period and relating to the father and mother seem normally to find their outcome in an identification of this kind, and would thus reinforce the primary one" (21).

Freud acknowledges the complicated nature of this "whole subject," but his primary point is clear, namely, that the boy has experience of an identification with a prehistoric father before his object-choice of his human or natural father has had a chance to form. In addition, the temporal and thus psychic priority of this identification with a prehistoric father over the boy's object-choice of his natural father is what enforces or makes necessary his abandonment of this object-choice. Thus, the "father in his own personal prehistory" provides an explanation for why the boy feels it is necessary to abandon his object-choice of his father and, in thus abandoning it, to relate to his mother as his exclusive object-choice.

But who is this father of personal prehistory? Freud's discussion of the development of the two forms of the Oedipus complex, which we have reviewed in detail, was intended, in part, to provide an answer to this very question. Following his review of these two psychic processes, he turns, in the concluding paragraphs of his chapter on "The Ego and the Super-Ego (Ego-Ideal)," to a brief discussion of religion and morality. Here he cites the hypothesis he put forward in *Totem and Taboo* (originally published in 1913), that both religion and morality "were acquired phylogenetically out of the father-complex" (Freud 1950, 27). The word *phylogeny*, coined by Ernest Haeckel, a German biologist and philosopher, refers to the lines of descent and evolutionary development of a plant or animal species. It is distinguished from *ontogeny*, which refers to the life cycle of a single organism or the biological development of the individual. A detailed discussion of the hypothesis presented in *Totem and Taboo* would take us too far afield, but Freud's essential point for our purposes here is that the human species has a phylogenetic father who is imprinted in the psyche of each and every individual. Being phylogenetic, this father is there, as it were, from the beginning of every individual's existence, whereas the father of the individual—the father of ontogeny—is a later acquisition. The boy "knows" the phylogenetic father before he "knows" the ontogenetic father.

Thus, while Freud, as he points out in *An Autobiographical Study* (originally published in 1925, with a postscript added in 1935), did not believe that religion possesses a "material truth," it does have a "historical truth" (Freud 1952, 138). That is, religion is "true" in the sense that it lives phylogenetically. Freud also believed that Judaism—and, by extension, Christianity—were "truer" than religions based on polytheism, because their emphasis on a single God was more accurate phylogenetically (see *Moses and Monotheism*, 1939).

We can say, therefore, that "the father of personal prehistory" is the boy's mnemonic (or remembered) image of the deity (see Rizzuto 1979, 17), and that this image is the nucleus of the boy's subsequent and more nuanced image of the heavenly Father of the Judeo-Christian tradition. Against this phylogenetic image, the boy's object-choice of his natural father, a later acquisition, does not stand a chance. It is true that Freud asserts in *Totem and Taboo* that "the psychoanalysis of individual human beings" teaches us "that the god of each of them is found in the likeness of his father" and "that his personal relation to God depends on his relation to his father in the flesh," which "oscillates and changes along with that relation." Yet Freud also asserts that "at bottom God is nothing other than an exalted father" (Freud 1950, 147), or even, as he puts it in *Civilization and Its Discontents* (originally published in 1930), "an enormously exalted father" (Freud 1961, 21). It is doubtful that this image of God is so "exalted" merely because the small boy experiences his father as towering over him. Moreover, because this image originates *before* the boy has aggressive and hostile feelings toward his own father, this exalted image would not be the consequence of his fear of his father's retaliation against him. I suggest, therefore, that what exalts this image of God is precisely the element in it that derives from "the father of personal prehistory."

The Phobic Power of the Maternal Grandfather

If this father of personal prehistory comes to have an association with a human father in the boy's psychic development, I suggest that he is more likely to be the grandfather than the father, and, as I now want to show, this has direct bearing on the role that religion plays in devaluing the boy's object-choice of his own father. While the following may appear, at times, to be a rather tendentious argument, I hope that the reader will bear with me, as it involves several steps. First, Freud and his early associates were greatly interested in the psychology of grandparents (see Rapaport 1958). Karl Abraham wrote "Some Remarks on the Role of Grandparents in the Psychology of Neuroses." Sandor Ferenczi wrote "The Grandfather Complex." Ernest Jones wrote "The Significance of the Grandfather for the Fate of the Individual." All three of these essays appeared in 1913, the same year that Freud's *Totem and Taboo* was published. Concerning the grandfather, Abraham's comment is typical: "In the associations of a neurotic the figure of the father is accompanied constantly by the figure of the grandfather (on the maternal side) like a shadow" (cited in Rapaport 1958, 534).

In "The Occurrence in Dreams of Material from Fairy-Tales" (also published in 1913), Freud relates the case of a man who was later to gain notoriety in his "Wolf Man" case (originally published in 1918). This man recalled his first anxiety dream when, according to his own account, he was "three, four, or at most five years old at the time. From then until my eleventh or twelfth year I was always afraid of seeing something terrible in my dreams" (Freud 1958a, 80). The dream involved his being terrified to see six or seven white wolves sitting on a large walnut tree that was visible from his bedroom window. They were sitting quite still, with their whole attention riveted on him. He awoke in terror, evidently of being eaten up by the wolves. His initial recollection was that the dream was related to his older sister taunting him with a fearsome picture of the wolf in "Little Red Riding Hood." Further exploration revealed, however, that the dream was the conflation of a wolf story his grandfather had previously told him and the story of "The Wolf and the Seven Little Goats." Freud's primary interest in the essay is to demonstrate how material from fairy-tales reappears in dreams. He also points out, however, that in this particular case, the effect of these stories was reflected in the boy's development of an animal phobia, a phobia that "was only distinguished from other similar cases by the fact that the anxiety-animal was not an object easily accessible to observation (such as a horse or a dog), but was known to him only from stories and picture-books" (82).

Freud says that he will defer an "explanation of these animal-phobias and the significance attaching to them," but assures the reader that this explanation for the animal phobia in this case will be "in complete harmony with the principal characteristics shown by the neurosis from which the present dreamer suffered in the later period of his life" (82–83), namely that "fear of his father was the strongest motive for his falling ill, and his ambivalent attitude towards every father-surrogate was the dominating feature of his life as well as of his behavior during the treatment" (83). Freud concludes the essay by observing that the wolf in his patient's case was a "father-surrogate," and he guesses that "the hidden content" in the fairy-tales was, quite simply, "infantile fear of the father" (83). In support of this speculation, he notes that his patient's father "had the characteristic, shown by so many people in relation to their children, of indulging in '*affectionate abuse*'; and it is possible that during the patient's earlier years his father (though he grew severe later on) may more than once, as he caressed the little boy or played with him, threatened in fun to 'gobble him up'" (83). In support of this educated guess, Freud mentions another patient telling him "that her two children could never get to be fond of their grandfather, because in the course of his affectionate romping with them he used to frighten them by saying he would cut open their tummies" (83).

Freud makes no direct comment in the essay regarding the fact that it was the patient's grandfather who told the story of the wolves, a story which, in Freud's view, "contains an unmistakable allusion to the castration-complex" (81). He does note, however, that the story the patient's grandfather told clearly informs the dream, so that, while the patient could not remember whether he heard it before or after the dream, "its subject is a decisive argument in favor of the former view" (81). This suggests that, whatever ambivalences the boy had toward his own father, his animal phobia was more closely associated with his grandfather. Freud's concluding comment about the two children who could never get to be fond of their grandfather, as well as his observation that the patient's "ambivalent attitude towards every father-surrogate was the dominant feature of his life," supports this judgment.

Freud reserved the explanation of these animal phobias for another occasion. This explanation is, in fact, presented in *Totem and Taboo*, which, as I have indicated, was published the same year as this essay on fairy-tale material in dreams. In his chapter on "The Return of Totemism in Childhood," he takes up the claim of several students of ancient religions that a large number of customs and usages in modern societies may be explained as remnants of a totemic age. A detailed discussion of the features of totemism is unnecessary here, but, in essence, a totem is an animal or natural object considered to be ancestrally related to a given kin or descent group and taken as its symbol. An image of this totem may itself become an object of devotion (the totem pole of ancient tribes of the northwest coast of North America being perhaps the most familiar example).

Freud's primary argument in *Totem and Taboo* is that the totem originates from the murder of the father of the clan by his sons, and that it represents their guilt and desire for expiation. This works psychodynamically because there was no tendency among primitive societies to draw the "hard-and-fast line between their own nature and that of all other animals" that is reflective of premodern and modern societies. In his chapter on the return of totemism in childhood, Freud notes that children are more like their primitive than their modern ancestors in this regard, in that they too "have no scruples over allowing animals to rank as their full equals. Uninhibited as they are in the avowal of their bodily needs, they no doubt feel themselves more akin to animals than to their elders, who may well be a puzzle to them" (Freud 1950, 127).

Quite frequently, though, a strange rift will occur in the excellent relations between children and animals: "A child will suddenly begin to be frightened of some particular species of animal and to avoid touching or seeing any individual of that species" (127). The clinical picture of an animal phobia thus emerges, "a very common, and perhaps the earliest, form of psycho-neurotic illness occurring in childhood" (127). While these phobias may involve animals in the child's own neighborhood, the "senseless and immoderate fear shown in these phobias is sometimes attached to animals known to the child from picture books and fairy tales" (127).

Freud acknowledges that no detailed analytic examination of children's animal phobias has been presented as yet, but in the few cases of this kind directed toward the larger animals there has been one thing in common: "Where the children concerned were boys, their fear related at bottom to their father and had merely been displaced on to the animal" (127–28). He relates several cases, one in which a nine-year-old boy begged any dog that he encountered not to bite him, promising that he would not "play with his fiddle" (i.e., masturbate), having been forbidden by his father to engage in this practice. Of particular interest here, however, is Sandor Ferenczi's case (summarized by Freud) involving a two-and-a-half-year-old boy, who, on summer holiday, had tried to urinate in the chicken house, whereupon a chicken had either bitten or snapped at his penis. The next summer his "one interest was in the fowl-house and in what went on there and he abandoned human speech in favor of cackling and crowing" (130). By the time he was five years old, he had recovered his speech, but his sole interest were chickens and other kinds of poultry. They were his only toys and he sang only songs that had some mention of fowls in them.

Freud observes that the boy's "attitude toward his totem animal was superlatively ambivalent: he showed both hatred and love to an extravagant degree. His favorite game was playing slaughtering fowls." The slaughtering of fowls was a regular festival for him. He would dance around the animals' bodies for hours at a time in a state of intense excitement. But afterwards, "he would kiss and stroke the slaughtered animal or would clean and caress the toy fowls that he had himself ill-treated" (130).

Ferenczi's own interpretation of the boy's interest in fowls centers on the Oedipal theme. In his view, the boy's interest in the poultry yard gratified his sexual curiosity. At this time (five years old) he spoke of his desire to marry his mother. Freud contends, however, that the boy's "totemic interests did not arise in direct relation with his Oedipus complex but on the basis of its narcissistic precondition, the fear of castration" (130). Freud suggests that there is ample evidence in this case that he feared his father in this regard, who is the "dreaded enemy to the sexual interests of childhood" (130).

He concludes from his discussion of Ferenczi's case that the boy's "complete identification with his totem animal and his ambivalent emotional attitude to it" justify "substituting the father for the totem animal in the formula for totemism (in the case of males)" (131). In his judgment, there is really nothing new or particularly daring in this view because "primitive men say the very same thing themselves, and, where the totemic system is still in force today, they describe the totem as their common ancestor and primal father. All we have done is to take at its literal value an expression used by these people, of which anthropologists have been able to make very little and which they have themselves been glad to keep in the background" (131).

Ferenczi's case is especially interesting for our purposes here, however, because it concerns a boy who was two-and-a-half years old when he had the initial traumatic experience that precipitated his phobia, and then follows the course of his phobia to his fifth year. As Freud indicates, the onset of the phobia preceded the formation of his Oedipus complex; thus it occurred before he had reason to fear his own father. Subsequent developments of the phobia, especially those that evoked his fascination with the slaughter of the fowls and with their sexual activities, *were* associated with the Oedipus complex, and these clearly indicated an association of his phobia with his own father. But these developed later, and were not the basis for the original formation of the phobia. I question, therefore, whether the boy's own father was the focus of his castration anxiety, for the original traumatic episode that led to a phobic reaction occurred at the time when his father was his object-choice. More likely, the focus was his maternal grandfather, who was, in turn, a living representation of the father of personal prehistory.

While there is no reference to the grandfather in Freud's account of Ferenczi's case, it may not be a coincidence that Ferenczi's essay on "The Grandfather Complex" was published the same year (1913) as his case of the boy with the fowl phobia ("A Little Chanticleer"). Freud's view that the boy's fear of castration precedes the Oedipus complex itself—that this fear does not arise from the boy's fear that it is in retaliation for his object-choice of his mother—also supports the view that "the return of totemism in childhood" is likely to relate to dynamics between the boy and his grandfather.

The Mythohistorical Power of the Maternal Grandfather

Otto Rank's *The Myth of the Birth of the Hero* (originally published in 1909), provides considerable mythological support for this view. In his editor's introduction to Rank's major work, Philip Freund makes the interesting observation that Rank came to believe that "the cult of Freud was colored too much by the personality of Freud himself, a patriarchal figure who in youth had been the victim of an Oedipus complex (wherefore he greatly exaggerated its importance in others); for Freud had been the adoring child of a young mother nearer in age to her son than to her husband—*Sigmund Freud's father had been old enough to be his grandfather instead*" (Rank 1964, viii, my emphasis). Freud's mother was twenty-one years old when he was born, while his father was forty-one years old, and previously married. While his father ignored virtually all religious observances, he continued to read the Bible (i.e., the Old Testament) at home, and in Hebrew (Gay 1988, 6). This suggests that Freud was more likely to ascribe to his own father the grandfatherly traits that other boys, with fathers whose age was nearer that of their mothers, would have ascribed to their grandfathers instead. His association of his father with the Bible would have reinforced the connection in his mind between his own father and the father of personal prehistory (as represented, for example, in the figure of Moses). Other members of the psychoanalytic community were more disposed than Freud to maintain a stricter separation between the grandfather and the father.

In any event, Rank cites several myths in which the threat posed to a young boy who was destined to become a hero was his maternal grandfather's infanticidal intentions. For example, the myth of Perseus concerns Acrisius, the king of Argos, who had reached an advanced age without having a son. He consulted the Delphian oracle, who warned him against male descendants and informed him that his daughter Danae would bear a son through whose hand he would perish. Danae conceived through the direct agency of Zeus and gave birth to a son, Perseus. On learning of the birth, Acrisius killed the nurse and, refusing to believe that Zeus was the father, placed his daughter and her newborn son in a box and cast them into the sea. The box was carried by the waves to the coast of Seriphos, where a fisherman drew it out of the sea with his nets. He kept the mother and child as his relations. But when King Polydectes, the brother of the fisherman, became enamored of the mother, he sent Perseus away. Various heroic deeds by Perseus followed, but in throwing the discs during a contest, he accidentally killed his grandfather, and succeeded him on the throne (Rank 1964, 25–26). What is especially striking about this story is that, unlike the story of Oedipus, the theme of marrying the mother is absent. The only issue is the death of the grandfather at the hands of the grandson. In this sense, the story may be viewed as pre-Oedipal.

In a Celtic saga, Habis, the illegitimate son of a king's daughter, is persecuted in all sorts of ways by his royal grandfather, Gargoris, but is always protected by divine providence, leading his grandfather finally to recognize him as his successor (56). Another example is the story of Moses. Citing the view of Eduard Meyer that the version of the story recounted in Exodus 2:1–10 is the work of a later author, Rank contends that Moses' biological mother is the Pharaoh's daughter, and that she circumvented his decree that the infant was to be drowned in the river Nile by giving him to her handmaiden to rear as her own son. Here, Rank notes, we have "the familiar theme (grandfather type) of the king whose daughter is to bear a son, but who, on being warned by the ill-omened interpretation of a dream, resolves to kill his forthcoming grandson" (83).

Rank believes that these myths are essentially a displacement of hostile feelings felt toward the father onto the grandfather (78–79). It may be argued, however, that a small boy, prior to the emergence of the Oedipus complex, will in fact find his grandfather to be a daunting, even threatening figure. If he is not yet disposed to distinguish between animals and humans, why assume that he would be able clearly to distinguish the one father from the other? And, between the two, would he not find the older one more patriarchal and thus more foreboding? This father may also be experienced as more remote, as the man who makes occasional visits to the boy's home and who is therefore more similar to the father of personal prehistory and more remote than the father who lives in the same household. At the very least, as Karl Abraham suggests, these myths confirm that the maternal grandfather is the shadowy figure behind the father, and the shadow he casts is very long indeed.

In his essay "The Nature of Clinical Evidence," Erik Erikson reports the case of a young seminarian of Nordic heritage whose identity crisis centered on his maternal grandfather, "a rural clergyman of character, strength, and communal esteem" (Erikson 1964, 66). Erikson indicates that this man represented God to the patient when he was a small boy, and was deeply implicated in the boy's formation of an unusually demanding and cruel superego. Henry Murray, head of Harvard's psychological clinic for many years, makes an explicit connection between his maternal grandfather and the father of personal prehistory. In a brief autobiographical essay, he writes: "Of all these progenitors I was acquainted only with my daughter-venerated grandfather, aloof toward me, but a kindly gent whose white bearded visage resembled God's as painted, say, by Tintoretto. Remembering him I have been led to surmise that the image and concept of Yahweh must have come not from the all-too-familiar father figure, but from the more remote and lordly grandfather, the overruling patriarch of the clan" (Murray 1967, 296). In his reflections on the American identity in *Childhood and Society*, Erikson notes that, at least historically, the American boy's "male ideal is rarely attached to his father, as lived with in daily life. It is usually an uncle or friend of the family, *if not his grandfather*, as presented to him (often unconsciously) by his mother" (Erikson 1963, 312, my emphasis). Thus, there is a long tradition in psychoanalysis of identifying the maternal grandfather as the shadowy figure with whom the boy's original father identifications are connected. This figure, however, is the living (or remembered) representative of a much deeper, historical-psychic phenomenon, the father of personal prehistory, the Father God of the Judeo-Christian tradition itself.

As Freud points out in *Moses and Monotheism*, this father God is noteworthy for his jealousy of other gods and his insistence on his own singularity. In the terms of our present discussion, this father of personal prehistory ensures that boys will intensify their identifications with their fathers, thus consolidating their masculinity. The price he demands for this, however, is that the boy will forgo his object-choice of his own father. The boy will relate to his father as a model, however imperfect, of what he is to be and become, but not as one whom he may have as the object of his love. Thus, when the adult male makes confession to the eternal Father—the father of personal prehistory— he is, in effect, confessing the "lapses" that occur throughout his life when he experiences a deep love for his father and a longing to be loved by him in return. The confessional mode implies that there is something inherently wrong with this desire to have, not merely emulate, his father, for what he is confessing is his *inability* to eradicate his "lower nature," which gives priority to the desire to have and to hold over the necessity, reflected in his "higher nature," to be and become. A secondary effect of this arrangement is that an excessive demand is placed on identification as the only basis on which a boy relates to his father. If he were allowed to love his father, he would experience less guilt when he finds that, in order to develop his own individuality, he is unable to identify with his father as fully as this arrangement requires.

From this discussion of the role of the father of personal prehistory in the demolition of the Oedipus complex, we are in a position to understand not only why the expectation that the boy will both identify and bond with his father is inherently problematic, but also why religion, through the phylogenetic process, is able to ensure that identification with the father will take precedence. Thus, against the popular view that men are not very religious, Freud's analysis suggests that they are, in fact, incurably religious, and whether they consciously view themselves as religious is, in a sense, irrelevant.

In *The Varieties of Religious Experience*, William James notes that because we are "in the end absolutely dependent on the universe," sacrifice and surrender are unavoidable. In "states of mind which fall short of religion, the surrender is submitted to as an imposition of necessity, and the sacrifice is undergone at the very least without complaint" (James 1982, 51). In the religious life, however, "Surrender and sacrifice are positively espoused; even unnecessary givings-up are added in order that the happiness may increase. *Religion thus makes easy and felicitous what in any case is necessary*" (51, James's emphasis). Suggesting that religion is the only agency that is able to accomplish this result, James concludes that its vital importance as a human faculty is vindicated beyond any dispute.

On the basis of what we have discussed here, one could augment James's point by saying that the individual male might just as well claim to be religious, since his sacrifice, as James points out, is necessary anyway. On this point, however, Freud personally disagreed. In his view, the positive espousal of sacrifice and surrender does not make men any happier, and, if this is the case, "religion cannot keep its promise" (Freud 1961, 31). For men, of course, this is an especially serious indictment of religion, for it goes to the very heart of their sense of honor (that a man makes good on his promises) and hope (that a young man of promise lives up to the expectations that others have of him). Thus, ironically, for Freud, religion invalidates itself.

The Neurosis of Father Hunger

Frank Pittman suggests in *Man Enough* that men today are "suffering from father hunger" (the theme of the chapter he locates between "Growing Up Male" and "Mother Love"). Citing the film *Field of Dreams*, he points out, "The theme in this or in any other movie that draws the most tears from young men is unquestionably the lifelong mourning for the father they couldn't get close to" (Pittman 1993, 139). In light of our discussion in this chapter of the father of personal prehistory, it is interesting that Pittman traces this affliction from father hunger back to the creation of patriarchy as described in the Old Testament and contends that "in patriarchy, men's dominance is a gift from God to reward their willingness to die for [their] masculine authority" (120). He believes, however, that patriarchy is showing signs of fading away, as are "the myths based on patriarchal relationships with the dangerously powerful fathers boys need to escape or overturn" (133). These myths, he believes, no longer make sense, for "how can you escape a father who has already run away, who might not know you, might not remember you, or perhaps is just too busy for you?" (133–34).

He faults in this connection the poet Robert Bly, "the patron mentor of the men's movement" at the time he was writing this book, for emphasizing that one of the stages in a boy's initiation into manhood is "bonding with and breaking away from the father" (132). This breaking away is necessary, Bly asserts, because a boy needs to pass "beyond the realm of the personal mother and father" to achieve "spiritual unity with the universe" (quoted in Pittman 1993, 132). However, Pittman thinks that Bly, in struggling to escape an alcoholic father who was too present in his life, "may be closer to patriarchal times than many of us. Most men of recent generations are trying to get closer to the remote father, rather than trying to break away from the oppressive one" (132). Pittman acknowledges having "a couple of friends and a few patients who don't cry when they see movies like *Field of Dreams*, about finding the lost father," but, like Bly, the reason for this was that "their fathers were psychotics or alcoholics who presented an ominous presence they couldn't escape" (132). In his view, these men are the exception that proves the rule that the patriarchal father has become an anachronism. Men are not trying to escape their fathers, but to relate to them.

Pittman's observation that men are "suffering from father hunger" is certainly consistent with the argument presented in this and the preceding chapter. How, indeed, are boys or young men to break away from their fathers if they have not bonded with them in the first place? My argument here, however, would certainly call into question Pittman's view that "patriarchy is showing signs of fading away," for this is to focus solely on what one believes is happening on the sociocultural level and to ignore the phylogenetic process to which Freud gives such careful attention. In addition, it calls into question Pittman's tendency to place the onus for the failure of emotional bonding on the individual father, as if the neurosis of father hunger can be accounted for by noting difficulties or problems in individual father son relationships. If so many young men suffer from father hunger, then surely the causes are to be sought in historical processes. In fact, this is precisely what Pittman himself argues when he traces this father hunger to ancient times. To suggest that the "fading away" of patriarchy is occurring in our own times is to engage in a kind of cultural narcissism, the claim that, culturally speaking, our times are dramatically different from all previous eras known to humankind. This claim seems dubious at best, as it involves, for example, making the questionable claim that Bly's family circumstances—an alcoholic father who was too present in his life—are also fading away.

Most important, Pittman says nothing about the son's ambivalence, as a small boy, toward emotional bonding with his father. He emphasizes the efforts of men to try "to get closer to the remote father," but says nothing about the effort of the small boy to overcome his object-choice of his father under the pressure of the father of personal prehistory and his human surrogates. However, this too is the effect of a very long historical process that has been internalized, and it would be foolish to suggest that each and every small boy is responsible for it, or that if parents could somehow train their boys differently, this phenomenon would also begin to fade away.

My point, of course, is not that fathers should not try to maintain an emotional bond with their small boys after these boys have made their mothers their object-choice. After all, as Freud points out, the boy is ambivalent toward his father, and fathers should reciprocate their love and not give their sons cause for the hatred they also feel. The point, rather, is that fathers' best efforts to care for their small boys will come up against a tradition rooted in the phylogenetic structure of the human species, and both father and son are powerless to demolish this.

If Pittman's argument against Bly is irrelevant to the small boy in the throes of the demolition of his Oedipus complex, is it, however, relevant to the *adolescent* boy? Is Bly wrong to emphasize "bonding with and breaking away from the father" in adolescence, or late puberty? As Pittman puts it, "According to Bly's formula, the boy who would be a man must feel his mother's love and her blessing and then he must leave her. He must feel his father's love and his blessing, and then he must leave him and go alone into the forest, or the unconscious, or the unmapped world, and find his manhood" (132). Pittman is critical of Bly's formula on the grounds that the "impasse in Bly's formula comes when there is no longer a father to bond with the boy and anoint him and let him go. The boy can't escape his father if there is no father to escape" (132). Freud's view that adolescence is the time for a son to achieve independence from his father would seem to be vulnerable to the same critique.

While Freud, like Bly, is certainly "closer to patriarchal times than many of us," his position, however, is actually quite different from Bly's (as represented by Pittman). While it is certainly true that Freud emphasizes the need for the adolescent boy to "free himself" from his father, this "freeing" is to be understood in light of his earlier "infantile revolt" against his father, which either caused him to remain antagonistic toward his father throughout childhood, in which case there is now a chance for reconciliation, or caused him to lapse into subservience to his father, in which case there is now a chance to liberate himself from his father's domination. The primary way in which he accomplishes this reconciliation and/or liberation is by transferring his libidinal desires for his mother to an external love-object.

Freud, then, looks to a man's "lower nature" as the means toward reconciliation of son and father instead of his "higher nature," as Bly's "spiritual unity with the universe" implies. In Freud's own terminology, the issue is the adolescent boy's ability to redirect his libido (his sexual desire) from his mother to an external sexual object. With this, the "infantile revolt" is over, and, in a very real sense, the reconciliation has occurred, whether or not there is explicit acknowledgment of this fact by the young man's father. To put it in Pittman's language of blessing and anointing, the son who has transferred his object-choice from his mother to an external sexual object *has* his father's blessing. He has been anointed whether or not there is ceremonial recognition of this fact.

This way of viewing the reconciliation between father and son also sheds light on William Pollack's view that the adolescent period is the second time a boy experiences a separation from his mother. In my terms, this is a period in which his melancholy self reasserts itself, in both its sadness over the fact that he and his mother are separating for good, and anger over the fact that she is a complicating figure in this final separation. This heightening of the melancholy self can go on for years, with the boy's ambivalent feelings of love and hate toward his mother serving to confuse an already difficult task of finding a compatible love-object. This is one of the prices he pays, however, for ending his infantile revolt against his father, which, as we have seen, may take either the form of reconciliation or liberation, depending on the circumstances of the relationship that developed between himself and his father after the demolition of the Oedipus complex.

My primary concern in this chapter, however, is with the small boy and the phylogenetic factors that inhibit an emotional bond between father and son. As indicated earlier, Pittman follows his chapter on "Father Hunger" with one on "Mother Love," in which (as we saw in chapter 2) he suggests that the boy's relationship to his mother is overburdened with guilt. In terms of the argument presented in this chapter, the juxtaposition of these two chapters in Pittman's book is perfectly understandable. When loving the father is proscribed, the boy's desire for his mother will become an obsession—he needs her too much—and his loss of her affections will cast him into the depths of melancholic despair, where she (and her future surrogates) may become the objects of his callous neglect and subterranean revenge. The demolition of the Oedipus complex carries a heavy price indeed, and religion is deeply implicated in the resulting wreckage.

Christopher Lane notes that Freud "consistently criticized modern Western societies for compelling their subjects to live 'beyond [their psychic] means.'" He cites Freud's early essay entitled "'Civilized' Sexual Morality and Modern Nervous Illness" in which he contends that "for most people there is a limit beyond which their constitution cannot comply with the demands of civilization. All who wish to be more noble-minded than their constitution allows fall victims to neurosis; they would have been more healthy if it could have been possible for them to be less good" (quoted in Lane 1999, 14).

I have already noted the boy's vain hope that he may win his mother back by "being good." It is doubly ironic that, as far as his relation to his father is concerned, "goodness" means being able to relinquish his love for his father so that he may learn to emulate him instead, thus consolidating his masculinity. I suggest that Freud's analysis of the situation in which we now find ourselves—suffering from the neurosis of "father hunger"—explains why relations between sons and fathers have the emotional tenor of *unrealized* affection and love, that is, why love between fathers and sons seems so desirable yet elusive. It has little to do with how individual fathers treat or mistreat, relate to or fail to relate to their boys. Instead, it is largely and essentially due to the phylogenetic fault line that has persisted for thousands of years and promises to continue to persist, notwithstanding Pittman's optimistic observation that patriarchy is "fading away."

If there is a consoling word in this sobering analysis, it is that the responsibility for this state of affairs does not lie with the individual father-son dyad. Rather, it is rooted in the history of monotheism itself, for at the center of the faith of our fathers is a jealous God. As Julia Kristeva writes:

> Those who believe in the God of the Bible do not doubt His love. God—who is impossible to represent, fleeting, and always there though invisible—eludes me and invites me to let go of my narcissism, to venture forth, to inflict suffering and persecution upon myself in order to earn His love. Does he not force these roots into that ineradicable, archaic, and deeply felt conviction that occupies and protects those who accept Him? That is, the conviction that a preoedipal father exists, a *Father of Personal Prehistory*, an imaginary father? (Kristeva 1995, 122)

Faced with such a challenge, the object-choice of one's own father seems facile and unheroic, like worshiping the golden calf (i.e., indulging one's lower nature) when one ought to be ascending Mount Sinai (i.e., making a spiritual ascent). Thus, it becomes the role of our own fathers to teach us how to climb in order that we may earn the love of an imaginary Father. The psychic price we pay for this transcendent love is the neurosis of father hunger, which has its roots in repression of object-choice for the father for the sake of a world of civilized men.

Conclusion

As we have reached the end of our theoretical discussion of the formation of the melancholy self, I would like to summarize its major points. I argued in chapter 2 that boys become religious as a consequence of their emotional separation from their mothers at age three or four. As this separation is the traumatic experience that causes them to develop a melancholy self, the forms this religiousness takes reflect this emotional separation. I proposed that there are three such forms: (1) the religious impulse based on being a "good boy" as a means to win his mother back, which leads to a religion of moral rectitude (a religion of honor); (2) the religious impulse based on a compensatory quest for other persons, objects, or ideals that might take his mother's place, which leads to a religion of searching and questing (a religion of hope); and (3) the religious impulse that stands over against the "good boy" religious impulse by challenging its sense of ultimate seriousness, leading to a religion based on the relaxation of the superego (a religion of humor or light irony).[1] This religious impulse of humor may also make light of the questing religious impulse, viewing the quest for a maternal substitute with a similar sense of humor or irony. Cervantes's *Don Quixote* is an excellent example of both, as it pokes fun both at Quixote's code of chivalry and his devotion to Dulcinea, the woman for whom he performs these heroic acts.

In this chapter, I have discussed Freud's view of how religion develops in the small boy, especially noting his emphasis on the father of personal prehistory. In effect, this view of religion's origins supports my argument that religion has its fundamental origins in the mother-son relationship, because it presents God the Father as having a claim on the boy prior to that of the boy's father and as being more clearly identified, among the boy's relations, with the maternal grandfather. If the boy's own father plays a role in his religious formation, it is an auxiliary one. For example, the father may assist the boy in his efforts to be a "good boy" (modeling and teaching the qualities of a man of honor), encourage his quest for substitute love objects (e.g., by modeling the boy's future decision to commit himself to another woman), and endorse the boy's inner need to relativize his own "good boy" and "questing" religious impulses (e.g., by treating them with humor or light irony). The importance of the father's role as "assistant" should not be minimized, but the emotional separation between mother and son—a traumatic experience—is the primary inspiration for the first two religious impulses (moral rectitude and quest). Because it is, we have the rather ironic situation where the boy's mother is the parent who is primarily responsible for sustaining a patriarchal religion (the Judeo-Christian tradition). While this conclusion may seem counterintuitive, it squares with the evidence that Ann Douglas provides, as discussed in chapter 2, that women have traditionally been more supportive of this tradition than have men.

Moreover, if, for the most part, this patriarchal religion has been one that fosters the first two religious impulses but not the third, this helps to explain why the psychic relief from humor and light irony has not been considered a religious impulse. In my own experience, while it was certainly true that my father endorsed the first religious impulse of moral rectitude, he also endorsed the contradicting religious impulse of humor and light irony. (Personal and sociocultural circumstances caused him to be less obviously supportive of the religious impulse of questing, or the religion of hope.) Because his endorsement of the third religious impulse was not, I believe, atypical, the widespread belief that men are not as "religious" as women—that they take it less seriously—is not surprising. In my view, however, this third religious impulse is not inherently inferior to the other two, and, this being the case, it supports the idea that men's religion is something of a paradox. Owing to its claim to be concerned with ultimate matters, religion must be taken with the utmost seriousness. Yet this very claim causes it to become stuffy and pretentious, and the debunking of these pretensions is itself a vital religious impulse.

The melancholy self, then, is the locus of a man's deepest and most enduring religious impulses, and these impulses are threefold: the impulse of moral rectitude (manifest in a religion of honor), the impulse of searching and questing (manifest in a religion of hope), and the impulse that challenges the seriousness of the other two (manifest in a religion of humor). As we saw in our discussion of Freud's "Mourning and Melancholia" in chapter 1, melancholia expresses itself in sadness and internalized rage. The first two religious impulses reflect and address these two fundamental emotions resulting from the loss of the loved object. But melancholia also gives rise to a cluster of emotions that ranges from bitter sarcasm (as reflected in James's example of the French patient) to the mechanism of emotional detachment found in humor and irony. As the first two religious impulses help the boy to cope with his loss, converting rage into honor and sadness into hope, so the third impulse helps him to cope, through an amused detachment, with the inevitable failure of these other impulses to overcome his sense of loss.

Notes

1. While I will continue to use the word *humor* in my discussion of the third impulse, I introduce the word *irony* here because it helps to delineate the meaning of *humor* as I am using it in this study. Specifically, it precludes the inference that I am talking about joking, wittiness, clever repartee, and so forth. As D. C. Muecke points out in his book on irony, irony is concerned with observing incongruities or discrepancies between human aspirations, on the one hand, and human achievements on the other. Given this focus on the discrepant, those who are its prime victims are persons who act in "confident unawareness" of the situation in which they find themselves. That is, there is a discrepancy between what they naively or innocently believe to be the case and what is in fact the case. The more incongruous this discrepancy, the more ironic it is. Thus, if a novice swimmer dives into an empty pool and strikes his head on the bottom, we view this as a pitiable, perhaps even tragic occurrence. If, however, it is the swimming instructor who dives into an empty pool, we view this as ironic, no matter how much pain he may suffer from this unfortunate occurrence (Muecke 1970, 28). We say, "How ironic. If anyone should have had the presence of mind to check the water level before diving into the pool, surely it was the swimming instructor." The ironic point of view, then, is manifest in a certain emotional detachment

(the swimming instructor's suffering is not the primary focus) so that the incongruity of the situation can be noted instead. If the swimming instructor is arrogant and demeans his students, the ironist may then find the instructor's mistake amusing, funny, or even downright pleasurable.

While one may view another person from this perspective of ironic detachment, Muecke also discusses self-irony, that is, when the ironist and the victim are one and the same person. The emotional distance in this case may vary, ranging from an attitude of superiority to one of sympathy and understanding. Self-irony is the ability to view oneself and one's actions and beliefs with a degree of emotional detachment. I contend that, as long as this detachment does not succumb to sarcasm, bitterness, or vindictiveness toward one's vulnerable self, it is a religious impulse. Thus, humor has a place in religion, namely, between the solemn and the snicker (James 1982, 38).

II.
Two Melancholy Selves

CHAPTER 5

❧

Goliath Meets His Inner David
Melancholic Religion as Moral Rectitude

In the foregoing chapters, I have presented the argument, based on Freud's own writings, that a boy's religious orientation to life is an expression of the melancholy self that emerges when he suffers the trauma of emotional separation from his mother at the age of three or four. I want now to turn to the contemporary context, and to focus in this and the following chapter on two contemporary portrayals of men afflicted with melancholia.

These portraits, derived from Ana-Marie Rizzuto's well known book, *The Birth of the Living God: A Psychoanalytic Study* (1979), are of somewhat extreme cases of male melancholia, as both men were studied by Rizzuto and her research team when they were psychiatric patients. By focusing on these two men, however, I am invoking William James's view that we are able to gain insight into the more "normal" forms of a psychological affliction by studying its more extreme, more pathological forms. My assumption is that men who deem themselves "normal" will see *something* of themselves in one or both of these portraits. But even if the reader sees little similarity between himself and either of these two men, these cases will provide insight into the melancholy self with which each of us is afflicted to a greater or lesser degree. As noted in the introduction, this is not a book for or about male depressives. Rather, it is about the melancholy self that we all share, one of the various selves that comprise our personal identity (or "sense of I"). We all have this self, though some of us are more aware of having it, some are more aware of its debilitating powers, and some have been more successful in coping with it, perhaps even making something positive out of it (a "blessing in disguise"). Most important, because it is an integral part of the male condition, it is not a pathology (though it can develop into one) but an aspect of "the male predicament" (Dittes 1985).

Rizzuto herself lends support for this use of more extreme cases to shed light on more typical or milder expressions of the melancholy self when she points out that in her pilot study prior to undertaking the final research for her book—a study that included five members of the staff at her hospital—she "found no differences of any significance between members of the staff and the patients in their way of relating to God" (Rizzuto 1979, 181). While this absence of a difference in terms of God-relating may seem to have no direct bearing on the question of the melancholy self, she does note that three of the four patients presented in the book (and both of the men whom I will be discussing in this and the following chapters) were indistinguishable from "more normal people" prior to the events that led to their hospitalization: "Fiorella Domenico, Douglas O'Duffy, and Daniel Miller may have appeared before their hospitalizations to be simply an average housewife, state police officer, and physician" (181). In this and the following chapter, I will first focus on Rizzuto's own presentation and analysis of the two cases, and will then bring to bear the views on the melancholy self and its role in the formation of a religious orientation to life presented in the preceding chapters.

Rizzuto's presentation of these four cases, two women and two men, is designed to explore her thesis that a person's representation of God is formed from parental representations (both mother and father) and also, though to a lesser degree, from their own self-representations. The central thesis of the book is "that no child in the Western world brought up in ordinary circumstances completes the oedipal cycle without forming at least a rudimentary God representation, which he may use for belief or not" (200). This representation may then be left "untouched as the individual continues to revise parent and self-representations during the life cycle." However, if it "is not revised to keep pace with changes in self-representation, it soon becomes asynchronous and is experienced as ridiculous or irrelevant or, on the contrary, threatening or dangerous" (200).

Rizzuto claims that the results of her study are essentially twofold. First, "Freud was basically correct in suggesting that God has his origins in parental images and that God comes to a child at the time of resolution of the oedipal crisis." This implies that "all children in the Western world form a God representation—one that may later be used, neglected, or actively repressed" (208). While I disagree with Rizzuto's view that the God representation comes "at the time of resolution of the oedipal crisis"—our discussion of Freud's views on the father of personal prehistory in chapter 4 suggests that it comes earlier—her point that "all children in the Western world form a God representation" is consistent with Freud's phylogenetic argument.

The second finding of the study is that it "reveals the ingenuity of the child in creating a God representation through experience and fantasy" (208). While it is true that "God is heavily loaded with parental traits," God "has other traits that suit the child's needs in relating to his parents and maintaining his sense of worth and safety" (208–9). Thus, while "either the father or the mother or both contribute their share, other primary objects (grandparents, siblings) may also provide some representation components" (209).

Unlike the first finding, the second one does not include any claim that all children in the Western world exhibit this ingenuity. In fact, Rizzuto's clinical studies give the impression that such creative ingenuity plays a relatively small role in the formation and maintenance of the God representation. Moreover, there is a greater tendency for this representation to become rather fixed and impervious to modification or change. As we have seen, this is because one's God representation has a phylogenetic core. As Freud notes in *Civilization and Its Discontents*, "The common man *cannot imagine* this Providence [which watches "over his life and will compensate him in a future existence for any frustrations he suffers here"] *otherwise* than in the figure of an enormously exalted father" (Freud 1961, 21, my emphasis). This suggests that the God representation is rather fixed and unchanging (i.e., it is difficult to "imagine" it in a new or different way), and raises the question whether the God representation formed in early childhood can in fact undergo fundamental revision in the course of life "to keep pace with changes in self-representation" (Rizzuto 1979, 200). We will explore this issue in relation to the two case studies.

As for Rizzuto's contention that the God representation may be maternal as well as paternal, or even exclusively maternal, it is worth noting that, in his discussion in *The Ego and the Id* of how the superego is formed, Freud suggests (as we have already discussed in the previous chapter) that behind the superego "there lies hidden an individual's first and most important identification, his identification with the father in his own personal prehistory" (Freud 1960a, 21). However, he adds in a footnote: "Perhaps it would be safer to say 'with the parents' [of his own personal prehistory] for before a child has arrived at a definite knowledge of the difference between the sexes . . . it does not distinguish in value between its father and its mother. . . . In order to simplify my presentation I shall discuss only identification with the father" (21) Thus, while the view that the God representation may have maternal aspects receives little attention from Freud in the writings we have discussed, he does not rule out this possibility in principle. On the other hand, the religious tradition that especially concerns him—the Judeo-Christian one—clearly favors, historically and thus phylogenetically, the paternal representation of God.

Rizzuto indicates that all the subjects in her study fit into one of the following four categories in terms of their relation to God. These are persons who either (1) have a God whose existence they do not question and with whom they have a significant relation, (2) wonder whether or not to believe in a God they are not sure exists, (3) are amazed, angered, or quietly surprised to see others deeply invested in a God who does not interest them, or (4) struggle with a demanding, harsh God they would like to get rid of if they were not convinced of his existence and power. Rizzuto places Douglas O'Duffy in category 2 and Daniel Miller in category 3. This means that the two men in her study are more questioning of the existence and/or importance of God than the two women, who belong to categories 1 and 4. Rizzuto does not provide data indicating whether this gender difference was representative of the whole subject group. Nonetheless, the fact that the two men are less convinced of God's existence or importance in their lives points to a significant difference in the way in which men are religious.

As we move into our discussion of the two case studies, it should be noted that Rizzuto's psychiatric diagnoses of the two men provide no indication that they are melancholic. She does not, for example, use the "melancholic specifier" when she states that Douglas O'Duffy's diagnosis was "reactive depression to occupational trauma (car accident) in an obsessive compulsive personality" (Rizzuto 1979, 111). Nor does melancholia appear in her statement that "in APA [American Psychiatric Association] terms Daniel Miller is a schizoid personality" (134). The fact that she does not view these two men as melancholiacs is not surprising, however, for the term *melancholia* is seldom used in contemporary psychiatric diagnoses. In addition, my argument that these two men are melancholiacs will be based on the mother-son relationship. While Rizzuto gives considerable attention to this relationship, she does not have the same agenda as I have here, that is, to establish a connection between this relationship and these men's melancholic condition.

I will take up Douglas O'Duffy first, on the grounds that he was diagnosed as having a less severe disorder than Daniel Miller and that he reflects the first of the three religious expressions identified in chapter 2 that follow from the mother-son separation. This is the religious impulse, based on conscience, of moral rectitude, which leads to the development of a religion based on personal honor. (In the following summary of Rizzuto's presentation of this case, I will forgo citing page numbers, as all quoted material is from her seventh chapter, which is comprised of pages 109–29 of her book.)

Douglas O'Duffy's Personal Story

Rizzuto depicts Douglas O'Duffy as "a giant of a man" who is "an officer of the Pennsylvania state police" and describes himself as an "honest cop." This claim is supported by "numerous citations for courageous service above and beyond the call of duty." At thirty-nine, he is "a well-established, middle-class, Roman-Catholic Irish-American, righteous, determined, and intensely frustrated by the evils of a society where corruption is rampant. He boasts about his own contrasting brave actions and his incorruptible behavior. He is also a tender, loving man very much in love with his wife of seventeen years and his three children."

In psychiatric terms, his "psychic decompensation" was diagnosed as a "reactive depression [related to] occupational trauma (car accident) in an obsessive compulsive personality." In psychoanalytic terms, it may be described as "a reactive depression following the shattering of a sustaining, admired, and admirable self-image which maintained his narcissistic balance in his dealings with society as a maternal substitute."

When Rizzuto met O'Duffy, he was suffering from intense nervousness manifested in facial tics, headaches, and pain in the back of his neck: "He was obviously depressed and extremely angry. He had lost weight, was unable to sleep, and had not worked for six months." His symptoms began after an accident that occurred when he was driving a patrol car and was hit by another car. While he was knocked unconscious for a few minutes, he was examined and released by the physician because he had no injuries. He went immediately to bed, however, and remained there, "waited on hand and foot by his wife. His headache required constant use of Demoral." His personality underwent a noticeable change: "He became bitter, depressed, angry, intensely afraid of going back to his duties; he ruminated constantly on his life, the accident, and, most specifically, on the ungrateful public and the lack of concern of his superiors and fellow officers."

A neurological evaluation revealed no consequences from the trauma, but family and friends agreed that he was "not himself" since the accident. One major change was that he "had reversed roles with his wife: he was now cooking and taking care of the children while she worked to balance their income." The marital tension created by this situation prompted O'Duffy and his wife to accept psychiatric help.

Douglas was the tenth and last child born to an Irish family in Philadelphia. Two brothers had died in infancy and both children "remained very much alive in the mother's constant thinking about them." His surviving siblings were three boys and four girls, in that order. One of the deceased boys was the second-born son, while the other was apparently born between two of the sisters. The family never mentioned the second dead boy's name, the details of his death, or when he was born. Douglas was a normal child at the time of delivery, but he became, according to himself, a "skinny, sickly, ungainly, awkward little ferret" who contracted rheumatic fever sometime between the ages of three and six. In the first or second grade, he was confined to bed for three months, and to help him recover, his mother (accompanied by her sister) took him to a Caribbean island for two months of recuperation.

He was lonely and unhappy as a child and felt "very different from his admired and athletic brothers." He resented the shots his mother gave him for his ailment and "felt that he hated her during most of his early childhood," in large part because of her "constant involvement with religion." On the other hand, he admired his father "to the point of hero worship." His father was also a state policeman who was "much loved by officers, bums, and crooks alike," a "jolly, efficient, caring man always personally interested in anyone he met."

When he was nine years old, a playmate, a boy his own age, died of pneumonia. This chum had also been a sickly child who, in Douglas's view, "simply couldn't make it." At the funeral, he saw his dead friend's face, and in his shock he began to reflect on his dead brothers, especially the first boy, whose death had especially upset his parents and whose memory his mother kept alive through the years. Two other deaths at this time—a woman neighbor who had visited him frequently during his illness, and her son, a young soldier who was killed in the war—added to his grief.

By age eleven, however, his rheumatic fever had been controlled, and he decided he would undo the image of a sickly child by succeeding in sports like his three older brothers. Despite the doctor's warnings that this would place undue strain on his heart, he was determined to be an all-around athlete (football, basketball, and baseball) and practiced "to the point of exhaustion." He achieved his goal of total mastery over his body (symbolized in his habit of staring directly at the sun even though he knew how harmful this could be), and he developed into a very tall, well coordinated, aggressive, competitive athlete. His intense frustration about feeling different from his brothers, however, did not subside. With the exception of his father, he felt his family was uninterested in his achievements, and they continued to treat him as "the kid brother." No matter what he did or how well he performed in sports, he could never win the accolades his older brothers received.

At this point Douglas accused his mother of having only enough time for eight children (his seven living siblings and the first of the two dead brothers) and not for all ten (himself and the other dead brother). As Rizzuto puts it, "He brooded on the idea that he should not have been conceived because his mother did not realize she had a younger son." Referring mainly to himself but also the other dead brother, he "could not understand why anybody would conceive another child if they did not feel enough 'compassion' for that child."

His criticisms centered on his mother, who seemed so unaware of him "as the person he was," despite the fact that she was very conscious "of whatever was going on in the family." She was omnipresent, the one, as he put it, "who would read the riot act, or take away TV-radio privileges, assign work details, be waiting up when you came home stoned, or knew when you were going hot and heavy with the girl next door." His resentment became focused on the intense religious atmosphere his mother created in the home, with crucifixes, holy water, prayers, the Bible, and her demands that the children attend church. While he traces his ambivalence toward religion and God to childhood, it was in his early adolescence that he decided to prove that priests and religious people are "hypocrites who impose moral rules on others to control them while they do what they please." He began to spy on priests and to collect stories about their sexual escapades and their greed for money. He followed priests around in order to witness their escapades with "little dolls" and was delighted when he discovered a priest having an affair. Rejecting his mother's view that a person without "blind faith was nothing," he felt that reason would prove religious people wrong, concentrating these efforts on the dogma of the virgin birth, the idea that salvation outside the church is impossible, and life after death.

On the other hand, he surprised himself by singing in the church choir and becoming friendly with one particular priest. In addition, he was doing well in high school and began dreaming of an athletic college scholarship. His brothers had gone to Yale and Princeton and were now in high government positions. While his parents had paid for their educations, he was determined to be totally independent. His desire to compete successfully with his older brothers was crushed, however, when his athletic coach broke his promise to recommend him to Princeton and recommended a relative instead. Feeling cheated and let down, he reluctantly accepted a scholarship from a local Catholic college.

At twenty-one, he met his future wife. While observing that they "hit it off" and he "pretty much wanted to marry her," he also confesses that "it was not exactly what you call love." His marriage plans were interrupted when his father developed a fatal illness. With the exception of one brother, his older siblings were well established and living in other states, and he felt that he "had to terminate" his college education to help repair his father's finances. His father's last days were clouded by a major scandal in the state police department. He was found guilty of accepting bribes. Douglas was profoundly shocked by these disclosures, and had to come to terms with the fact that his father had "a flexible conscience," something his need to admire his father had not allowed him to see. In his grief after his father's death, he relinquished his dream of becoming a lawyer and joined the state police, because it would provide him "the security of a steady job." Rizzuto believes that his deeper reason was "the determination to be the ideal public servant he had thought his father was, admired, beloved, incorruptible."

Douglas married, had children, and tried as hard as he could to be a good state trooper. He had difficulties with his supervisors, however, because he was impatient with their frailties and limitations. He saw himself as setting an example for others to follow. He would be the first man on the spot in an emergency, the first to extend help, and the last to leave the scene. He used his free time to protect the poor and lonely. His superiors recognized his exemplary actions and gave him many citations. They would not promote him, though, because he was impossible to work with.

Several members of his extended family died when he was in his late twenties. He was able to relate the exact date, hour, and details of each death. He was unable, however, to remember the dates of his father's and mother's deaths. He was thirty when his mother died. While she had rejected his offer for her to live with him and his family, he had visited her frequently prior to her death and had engaged in "serious conversations" with her. In her last hours he felt close to her and realized, with relief, that "she was human too" when she complained of pain and discomfort.

In his thirties he was devoted to his work and family. For several years his life was largely uneventful, marked only by other family deaths and two minor on-the-job accidents that sent him to the hospital for a few days but had "neither psychological nor physical consequences." The children were growing up, and he was proud of his roles as husband, father, and provider. He decided to raise his children as Roman Catholics, reasoning that this "may save them some little doubt and make it easier for them," though he did not want to "coerce them." According to Rizzuto, his wife "obviously loved him," and she felt that he had "good communication" with her and his children, that he was "warm and friendly" in his relations with them. She did feel that he worked too much.

The auto accident that led to his psychological problems had been preceded by a series of tragic events. Two months earlier, two troopers had been killed on duty and an officer friend had committed suicide, using his own revolver. His own accident, Rizzuto suggests, was "the final straw."

Rizzuto outlines a series of events that led to his "psychic decompensation." The accident in which he was knocked unconscious for the first time in his life was followed by a violent psychosomatic and emotional reaction characterized by (1) intense rage at the public and the police for their failure to give him the recognition he deserved; (2) intense headaches and irregularity in his biological rhythms, including sleep, appetite, and his sex drive; (3) a depressed mood centered around intense brooding over his having been a "tin Jesus," thinking he could do something for others but finding himself rebuffed by those on whose admiration and gratitude he had counted; (4) brooding and regret about having invested so much of his heart and time in the public rather than in his family; and (5) retreating into bed, needing to be totally cared for by his wife. The period he remained in bed—three months—was exactly the amount of time he had spent in bed at age six with rheumatic fever. Rizzuto suggests that this "psychic decompensation" period of his illness was "a regression to a childhood state."

The stage of recovery comprised two moves: (1) a spontaneous decision to get out of bed, take over his wife's duties in the house, declare himself incapable of returning to work, and accept his wife's financial support; and (2) the realization that he needed help, to rededicate himself to his role of father and husband, and to resign from his job and secure a civilian job, which would allow him more time with his family. Rizzuto views the first move as "a transitional period of identification with his mother" and the second as a renunciation (after failing to attract the admiring public his father enjoyed in his final days) of his identification with his father as a well-liked man, together with a conscious decision to identify instead with his father as the loved and loving family man: "This move seemed to provide him sufficient self-esteem and satisfaction to restore his emotional equilibrium."

Douglas's Maternal Image

Lack of Maternal Recognition

In her discussion of Douglas O'Duffy's parental images and relationships, Rizzuto begins with his mother. Her discussion of his maternal relationship and image frequently shades into an exploration of his own grandiose self-representation, because the two of them are intimately linked. Her account of this maternal relationship begins with Douglas's frustration that his mother's inability to appreciate him and what he did for her was never resolved: "He tried to the end, but his mother died without giving him any satisfaction about this." Thus, when he complained about the lack of recognition he received in his family, "he was referring exclusively to his mother." He never felt that "his mother was aware of him, not even when, in her last days, he did everything he could to gain her recognition. His profound bitterness originates in her lack of recognition of his existence."

Rizzuto notes, however, that Douglas's mother was "in reality responsive to his needs for attention and for time with her, the best example being the [two] months she spent with him in the Caribbean during his recovery from illness." Why then did he have such a strong perception that his mother ignored him? For Rizzuto, the clue to this perception is in the fact that his mother was so preoccupied with the second dead baby that she had difficulty in fully relating to her new baby Douglas, whose first name was the middle name of his two deceased brothers (both named Paul). "She had warmth and was capable of loving," being very much involved with her children and husband, but may not have been able to respond in a similar way to little Douglas, having had "a problem in making full contact with the little boy." In addition, the fact that he was sickly throughout childhood "could have fed his mother's fear of losing him too, thus distracting her." While the shots he received from his mother might be evidence of her appropriate concern for him, Douglas felt that they were excessive, and "hated his mother giving him injections and keeping him in bed while the others were playing." His involvement in sports in adolescence despite the doctor's warnings suggests his determination to prove that her concern for his physical welfare was excessive, due, perhaps, to her own determination to see that no other son of hers would suffer death.

In her chapter in *The Untouched Key* on the painter Käthe Kollwitz, enti-tled "A Mother's Dead Little Angels and Her Daughter's Activist Art," Alice Miller discusses the fact that Kollwitz was one of four of six children to live beyond childhood. Her mother's first two children died at a very early age. While the death of a child at any age plays a very important role in a mother's life (Miller 1990, 27), Miller contends that there are special circumstances involved when the child dies soon after birth, "before the parents' expecta-tions are disappointed by the child's desire for autonomy" (28). In this case, "the mother may idealize her lost child and thereby preserve its central impor-tance for the rest of her life. Often after the death of an infant, there is no real period of mourning that runs its course; instead, the parents' hopes become attached to an 'if': if only the child had lived, the parents think, then expec-tations would have been met" (28). Thus, "The belief in the fulfillment of all their hopes, originating in their [own] childhoods, is associated with the memory of this child, whose grave they visit and tend for decades later" (28).

What is the impact of this loss on the other children? If "superhuman, even divine, qualities are attributed to the dead child," then "the other chil-dren in the family grow up in the shadow of this cult. They must be dutifully cared for and raised in a way to rid them of their bad behavior and make them acceptable in the future. To be affectionate [toward them] would be danger-ous, for too much love would ruin them" (28). Thus, the parents seem to believe that "affection and tenderness should be carefully measured out in the child's best interest. And so the poor well-raised mother feels a duty toward her living children to train them well and to suppress their true feelings" (28).

It is a very different matter, however, in the case of her dead child, for this child "needs nothing from her and does not awaken any feelings of inferior-ity or hatred, does not cause her any conflict, does not offend her." Nor need she be afraid of spoiling the child with her love. Being with her other children can also make her suffer "because they clearly do not measure up to the dead child and its fantasized goodness and wisdom. Their vitality, their demands and claims on her can make a mother in love with her dead child feel dis-tinctly insecure. They can cause feelings of helplessness and despair if she sees her pedagogical principles called into question" (29).

In addition to measuring out her affection and kindness, she is "anxiously concerned that nothing happen to them; she paints them a picture of the con-stant danger threatening them, and she is apparently right about the danger, for something terrible has already happened. She must always keep an eye on her children, plaguing them with her close supervision and restricting their freedom. As a result, she has long since unavoidably forfeited her own vital-ity and spontaneity and her depressed state is ultimately serving death" (29).

Miller's analysis of the consequences of the death of a sibling in infancy or early childhood for the living children provides an accurate picture of what occurred in Douglas O'Duffy's relationship to his mother. He experienced a combination of close supervision and restriction of freedom, on the one hand, and a careful measuring out of affection and tenderness on the other. While he felt he was the living child most victimized by this—believing that there was sufficient love for his other living siblings—the fact that (with the exception of his brother Peter) the others were "well-established persons living in other states" when his father developed his fatal illness and were not much in evidence in the period prior to their mother's death suggests that they too felt deprived of love.

In a poem about her sister who died in infancy, Louise Glück says that "when my sister died my mother's heart became very cold, very rigid, like a tiny pendant of iron. Then it seemed to me my sister's body was a magnet. I could feel it draw my mother's heart into the earth, so it would grow" (Glück 1990, 27). She also writes about the relationship between herself and her other living sister, who "were never allies" but, at the same time, "never turned on our parents." They did, however, have "other obsessions: for example, we both felt there were too many of us to survive. We were like animals trying to share a dry pasture. Before us, one rice, barely strong enough to sustain a single life" (48). Thus, the living children struggle to survive on the limited love remaining after so much of it has been drawn into the grave of their dead sibling. This sense of scarcity that Glück experienced would surely be multiplied in the O'Duffy family, with its eight surviving siblings and two dead children.

Miller's comment on "the cult of the dead children" is especially relevant to Douglas O'Duffy's resentment of "the intense religious atmosphere in the house." With crucifixes, holy water, prayers, and the Bible so omnipresent, the home may well have seemed to young Douglas to be a shrine to his dead brothers, especially the one who was constantly referred to by name. (Of course, because they were both named Paul, it could be that the dead child to whom his mother had reference on any given occasion was unclear to the others.) Perhaps his reaction against his mother's view that a person without "blind faith was nothing" was also linked to her maintenance of this cult of the dead children, for her practice of "blind faith" may have been the only way that she could come to any terms with these losses. After all, the fact that she was doubly bereaved would be beyond comprehension to a devout believer. Conversely, Douglas's challenges to the doctrine of the afterlife and, specifically, his view that "a dead person is in the category of your dog" may be a reflection of his bitter resentment of this cult of the dead children, an irreverent consignment of his mother's beloved dead children to the fate of a lowly canine.

In Rizzuto's view, young Douglas's determination to prove his physical indestructibility was "counterphobic," citing the following as evidence: (1) During his high school summers he always took high-risk jobs, such as being a tree surgeon, and felt exhilarated by the experience; (2) in college he collapsed from a ruptured appendix and was operated on under dangerous conditions, but he denied any fear of dying; (3) as a state trooper, he noted that "like a compulsive drinker or addict, I would be the first one in an accident or a fire. I went overboard"; (4) with the exception of his parents, he remembered the exact date of the death of any person who had meant anything to him; and (5) the accident that prompted his psychological problems seems to have been the equivalent of death, as this was the first time in his life that he had been knocked unconscious. (His wife had often said to him that he was so pugnacious and independent because he had never been knocked unconscious.)

Rizzuto contends that this counterphobic behavior was based on "a grandiose self-image of being invulnerable and capable of defying death itself." Having viewed his behavior as motivated by a willingness to risk himself for others as the perfect servant of society, his rage at the ungrateful public after his accident awakened him to other motives for this behavior. He acknowledged, "If I become angry I do not stop until the person is down on the floor. I am full of bitterness and resentment. I will meet violence with violence. If somebody crosses me I pull out my .38 and shoot. I have no warmth for society and the public." Rizzuto concludes, "One may see here the connection between death, dead siblings, denial of recognition and warmth, and the psychic imbalance produced by the failure of the grandiose self-representation (powerful, immortal, and admired by others) to protect him from the risk of dying and the absence of public respect and admiration."

The accident precipitated the downfall of his grandiose self-representation. Rizzuto sees this event as a "painful repetition of his childhood anguish with his mother," the repeated event being his childhood illness. He went to bed for exactly the same period of time he had been in bed as a child with rheumatic fever, and demanded that his wife take care of him: "While this was happening, his mind's eye was on the public and his superiors. He wanted recognition and care from them in return for his intense commitment, but they failed him. The public did not even notice what had happened to him, and his superiors looked at his accident matter-of-factly." Still, he expected "'the accolade of attentions' he never received from his mother, waiting and waiting, with his headaches and anguish, in his post-trauma bed."

This recognition never occurred. He experienced tremendous rage ("I am extremely bitter"). His voice rose to a shout: "I am extremely hurt with the public per se. Since I've been out, my officer friends have not been near me. For fifteen years I was a good officer. I have delivered thirty-five youngsters and got thirteen citations, and they are as useless as the public I've saved. . . . I must have been a damn fool." Note his use of the word "saved" (a person with a less grandiose self-image would surely have said "served") and the fact that he knows the exact number of the babies he delivered and the citations he received. These, together with his ability to remember the exact dates on which persons who had meant "anything to him" died, are also reflective of his obsessive-compulsive personality, a point to which I will return in my discussion of his melancholy self.

As Douglas's grandiose self image unraveled following the accident, his capacity for great affection and tenderness reemerged. Rizzuto describes him as an "imposing giant of a man" who "could now easily turn into the soft-hearted protective giant in need of affection. During those moments his voice would become soft, his face smooth with a faint smile, and his longings for warmth and affection would be undisguised." From this evidence, Rizzuto suggests that he "did have tender exchanges with his mother," as when she took him to the Caribbean for his recovery. There was also his "tender care of her when she was dying" during which they had "long conversations." On the other hand, while he felt then that *he* had gotten close to *her*, perceiving that she "was human too," there is less evidence that she moved any closer to him.

The Mirror-Hungry Personality

Rizzuto concludes from this that "it was not that the mother denied him care and warmth but that the child did not find in her the mirroring, the recognition he felt he needed in his own right." She makes reference here to a psychoanalytic concept—mirroring—introduced by the French psychoanalyst Jacques Lacan and applied by D. W. Winnicott to the mother's face. She quotes from Winnicott's essay, "Mirror-Role of Mother and Family in Child Development" (originally published in 1967): "What does the baby see when he or she looks at the mother's face? I am suggesting that, ordinarily, what the baby sees is himself or herself. In other words, the mother is looking at the baby and *what she looks like is related to what she sees there*" (Winnicott 1971, 131, Winnicott's emphasis).

Winnicott adds, "All this is too easily taken for granted. I am asking that this which is naturally done well by mothers who are caring for their babies shall not be taken for granted" (131). Consider, by way of contrast, "the case of the baby whose mother reflects her own mood or, worse still, the rigidity of her own defenses." What then does the baby see? What is mirrored back to him? Not the baby's own face, with whatever expression (discomfort, joy, etc.) he presented to the mother, but the mother's own preoccupations or defenses. If this is merely a single occasion, no lasting damage has been done. But many babies have "a long experience of not getting back what they are giving. They look and they do not see themselves," and "the baby gets settled into the idea that when he or she looks, what is seen is the mother's face," in which case her "face is not then a mirror," for when the mother's face is unresponsive, "a mirror is a thing to be looked at but not to be looked into" (132). Mirroring is crucial because babies have a fundamental need to get "something of themselves back from the environment." Mirroring is therefore "the beginning of a significant exchange with the world, a two-way process in which self-enrichment alternates with the discovering of meaning in the world of seen things" (132).

Winnicott cites the case of a patient of his who had a perception of herself as a baby who "would look at the mother and see her talking to someone else" (137). His work as a psychotherapist is "a long-term giving the patient back what the patient brings. It is a complex derivative of the face that reflects what is there to be seen. I like to think of my work in this way, and to think that if I do this well enough the patient will find his or her own self, and will be able to exist and feel real" (138). While Rizzuto does not make a similar claim for her own psychotherapeutic work with Douglas O'Duffy, this is certainly an implication of her observation that there were moments when he would abandon his defensive shield—the grandiose self-representation—and his voice "would become soft, his face smooth with a faint smile, and his longings for warmth and affection would be undisguised." Rizzuto was able to see this face and hear this voice in a way that his mother, worried that he might suffer the same fate as her two dead sons, could not. In effect, what his mother had mirrored to him was the face of a mother who was preoccupied with her dead boys.

Heinz Kohut has expanded on Winnicott's association of the mirror and the mother's face in his formation of "a psychology of the self." I will not discuss his views in detail, but I want to comment on his idea that children who are inadequately "mirrored" are likely to develop a grandiose self-representation (an important theme, as we have seen, in Rizzuto's own interpretation of Douglas O'Duffy's problems). Kohut argues that the child looks to the parental environment (comprised of both mother and father) for two things: (1) for confirmation of his own innate sense of vigor, greatness, and perfection; and (2) for persons to whom he can look up and with whom he can merge as an image of calmness, infallibility, and omnipotence (Kohut and Wolf 1986, 177). He calls the former the "mirroring selfobject" and the latter "the idealized parent imago." (By *selfobject* he means objects in the external environment that we experience as part of our own self; the infant and small child look primarily to the parental environment for such objects.)

"Mirror-hungry personalities," then, are persons who "thirst for selfobjects whose confirming and admiring responses will nourish their famished self. They are impelled to display themselves and to evoke the attention of others, trying to counteract, however fleetingly, their inner sense of worthlessness and lack of self-esteem" (188). Some of these mirror-hungry personalities "are able to establish relationships with reliably mirroring others that will sustain them for long periods," but "most of them will not be nourished for long, even by genuinely accepting responses. Thus, despite their discomfort about their need to display themselves and despite their sometimes severe stage fright and shame they must go on trying to find new selfobjects whose attention and recognition they seek to induce" (190).

As for Douglas O'Duffy, his mirror-hunger was reflected in his need to display himself in heroic actions in a desperate effort to find new selfobjects who would nourish his flagging self. The "public" afforded an unlimited number of such temporary selfobjects. If he delivered "thirty-five youngsters" in unusually risk-filled situations, he won the appreciation and admiration of thirty-five new mothers. The fact that there were thirty-five such mothers, however, illustrates how temporary and fleeting this admiration was. Also, because his superiors refused to promote him because he was not a team player, the thirteen citations they awarded him rang hollow. As he bitterly concluded, these citations were "as useless as the public I've saved." Unlike promotions, which would have brought tangible benefits, the citations had temporary, ephemeral value, a ceremonial recognition providing a brief inner glow but not enduring nourishment for his famished self.

Kohut had a patient, Mr. X., a mirror-hungry personality who made "insistent claims for attention and praise" and exhibited an "arrogant superiority" (189). While his mother's "approval of him had indeed been excessive, the focus of her mirroring had not been selected in accordance with *his* needs—but in accordance with *hers*—namely, to keep him dependent on her, indeed to retain him within her own personality organization, in order to brace up her own, precariously constituted self" (190). Douglas, too, made "insistent claims for attention and praise" and exhibited an "arrogant superiority." This "arrogant superiority" reflected a defensive self-structure that he could present to others in order to disguise his inner sense of worthlessness and lack of self-esteem. As Kohut and Wolf explain, "It is not so much what the parents *do* that will influence the character of the child's self, but what the parents are. If the parents are at peace with their own needs to shine and to succeed insofar as these needs can be realistically gratified, if, in other words, the parents' self-confidence is secure, then the proud exhibitionism of the budding self of their child will be responded to acceptingly" (182). Then, no matter how "grave the blows may be to which the child's grandiosity is exposed by the realities of life, the proud smile of the parents will keep alive a bit of the original omnipotence, to be retained as the nucleus of the self-confidence and inner security about one's worth that sustain the healthy person throughout his life" (182).

If, however, the parents are preoccupied with "the needs of their own insecurely established self," the child's natural grandiosity will not evolve into the nucleus of self-confidence and inner security about his worth but will instead become a defensive grandiosity, reflected, for example, in the arrogant superiority that both Mr. X. and Douglas manifest. Like Winnicott, Kohut and Wolf emphasize the difference between a parent's "unavoidable *occasional* failure" in this regard and a "*chronic* attitude" (183–84, their emphasis).

As Rizzuto notes, Douglas's grandiose self-representation emerged in early adolescence, when he reacted against his mother's need, similar to Mr. X.'s mother, to keep him dependent on her, even to retain him within her own personality structure. This dependence was symbolized by the fact that she insisted on giving him shots which, in his view, he did not need. His program of "total control over his body" was designed, in part, to prove that he was right, as well as to achieve his independence from his mother in the one area—his physical body—where her attentions were the most emotionally suffocating.

Douglas's Paternal Image

While Rizzuto's discussion of Douglas's parental images focuses to an overwhelming degree on his mother, she turns to his father to identify the source of his grandiose self-representation. It was based, she suggests, on "an idealized father," the father he had "hero-worshiped" as a boy. In response to her question about his ideal father, Douglas stated without hesitation: "The one I got. I would not change a thing." He is not troubled by the fact that his father hit and punished him, for what especially came through to him was his father's "infinite perceptivity to know when you needed help, to know when you needed to talk; to know when to scold and when not to scold and give you a pat on the back and say: 'what in the hell has happened?'" During his protracted illness with rheumatic fever, his father "made me feel that even though I felt sick and rotten that in time I would feel better. He always sensed when I needed a boost or knew when to encourage and praise. He always was there when I needed him or needed advice. He was lovable."

Rizzuto suggests that Douglas's grandiose self-image was formed mostly to deal with a mother incapable of nurturing him. Throughout his life all "his extraordinary efforts and deeds were aimed at being noticed by his mother (his father noticed him even before he said anything) or to convince himself that he was good enough to deserve being noticed by her." We may surmise that his decision to terminate his college education "to help repair his father's finances" and subsequent decision to abandon his dream of becoming a lawyer and to join the state police force were designed to secure his mother's notice, because he would thereby both save her from financial insecurity and rehabilitate his father's (and the family's) reputation and honor. He would be the man in her eyes that his father, with his "flexible conscience," could not be.

With the downfall of this grandiose self-representation following his accident, his identification with his idealized father changed into one in which he identified with the father that others knew him to be, the man who was "well-liked" in his professional life and who was "the loved and loving man" in his family life. Thus, the real—not the idealized—father provided Douglas with a model that he could emulate now that his grandiose self-image lay in tatters.

Rizzuto's presentation of Douglas's parental relationships and images is largely based on his relationship with his mother and the grandiose self-representation that he constructed—defensively—in order to gain his mother's recognition. If his paternal relationship plays a relatively small role in her presentation, this undoubtedly reflects the fact that his mother was the dominant figure in the O'Duffy household and was largely responsible for creating its religious atmosphere. The same predominance of his maternal representation and grandiose self-representation is reflected in his God representation.

Douglas's God Representation

Rizzuto makes several propositions regarding Douglas's God representation. These may be broken down as follows:

1. It derives its characteristics mainly from his mother.

2. In descriptive terms, it belongs developmentally to the last stages of separation-individuation in early childhood. In psychoanalytic terms, it belongs to the anal-retentive phase with its narcissistic ambivalent attachment to the maternal object. As such, it belongs to a late stage of the need for mirroring and admiration of the exhibitionistic child.

3. Defenses used against believing in it include repression, reaction-formation, and a grandiose self-image. By repressing, he refuses to make himself aware of the God he has, and by reacting violently against his need for a God, he makes himself exceedingly independent and self-sufficient.

4. It is used as an object for displacement of his narcissistic rage toward his mother, thus enabling him to have a less painful experience with her and to remain on relatively good terms with her until her death.

5. Its elaboration and transformation of the maternal representation is minimal, that is, God is a direct continuation of the maternal representation and its ambivalent attachment. Such elaboration and transformation were impeded by his mother's limited ability to respond to his need for recognition and admiration and his natural grandiosity, and by his own fear of narcissistic exposure and acknowledgment of his need for his mother and her care. Acceptance of both impediments would require working through his narcissistic expectations and the rage that followed their frustration.

Rizzuto adds that the God offered by his current local parish—one who is kind and appealing—coincides with the God he *might* believe in, that is, the unconscious component of his God representation. If brought to consciousness, belief in this God would give meaning to his life and worldview.

Rizzuto's strategy with all four clinical portraits is to intersperse commentary on the parental images with their God representations, thereby demonstrating the psychodynamic connections between them. In addition, she provides a table of roughly two to three pages in which she juxtaposes the patients' statements about one or both parents with similar statements made about God. Focusing on the interactions between Douglas's composite God representation and maternal representation, she suggests that four elements are especially noteworthy. In order of importance, there is (1) the *frustrating mother* who failed to offer sufficient narcissistic enhancement; (2) the *caring mother*, colored by the wish that she also recognize and value him; (3) the fantasized and acted-out *grandiose self-representation* that compensates for narcissistic injury; and (4) the God his mother presented to him in words and actions as an existing being who is omnipotent, omniscient (capable of knowing one's inner thoughts), and all-merciful. In the table juxtaposing his statements about his mother, his grandiose self-representation, and God, Rizzuto makes a division between "the frustrating mother" and the "caring and wished-for mother." The "frustrating mother" statements outnumber the "caring and wished-for mother" statements (with corresponding God representation statements) by a ratio of six to one, indicating that his God representation is itself dominated by a sense of profound frustration. Even the statements that correspond to the "caring and wished-for mother" are ones that view God as one who does *not* meet such expectations.

God as the Frustrating Mother

In her discussion of Douglas's God representation, Rizzuto says that "God never had the appeal his father had. He experienced God as opposed to him, frustrating, controlling, deceptive, and unresponsive, just the opposite of his tender description of his father, but identical with his perception of his mother." Typical statements about God that support this summary include: "The feeling I get from my relationship with God is one of total, complete, utter frustration because of double standards"; "For me my love for God is not important because hypocrisy and deceit is not the cornerstone of trust"; "I think that God wants me to be good because he says it is compatible with his own ideas of how you ought to behave"; "What I resent the most about God is that it is like an opiate that saps, controls people's minds, and inhibits them with utter phantasy. That is great until tested. People have blind faith and lose their ability to think"; "He wants us to believe so that we can lead our tough little lives and not make waves"; and "I think that as a person I have dissatisfied God because according to his standards, I haven't taken all he has offered me on blind faith."

While Rizzuto suggests that these are all reflective of "the frustrating mother" representation, several seem more reflective of the God his mother explicitly taught him to believe in by her words and example. Those are the ones that allude to blind faith and the requirement that one relinquish one's "ability to think" in order to believe in God. For Rizzuto, however, the statements about God that are most reflective of his *experience* of his mother as unresponsive to him are ones about prayer: "Prayer is not important to me because it is like one crying in the wilderness. Nobody hears them or even listens"; "I do not pray because I feel that God will not answer because he does not exist as I know him"; and "God is closest to those who believe and accept him (if you acknowledge his existence)." As Rizzuto notes, this sense that God "does not exist for me the way I know he exists for others, from the way I see him behaving with them" reflects his experience as a child who "did not feel noticed as himself while he noticed his mother's capacity to respond to others (alive or dead) with affection and enthusiasm."

While Rizzuto does not make this particular connection between the frustrating mother and his God representation, there is a prominent moral theme in his statements about God. He states that God "wants me to be good because he says it is compatible with *his* own ideas about how you ought to behave" (my emphasis). He wrote "his" after striking out "my," which may suggest that his own views of how he ought to behave are not the same as God's views, as represented to him by his mother's rules and sanctions, which he seems to have found overly restrictive and punitive. He accuses God, however, of having a double standard, of being guilty of hypocrisy and deceit, and of expecting him to accept his offerings on blind faith. While he has not lived up to God's standards, however, he has no fear of God: "The fear of God is not important, because I have strong reservations as to his existence." I will discuss this moral theme further in my consideration of his melancholic condition.

God as the Caring and Wished-for Mother

As for the "caring and wished-for mother" and its contribution to Douglas's God representation, this is largely reflected in negative statements about God and his mother's belief in God. On being asked to describe the ideal mother, he responded, "An ideal mother for me is a mother interested in me as a human being more than a God-damned God in person. A mother who realized she had a younger son. More interested in me as a human being rather than one in a group, a number." His view that she would be "interested in me as an individual rather than a number" clearly refers to his statements about there being only enough love for eight, not ten, children. Corresponding statements about God are the ones about why he doesn't pray and about his agnosticism: "There may be a God or some being but his power, Glory, Warmth, reason, compassion have never manifested themselves on me." Continuing, he expresses both indifference and sadness about the absence of any such manifestations: "There may be a supreme being but where and who may it be I am not particularly interested. . . . I am sad about religion. The aesthetic approach is fine but there has got to be some meaning for your life." It may well be that his capitalizing of the words "Glory" and "Warmth" is significant, as these two attributes of God suggest the mirroring theme discussed earlier, that is, the desire of the small child to see a maternal face that glows and expresses tender warmth, thus reflecting back the glow and warmth he feels toward her.

Rizzuto emphasizes that the frustrating mother was such a dominating factor in Douglas's God representation that the caring and wished-for mother has little opportunity to assist toward the elaboration and transformation of this representation. The tender and caring side of God, however, is reflected in Douglas's response to a question about his wishes for an afterlife: "I would like to be with God after death because it is a nice idea and it would make life easier." When queried whether he would like to be united with God in the afterlife, his voice grew soft and tender: "Sure; I will enjoy that!" (Note his use of "will," not the subjunctive "would.") He elaborated on this response, noting that he wanted his entire family with him, his father, his mother, his dead brothers, his living siblings, and their spouses and children. When asked if he felt close to God as a child, his voice again became tender, "Yeah, when singing in the choir, going to mass, things like that."

Rizzuto views these statements as evidence for the caring and tender side of God, and thus as associated with the caring and wished-for mother. They could, however, be viewed instead as a tender reflection on himself as a young boy, an affection for the lad who wanted his family to live in perfect unity and who gave voice and expression to these longings and aspirations through acts of religious devotion.

Grandiose Self-Representation and God Representation

Rizzuto also contends that his God representation has elements of his grandiose self-representation. This is not the natural grandiosity of the small child that evolves into the nucleus of quiet self-confidence and inner security, but the defensive grandiosity that results from inadequate or flawed mirroring by his parents. Illustrative of this association is his statement that he "considers God as my conscience, the part of me that strives for perfection." It is also expressed in his tendency to view God with a degree of sarcasm, as when he says, "Emotionally I would like to have the prestige that God has so that I too could make profound (stupid) statements and not even be questioned." In a footnote, Rizzuto speculates that the suggestion of an unconscious *paternal* component to his God representation may be involved here, in that his mother "appreciated her husband's prestige, as did his family, friends, and the public." If so, Rizzuto indicates that it is not available to his conscious mind nor usable in his present psychic state.

There are other statements about God, however, that reveal the longings that underlie this defensive self-representation. These, it would seem, point to the possible locus of an elaboration or even transformation of his God representation. One is an eloquent statement about what religion can do for a person, namely, that it "is a very strong motivating force that keeps people from despairing—I mean, regardless if you believe in a chair or a tree it gives you personal solace *and holds you together when normally you'd fall apart*" (my emphasis). This view of religion reflects its etymological meaning—"binding together"—and applies it to the self. Douglas goes on to say, however, that "religion has neither been to me useful, helpful, or comforting in any way, shape, or manner." Another indication of the possibility of an elaboration or transformation of his God representation is the statement that he wrote beneath his drawing of God (see figure 1), which is the basis of Rizzuto's chapter title "A God in the Mirror" and the inspiration for her discussion of the psychoanalytic concept of mirroring. It reads, "I feel that God may be me in a mirror and that the only way I can open the Door is to know me completely and honestly." As he was drawing the picture, he explained, "I know that God is there inside me—I don't know what it is."

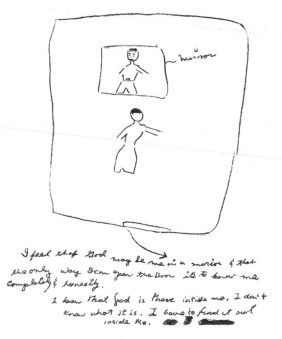

Figure 1

About the picture itself, Rizzuto notes that the "me" of the picture is a child of seven or eight wearing short pants. She also draws attention to his use of the pronoun "it" instead of "he" for God. His use of "it" may reflect his judgment ("God-damned God in person") against his mother's view of God and his comment that he considers "God as my conscience, the part of me that strives for perfection." On the other hand, by also assigning the pronoun "me" to God, he implies a self-identification with God. As he states, "If I have to describe God *according to my experience with him* I would say that he is what I find in me that is good; the part of me that finds contentment" (my emphasis). This is not an expression of defensive or vaulting grandiosity (as reflected, for example, in a nurse's judgment that his "most urgent emotional need throughout his life is to feel satisfied in living up to practically unattainable goals which he sets for himself. He has a need to be his own God") but of the natural grandiosity that lies hidden behind his arrogant self-presentation. If God is identified with "what I find in myself that is good," this is the natural grandiosity of a child who has not yet begun to intuit that his mother, especially, does not have the emotional capacity to respond to his own sense of warmth and inner glory. As Rizzuto points out, these statements indicate that "the narcissistically frustrated child was able to find some self-affirmation and worth in himself." She adds, "That he calls that aspect of himself *God* permits a further inference: when he was searching for his mother's mirroring of his felt goodness and perfection, he must have been thinking about God or at least used this experience in later speculation."

What does Douglas mean when he says that "the only way I can open the Door is to know me completely and honestly?" Is the Door a metaphor for his heart, or is he referring to someone? Rizzuto points out that when he was asked to indicate who was the most hated person in his life between ages three and six, he talked about the shots his mother gave him and then said, "She was the DOOR [his emphasis], my father was the janitor." This means, in her view, that "the entrance to self-knowledge, as well as his knowledge of God, may take place only after passing the maternal door." His mother stands between himself and the mirror that will not only reflect his own self but also enable God to reveal himself.

Rizzuto concludes that Douglas's God representation reflects "an early developmental period between the ages of one and three or four," and that it comprises those features that reflect what occurred in his relations with his mother at that time: her frustrating failure but also her benign approach to the child and tolerance of his anger, and his wish to be seen as he saw himself, with his perceived goodness and perfection and the developmental battle for control. God, then, has been a great disappointment to him, is not to be feared, but is viewed as a threat to his desire for independence in the use of his mind and in the way he lives his life. On the other hand, his God representation has

an element of longing, the desire for a God who would recognize his fundamental goodness. This God representation, which has been "repressed and
reacted against," has been "untouched by his good relations with his father and
brother or, at present, with his wife." The demolition of his Oedipus complex
was achieved as prescribed—intensified identification with his father and
diminution of his object-choice of his mother—but this further development
"did not touch his narcissistic problem," which related to inadequate mirroring.

If this is so, we need to ask how a consideration of Douglas O'Duffy from
the perspective of melancholia might shed light on the ways in which his understanding of God and of religion have continued to influence his adult life.

Douglas's Melancholy Self

Psychiatric Diagnosis

I will begin my discussion of Douglas's melancholic condition with his psychiatric diagnosis, a "psychic decompensation" viewed as a "reactive depression to
occupational trauma (car accident) in an obsessive compulsive personality."
"Psychic decompensation" indicates that compensatory structures—his defensive grandiose self—broke down as a consequence of the auto accident (which
had been preceded by the deaths of three state troopers, two by killers, the other
by his own hand). "Reactive depression" was the form this decompensation
took. In *DSM-IV* terms, he had suffered a "Major Depressive Episode" whose
essential feature is at least two weeks during which there is either a depressed
mood or the loss of interest or pleasure in nearly all activities. The person must
also experience at least four additional symptoms drawn from a list that
includes: (1) changes in appetite or weight, sleep, and psychomotor activity; (2)
decreased energy; (3) feelings of worthlessness or guilt; (4) difficulty thinking,
concentrating, or making decisions; and (5) recurrent thoughts of death or suicidal ideation, plans, or attempts. The symptoms must persist for most of the
day, nearly every day, for at least two consecutive weeks, and must be accompanied by clinically significant distress or impairment in social, occupational, or
other important areas of functioning (*DSM-IV* 1994, 320–21).

The mood in a Major Depressive Episode is often described by the person
as being depressed, sad, hopeless, discouraged, or "down in the dumps." In
some cases, sadness may be denied at first, but may subsequently be elicited
by his being informed, for example, that he looks as if he is about to cry. Some
individuals emphasize somatic complaints (e.g., bodily aches and pains)
rather than reporting feelings of sadness. Many individuals report or exhibit
increased irritability (e.g., persistent anger, a tendency to respond to events
with angry outbursts or blaming of others, or an exaggerated sense of frustration over minor matters). Loss of interest or pleasure is nearly always present

(i.e., one may report "not caring anymore" or not feeling any enjoyment in activities previously considered pleasurable). A sense of worthlessness or guilt may also be present, and there is a tendency to misinterpret neutral or trivial occurrences as evidence of personal defects. One may also exhibit an exaggerated sense of responsibility for untoward events. Thoughts of death and suicidal thoughts or attempts may also be present (321).

An untreated episode typically lasts six months or longer. In the majority of cases, there is a complete remission of symptoms. In some cases (perhaps 20 to 30 percent) some depressive symptoms may persist for months or years ("partial remission"). In another 5 to 10 percent the full criteria for Major Depressive Episode continue for two or more years, in which case the word *chronic* is added to the diagnosis.

Worthlessness and Guilt

Two features of this description of "Major Depressive Episode" stand out. One is *the sense of worthlessness or guilt*. If Douglas's "psychic decompensation" involved the breaking down of his grandiose self-structure, we may conclude that this uncovered the deep feelings of worthlessness that this structure was designed to overcome and disguise. The auto accident unveiled his physical vulnerability and brought him face-to-face with the fact that he was once "a skinny, sickly, ungainly, awkward little ferret." When he looked at himself in the mirror of his mind, he saw this rather pathetic boy, and he could not deny to himself that this boy remained a part of him. As Erik Erikson notes in *Childhood and Society*, "Every adult, whether he is a follower or a leader, a member of a mass or of an elite, was once a child. He was once small. A sense of smallness forms a substratum in his mind, ineradicably. His triumphs will be measured against his smallness, his defeats will substantiate it" (Erikson 1963, 404).

As Rizzuto points out, the picture Douglas drew of himself when asked to portray God was that of a seven- or eight-year-old. He had worked hard to eliminate this boy from his consciousness. It was not until he was confronted with his physical vulnerability that he needed to acknowledge this boy's continuing existence as an important part of who he was. Significantly, the experience of physical vulnerability involved being "knocked unconscious"; thus, it was one in which his consciousness was dethroned and a long-repressed awareness of himself as small and pathetic replaced it.

Regarding the matter of guilt, the killing deaths of two other state troopers and the suicide death of his "officer friend" were the "two straws" that preceded the "final straw" of his own auto accident. "Survivor guilt" was surely a contributing factor in his depressive episode. His other colleagues would also have experienced survivor guilt. For him, however, this was exacerbated by the fact that he had viewed himself as the "hero" of the force, the one who would place himself in greater harm's way than the others, thereby providing a protective shield for them. The suicidal death of his friend was especially frustrating, since this meant that, in his friend's case, the enemy was not "out there" but "in here." If, as Freud argues, the "lost object" of the melancholic has been internalized, then suicide means that the ego is not strong enough to counter the desire to kill this internalized object, thereby terminating the melancholiac's psychic ordeal.

I suggest that Douglas saw a great deal of himself in the friend who committed suicide—"There, but for the grace of God, go I"—but he was able to forestall suicide by means of the other "method" that Freud discusses in his "Mourning and Melancholia" essay. This is the method of mania. Such mania was reflected in acts of heroism that portrayed him as a man who was invulnerable. As Freud points out, "the content of mania is no different from that of melancholia," for both "disorders are wrestling with the same 'complex,'" but "in melancholia the ego had succumbed to it, whereas in mania it has mastered the complex or thrust it aside" (Freud 1963c, 175). In Douglas's case, it was more a matter of having "thrust it aside" than of having mastered the complex itself. This is not to say that he had "manic episodes" as defined by *DSM-IV*, which must last a full week (*DSM-IV* 1994, 328–32). There was, however, a manic quality to his counterphobic behavior as an adolescent and his subsequent heroic behavior as a state trooper who courted death by defying it. *DSM-IV* notes that one of the characteristics of a manic episode is "an inflated self-esteem or grandiosity." I suggest, therefore, that Douglas needed these periodic acts of heroism to sustain his defensive grandiose self. He was not suicidal in any technical sense, but, as Rizzuto points out, his behavior from adolescence through his auto accident was "based on a grandiose self-image of being invulnerable and capable of defying death itself."

In contrast to the events that preceded his auto accident, however, the accident was rather insignificant. Unlike the two state troopers who were killed in the line of duty—and who would have received posthumous citations and a state funeral—his accident was quite routine. This combination of circumstances perfectly replicated the deaths of his own brothers and his own experience of being stricken with rheumatic fever. While rheumatic fever is a very serious illness, the "heroes" in his family were the two boys over whom his mother grieved. They were the ones who warranted the "cult of the dead"—the holy water, the crucifixes—while he was the one who was subjected to humiliating injections. They were the ones who resembled the Christ figure on these crucifixes, while he was the "tin Jesus" whose affliction from rheumatic fever resulted in forced bed rest. His dead brothers were memorialized, the home turned into a shrine in their honor, while little Douglas looked on, sensing that the only way to gain his mother's admiration and accolades was to suffer death. There is a great gulf between a "dead little angel" and a "sickly little boy," and this gulf is bridgeable only by death itself. The only way he could live with this circumstance was to identify with the dead brother who, he believed, was not grieved over as much as the other dead brother.

I suggest, therefore, that the deaths of the two state troopers who were killed by the hands of others were reminiscent of the deaths of his two dead brothers who were also killed by another hand (Death? God?). The death of his officer friend by his own hand may, however, have struck even closer to home, as this death brought him face to face with himself. If not consciously, at least unconsciously, he cannot help but ask himself: "Am I, too, engaged in a form of suicide each time that I, in my grandiosity, play the role of the hero? And, if so, have I gotten a taste of how a suicidal death is viewed by my superiors, my fellow officers, and the public in the fact that no one has treated me as a hero?" Death suffered in the line of duty gains accolades; a suicidal death is embarrassing to all concerned and is quickly passed over in silence. In addition, however, I think that the suicide death of his officer friend was also reminiscent of the death of his playmate when the two of them were nine years old. As he said about this playmate, "He couldn't make it." The same was true of his officer friend. There was a vulnerability in him to which Douglas responded, with which he could personally identify, and that opened him up, once again, to the vulnerable self that he had tried to put to death through his counterphobic, defensive, grandiose self—the deliberately constructed self who could look directly into the sun and climb tall trees. Thus, if his three months in bed following the auto accident perfectly replicated the period in which he was bedridden from rheumatic fever, this period of psychic decompensation also took him back to the very circumstances of his childhood before he managed to recreate himself in the image of an invulnerable "giant of a man." Goliath met his inner David, and this David felled him, for Goliath was created from a false sense of his physical invulnerability. As Erikson puts it, a man's triumphs will be measured against his smallness, his defeats will substantiate it.

Experience of Sadness

A second feature of the *DSM-IV* description of "Major Depressive Episode" that stands out in Douglas's case is *the experience of sadness*, which may be denied at first. There is little, if any, discussion of Douglas's sadness in Rizzuto's case study, which focuses almost entirely on his resentments. This is consistent with the melancholic condition, which especially manifests itself in rage against the internalized lost object. Much of this rage comes out in his psychotherapy with Rizzuto. But melancholia also bears a relationship to mourning in that both involve the experience of loss, and it therefore invokes deep feelings of sadness as well. The difference between the two mental states is that sadness is allowed expression in mourning, while it is repressed in melancholia. In Douglas's case, this sadness was deeply hidden beneath the feelings of rage, which, while also repressed, were, through psychotherapy, more accessible to consciousness.

His sadness has both an adult and a childhood dimension. His sadness as an adult relates to the deaths of his parents. The fact that he cannot remember the dates of their deaths (when he can remember the death dates of many other relatives) reveals his difficulty in coming to terms with these two deaths. Both parents' deaths were troubling to him, his father's because he had so deeply identified with him and his mother's because he, not she, was the one who took the initiative toward an emotional closeness that had eluded him through the years. Her death thus meant that he would never experience her own "glory" and "warmth." At best, he came to know her as "human too."

The difference in the two deaths—and the reason, as I argued in chapter 4, why melancholia is not associated with the father—is that, in the wake of his father's death, Douglas could further intensify his identification with his father by becoming a state trooper, with the intention that he would redeem his father's honor. His mother's death, on the other hand, afforded no such compensating actions. As Rizzuto notes, "He tolerated her death well, though he is still a bit confused about it." I believe that this confusion was directly related to the emotional separation he experienced from his mother in early childhood ("Did this happen because of something I did or should have done?"). His mother's death thus reactivated this earlier psychological trauma, and he experienced a similar frustration and sense of failure. The fact that he "tolerated her death well" also points to this early separation, for this is precisely how a boy is "supposed" to respond to his emotional loss of his mother. This, in fact, is a boy's first experience in pain tolerance, and thus the first step on his way toward manhood.

But did little Douglas actually tolerate this loss well? Rizzuto tells us that he contracted rheumatic fever "between the ages of three and six" and adds that "the dates are not precise because the patient had trouble remembering this very emotional detail." While it is unrealistic to expect that he would remember the exact date of an illness that could have begun as early as age three, we have also seen that, for him, imprecise dates may be due to the emotional trauma involved. In any event, his rheumatic fever probably occurred about the same time as his emotional separation from his mother (Rizzuto assigns his God representation to "the last stages of separation-individuation," or when he was about three or four years old). We are justified, then, in wondering if his susceptibility to rheumatic fever may have been due to his emotional loss of his mother.

Rheumatic Fever and Emotional Loss

Rheumatic fever is a systemic disease of childhood, in many cases recurrent, that follows streptococcal infection. Physicians often need to allay parents' guilt feelings for failing to seek treatment for this infection because initially the illness seems no worse than a common cold. Long-term antibiotic therapy is typically rendered in order to minimize its recurrence, reducing the risk of permanent damage to the heart and eventual deformity of the heart valves. The shots that Douglas complained about were medically essential in this regard. Preventive treatment is recommended until age 21. Because very few children (0.3 percent) with streptococcal fever ever contract rheumatic fever, the child's reduced resistence is involved in its development or recurrence. While rheumatic fever tends to be familial, this may merely reflect contributing environmental factors, such as malnutrition or crowded living quarters. In more severe cases, the child may develop muscle spasms, poor muscle coordination, and weakness. Psychological symptoms include hyper-irritability, inability to concentrate, deterioration in handwriting, and purposelessness. As it generally strikes during cool, damp weather in the winter and early spring, and is more common in the northern U.S. states, Douglas's mother's decision to take him to the Caribbean for two months was excellent therapy. Even so, recovery is very prolonged, with occasional recurrences, and the parent who assumes primary care is likely to become frustrated both by the prolonged nature of the illness and by its effects on the child's lifestyle, while the child is likely to become extremely bored from spending so much time in bed. Primary symptoms are migratory joint pain, with swelling and redness accompanying the pain, which commonly affects the knees, ankles, elbows, or hips (*Professional Guide to Diseases* 1998, 1087–88).

With eight children and two parents, we may assume that the home in which Douglas grew up was crowded. Since the first boy died of diphtheria (also a communicable disease), the family living conditions were conducive to illness such as the one Douglas contracted. It is not inconceivable that the children were also malnourished, as the family was wholly dependent on Douglas's father's income as a state trooper. The fact that his father was susceptible to bribery is indicative of the family's financial state, as is the fact that Douglas left college to assist his parents in resolving their financial problems. It is not inconceivable, however, that an additional factor in Douglas's susceptibility to rheumatic fever was his silent despair over the emotional separation from his mother at this time, which was exacerbated by the fact that there were so many other children vying for her attention, and that she was preoccupied with the deaths of his two older brothers. Even the fact that rheumatic fever poses a continuing cardiac threat is at least metaphorically—

and, quite possibly, psychologically—significant, as the emotional separation from his mother was heartrending on a recurrent basis.

We may conclude, therefore, that Douglas did not tolerate the emotional loss of his mother well at all. Not only did he fall ill somewhere around the time of the separation, but also his illness continued for several years (e.g., it was during his first or second grade in school that the rheumatic fever confined him to bed for three months, and his recovery in the Caribbean took another two months). His illness might even be viewed as a bid to regain his mother's attention and to receive a measure of the same love and sympathy accorded his two dead brothers. Yet, while his mother did minister to him, she also inflicted pain—the shots that he so much resented—and, in time, he came to feel that she was becoming overly solicitous, frustrating his desires for independence and his need to live as normal a life as possible. While she no doubt was simply following the doctor's orders, she may have communicated excessive anxieties of her own, owing to the previous deaths of Douglas's two brothers. In any event, it was his perception of her excessive attention to him that caused him to feel that she did not take his desires and needs into consideration. She emphasized his patienthood more than his need to function as normally as possible under the circumstances. This in turn may be evidence of her ambivalent feelings toward him. For a mother already bereaved of two young sons, a sickly child could become the object of her own (repressed) rage. Conceivably, she unconsciously welcomed the opportunity to inflict pain on her sickly boy through doctor-prescribed injections, and perhaps he sensed that there was a certain amount of malice in her administration of them.

Image of the "Little Ferret"

This brings me to what I consider to be the very depths of Douglas's sadness, that is, his sadness for the "skinny, sickly, ungainly, awkward little ferret" from whom he had attempted to distance himself through "total mastery over his body." He viewed this "little ferret" of a boy as an "invalid" (in both senses of the term) and embarked on a program of remaking himself into a totally different boy—"well-coordinated, aggressive, competitive." Now, in his depressive episode, which recapitulated his earlier illness, he rediscovered the little boy of whom he had been ashamed, and his heart went out to him. Lying in bed for three months, felled by the auto accident, he regained emotional contact with the boy who lay in bed for three months with rheumatic fever.

The picture he drew of this boy—who, in Rizzuto's view, is about seven or eight years old—is rather indistinct and featureless. The boy is bereft of his lower legs and feet (thus, unable to seek out the company of others) and lower arms and hands (thus, unable to reach out to anyone). One cannot help but wonder if he has eliminated the very parts of his anatomy that caused him pain as a boy; as noted above, rheumatic fever affects the knees, ankles, elbows, or hips. Yet, because this boy is almost exactly replicated in the mirror, this is the "me" whom he seeks to know "completely and honestly," and this is the boy who also holds the key to knowing the God who "is there inside me." If, as Rizzuto suggests, his mother is the door standing between himself and the rediscovery of this little boy, the reason she is this door is that her ministrations, ambivalently motivated, prompted him to make himself into a very different boy—an aggressive, death-defying boy. This well-defended and defensive boy, now lying stricken and demoralized, a "tin Jesus," had stood between himself and the original "me," even as his mother's dead boys stood between her and her living boy. The adult Goliath, that giant of a man, has met his repressed David, a mere boy, and against all expectations, this David has proven the stronger.

I am not suggesting that Douglas is necessarily consciously aware of his sadness over the "little ferret" that he laid to rest when he set about his program of "total mastery" over his body. After all, the very reason Rizzuto asked her subjects to draw pictures of God was to gain access to their unconscious or, at best, preconscious thoughts and feelings about God. Even so, her case study provides considerable evidence of this sadness for the little boy who continues to live inside of him. Besides the picture itself, there is his account of his nine-year-old playmate who died of pneumonia and who was also "a sickly child." Rizzuto notes that when he saw the dead child's face he reflected, in his shock, on "his dead siblings, especially the first boy, whose death had upset his parents and whose memory the mother kept alive through the years." While I do not doubt that the death of his playmate caused him to reflect on his dead brothers, the fact that the playmate was a boy of his own age, and was sickly like himself, must have prompted even deeper feelings of his own identity with this boy (As William James said of the epileptic patient, potentially, "That shape am I"). As Douglas says of this boy, he "couldn't make it." It was not long after this that he made his decision to undo his own image as the sickly child. The "sickly child" is a potentially dead child, and Douglas was determined to live. The "shock" he experienced was the shock of self-recognition.

Another piece of evidence that he experienced sadness for the little boy who lives inside of him is the term he used to describe him—"little ferret." Coming from a tough and seasoned state trooper, his comparison of himself to a ferret conveys a sympathetic, even tender feeling for this boy. The ferret, close kin to the weasel, has a long, low-slung body of some 18–24 inches in length, and weighs only 18–22 ounces. Interestingly, in light of Douglas's determination to be competitive with his athletic brothers, the ferret preys on the prairie dog, which is shorter than the ferret but much heavier. It makes its way surreptitiously into the prairie dog's tunnel and quickly kills its prey with a bite to the base of the skull. It is then likely to take up residence in the prairie dog's own burrow (Whitaker 1998). Thus, this "little ferret" embarked on the bold and audacious plan of competing with his brothers in the very arena—athletics—in which they excelled. He would prove himself to be more than competitive with them, and, having proven his superior ability, he would dislodge them from their privileged position in the O'Duffy home, in which all the brothers competed for their mother's admiration.

This image of the "little ferret" may also, however, have relevance to the sense that he was also "competing" with one or more dead brothers—long since buried in the earth—for his mother's love. The fact that the ferret's prey is a prairie dog may have relevance to his claim that a dead person —epitomized by his deceased brothers—is "in the category of your dog" as far as the after-life is concerned. Perhaps it is also significant that the ferret is the most endangered species among mammals in North America due to the mass slaughtering of prairie dogs, the ferret's primary prey. If the prairie dog is dead, the ferret is endangered.

In any case, Rizzuto notes that Douglas was capable of great tenderness. As his recovery began, "his readily available warmth and tender feelings to his wife and children became the focus of his conscious attention." She also notes, however, that his voice took on "a very tender pitch" when he recalled his childhood experience of singing in the church choir and going to mass. While his tenderness toward the "little ferret" he laid to rest—but who con-tinues to live inside of him—may remain largely unconscious, the very fact that his motivation for deciding to have his children raised in his own child-hood faith—"To spare them the pain of doubt"—suggests his sensitivity to the emotional pain he suffered as a child, which his defensive grandiose self-structure was designed to counteract.

In effect, the original Douglas "died" in his late childhood, the victim, as it were, of a conscious, suicidal act whose purpose was to enable another Douglas to come to life. This secondary Douglas is now the one whose life is under threat, and O'Duffy has an intuitive sense that the next phase of his life depends upon his reconciliation with the original Douglas. As presented in the picture, this original boy is a pathetic figure—an amputee four times over—but what remains is his essential "me," the locus of his own divinity. With the demise of the "tin Jesus," the way is now clear for the adult Douglas to embrace this pathetic creature, thus initiating a process of self-reconciliation.

Douglas's Obsessive-Compulsive Personality

Rizzuto indicates that Douglas O'Duffy may be diagnosed as an "obsessive-compulsive personality." I now want to show how his obsessive-compulsive personality and his underlying melancholic condition are related. While Rizzuto does not say that he suffers from "Obsessive-Compulsive Personality Disorder" as such, the *DSM-IV* description of this disorder's characteristics provides valuable insight into the obsessive-compulsive personality.

The essential feature of this disorder is a preoccupation with orderliness, perfectionism, and mental and interpersonal control, at the expense of flexibility, openness, and efficiency (*DSM-IV* 1994, 669). Persons with this disorder manifest four or more of the following: (1) an attempt to maintain a sense of control through painstaking attention to rules, trivial details, procedures, lists, and so forth, to the extent that the major point of the activity is lost; (2) perfectionism which interferes with task completion (e.g., an inability to complete a project because the person's own overly strict standards are not met); (3) an excessive devotion to work and productivity (not accounted for by obvious economic necessity) to the exclusion of leisure activities and friendships; (4) overconscientiousness, scrupulosity, and inflexibility (not accounted for by cultural or religious identification) about matters of morality, ethics, or values; (5) inability to discard worn-out or worthless objects even when they have no sentimental value; (6) reluctance to delegate tasks or to work with others unless they submit to exactly the person's way of doing things; (7) a miserly spending style toward both self and others, money being viewed as something to be hoarded for future catastrophes; and (8) rigidity and stubbornness (669–70).

Three of these characteristics are clearly evident in Douglas's case. These include an excessive devotion to work; an overconscientious and inflexible attitude toward matters of morality, ethics, and values; and a reluctance to delegate tasks or to work with others unless they submit to his exact way of doing things. In addition, his ability to remember the dates when several relatives died suggest that he might have a tendency toward preoccupation with details. That Rizzuto herself points to his perfectionism may also indicate that he has difficulty completing projects due to excessively high standards for himself. Recall that he did not complete college. Not enough information is provided to make a conclusive judgment about these latter two criteria, but the three criteria that are clearly present go a long way toward offering an accurate and comprehensive picture of Douglas's professional life. They also characterize the young boy who in late childhood set out to "undo the image of the sickly child." The grandiose self-image that he began to construct at this time included an excessive devotion to the work of making himself into a young man who was physically invulnerable, and an overconscientious and inflexible attitude toward matters of morality, ethics, and values was reflected in his surveillance of the priests. His reluctance to delegate tasks or work with others, causing him to miss out on promotions in his professional life, was evident in his determination to remake himself without any assistance or interference from others. Thus, his coach's failure to recommend him for the scholarship at Princeton may have been because, even then, he was not a "team player."

If this tendency toward obsessive-compulsiveness was evident in his late childhood, I would suggest that it reflected a predisposition formed much earlier, one directly related to the emotional separation from his mother that he experienced in early childhood. This claim brings us to our consideration of his religiousness as an expression of his melancholy self.

Melancholic Religion as Moral Rectitude

I have suggested throughout this book that the religiousness of boys and men is a direct consequence and reflection of their emotional separation from their mothers in early childhood (age 3–4). Its two primary characteristics are the determination to win mother back through exemplary behavior (the religious impulse of moral rectitude leading to a religion of honor) and the search for the lost object or compensatory objects (the religious impulse of questing leading to a religion of basic hopefulness). A third characteristic is a counter-tendency to view the first two characteristics with amused detachment (a religion of humor). It isn't difficult to see that Douglas's religiousness takes primarily the first form. As I now want to show, this predominant form of his religiousness and his obsessive-compulsive personality are two sides of the same coin. (Freud explored this connection between the obsessive-compulsive personality and religion in his earliest writing on religion, "Obsessive Acts and Religious Practices," originally published in 1907.) His obsessive-compulsive personality is also related to his emotional separation from his mother and effort to win her back through good and virtuous behavior. As we saw earlier in our discussion of psychoanalytic views on why the conscience itself is formed, this emotional separation from mother and the formation of the conscience occur in the same developmental period. As Erikson especially emphasized in his early essays on children, the conscience that forms may be far more severe and demanding than the parents may desire, and thus can lead to a situation where the child accuses the adults of not living up to their own rules.

There is considerable evidence in Rizzuto's case study of Douglas's excessively stringent conscience. There were his accusations against religious people for being "hypocrites," which he set out to prove by spying on priests. There was also his dismay as a twenty-one-year-old when he learned that his father had "a flexible conscience," leading to his own determination to succeed in this regard where his father, in his eyes, had failed. These examples, however, derive from adolescence and early young adulthood. Is there evidence from childhood? I think the most convincing evidence—aside from his God representation, which I will discuss later—was his determination to achieve "total mastery" over his body. Rizzuto, of course, focuses on his determination to excel athletically, which relates mainly to his desire to compete with his older brothers, and thus to his aggressivity.

"Total mastery" over one's body, however, also means controlling one's sexual drives. This dimension of his "total mastery of his body" program does not receive any attention in Rizzuto's case study. Yet we may surmise from his adolescent habit of spying on priests for the purpose of collecting stories "about their sexual escapades (though they preached chastity)" that mastery over the body also implied controlling his own sexual urges and desires. Rizzuto's indication that he began this project at the beginning of puberty suggests that total mastery of his body had sexual implications, perhaps relating to autoeroticism, the "private sin" that, in a Roman Catholic boy's mind, would be associated with the fear of damnation itself.

But how is this project of total mastery over his body related to his emotional separation from his mother in early childhood? Aside from his God representation, the answer lies in the fact that Obsessive-Compulsive Disorder—as distinguished from Obsessive-Compulsive *Personality Disorder*—is classified in *DSM-IV* as an anxiety disorder. The difference between them is that the personality disorder "is not characterized by the presence of obsessions or compulsions and instead involves a pervasive pattern of preoccupation with orderliness, perfectionism and control" (*DSM-IV* 1994, 422). Thus, the personality disorder is "a pervasive pattern," whereas in Obsessive-Compulsive Disorder (1) recurrent and persistent thoughts, impulses, or images are experienced as intrusive and inappropriate and cause marked anxiety or distress; (2) these thoughts, impulses, or images are not simply excessive worries about real-life problems; (3) the person attempts to ignore or suppress such thoughts, impulses, or images, or to neutralize them with some other thought or action; and (4) the person recognizes that these thoughts, impulses, or images are a product of his own mind (not imposed from without as in thought insertion). *DSM-IV* indicates that it normally begins in adolescence or early childhood, but that it may begin in childhood (422–23).

I do not assume or believe that Douglas is afflicted with Obsessive-Compulsive Disorder. (Rizzuto is content to describe him as an "obsessive compulsive personality.") This disorder, however, sheds light on the fact that his religiousness took the moral rectitude rather than the questing form. As one of the anxiety disorders, Obsessive-Compulsive Disorder has roots in excessive anxieties or worries that one finds difficult to control precisely because they are not related to threats in real life. I suggest that a little boy's emotional separation from his mother is exactly the kind of experience that creates such anxieties because it involves an emotional—but not physical—sense of abandonment. If she had died, he could grieve his loss and attach himself to another object. Because she is still alive, she becomes the very object of anxiety and worry: Will she send me away? Will she leave me for good? To forestall these dire consequences, he tries to become a boy whom she would never consider sending away or leaving for good. Aggressive feelings toward her are controlled at all costs, and become self-directed instead. He must contain his aggressions, lest they provoke her to send him away. His sexual impulses toward her must be mastered, partly because he believes his father will send him away, but also because conscience tells him it is wrong for him to want her for his very own. Young Douglas does not search for his mother or some compensating object in the real world. He does not become a little quester. Instead, he remains focused on preventing abandonment by her, and this means determining to become a boy who gives her no cause for doing so.

Admittedly, we haven't much evidence to support the view that his tendency to be an "anxious child" may be traced to his early childhood, but succumbing to a chronic illness requiring his mother's attention points to the role of anxiety in a small child's susceptibility to physical illness and to the secondary uses of such an illness. This, together with the fact that he tried to achieve a total mastery of his body in later childhood, provides the grounds for suspecting that his obsessive-compulsive personality may be traced to his emotional separation from his mother. However, if Rizzuto's view that his God representation belongs, developmentally, to "the last stages of separation-individuation" is correct, the God representation itself provides the best evidence of all that Douglas was an anxious child in early childhood and that his anxiety centered especially on his fears of abandonment by his mother due to his own provocations. Because it does, it enables us to see that his religiousness has a deep melancholic core.

Douglas's God Representation as Evidence of His Religious Melancholia

As we have seen, Rizzuto believes that Douglas's composite God representation originated mainly from his interactions with his mother. The first two elements—the frustrating and the caring-wished-for mother—reflect this mother-child interaction. The third element is his own grandiose self-representation, and the fourth is the God that his mother presented to him through her words and actions. While this fourth element was essentially the God of his Roman Catholic heritage, Rizzuto believes that it was culture bound—a reflection of the era in which he grew up—and that the God of his current local parish is very different, in that this newer God image is "kind and appealing." Thus far, however, this image remains inaccessible to him, even though it would be congruent with his positive relationships with his father, his brother Peter, and with his wife.

As we enter into our discussion of his God representation as evidence of his religious melancholia, it should also be noted that Rizzuto believes he successfully resolved the Oedipus complex. This is reflected in his strong identification with his father, whom he in fact worshiped as a hero. His God representation does not have the negative paternal qualities that we would expect if there were serious Oedipal difficulties. In fact, the absence of such difficulties—both in his reports about early childhood (especially ages 3–6) and his statements about God—is a major reason why Rizzuto looked to pre-Oedipal experiences (hence his narcissistic aspirations and injuries) to account for his God representation. This does not mean, however, that the separation-individuation process, especially the emotional separation from his mother, was unproblematic. On the contrary, it was seriously troubled in its own right—this separation is inherently traumatic—with the complicating factor that his mother's love seemed to him to be directed primarily toward one of his dead brothers and secondarily toward his older living brothers.

His God representation therefore reflects the rage he feels toward his internalized mother. In this sense, it is inherently melancholic, for, as I have argued, melancholia manifests itself in rage against the internalized maternal object. Virtually every statement he makes about God has an element of rage, bitterness, or sarcasm. For him, God is ineffectual (a real God would do "a great deal more to prevent human suffering") and undeserving of the prestige he enjoys ("Emotionally I would like to have the prestige that God has so I too could make profound [stupid] statements and not even be questioned"); is basically immoral (i.e., uses a "double standard," supports "hypocrisy and deceit," wants Douglas "to be good" merely because this fits his own "ideas about how you ought to behave"); sustains belief in himself through "brainwashing"; and inculcates belief so that we will live "our tough little lives and not make waves."

On the other hand, the God that these critiques are leveled at is not a projection of his maternal representation as such. Instead, this is the God whom his mother presented to him in her words and actions, the God, in other words, whom she herself believed in. Therefore, we need to distinguish between the emotional feeling that he expresses toward this God—which reflects his rage against his mother—and the content of this God representation, which is largely based on the God presented to him by his mother (and, by implication, the Roman Catholic Church that she so faithfully served). This distinction enables us to differentiate, for example, his statements about this God's support of hypocrisy and deceit (which he felt the priests displayed) and desire to "brainwash me" (which is what he thinks his mother, with her endorsement of "blind faith," was herself the victim of).

The two features of his God representation that directly reflect his experience of his mother—and that are the primary source of his rage—are his statement about the fact that he does not pray to God and his description of God's attributes. About prayer he states, "Prayer is not important to me because it is like one crying in the wilderness. Nobody hears them or even listens," and "I do not pray because I feel that God will not answer because he does not exist as I know him." These statements reflect his emotional separation from his mother, who does not hear his cries or even listen to them, and who is not someone to whom he can talk because she cannot respond, owing to the fact that she does not exist as the mother he would like to have and know. His statement about the attributes of God—which, he says, "have never manifested themselves on me"—includes "power, Glory, Warmth, reason, and compassion," the key ones being those that he has capitalized. A resident psychiatrist noted that "the patient grew up with a chronic resentment of the lack of real warmth in his mother," and Rizzuto, as we have seen, notes the lack of mirroring that his mother afforded him, thus depriving him of the experience of basking in *her* glory and thereby having his own sense of inner glory confirmed. These statements then *do* reflect his maternal representation. Significantly, they all have to do with the absence of emotional closeness, and they all have a note of barely suppressed anger or rage.

What about the statements about God that Rizzuto ascribes to Douglas's grandiose self-representation? Are they also a reflection of his melancholic condition? I believe that they are. One of these—"I consider God as my conscience, the part of me that strives for perfection"—reflects the determination of the boy who has lost his mother emotionally to be a good boy so that she will want him back. Another—"I feel that God may be me in the mirror and that the only way I can open the Door is to know me completely and honestly"—relates to melancholia in the sense that his mother is the one who prohibits him from experiencing the divinity inside of him that continues to struggle for life itself. The God that she represents continues to be such a powerful image in his mind that he cannot fully entertain the God who is "me in the mirror."

In Rizzuto's view, this reference to the "God who is me" is a reflection of Douglas's defensive grandiosity. A Roman Catholic herself, she wishes that he would embrace the "kind and appealing God" made accessible to him by his local Roman Catholic parish, who seems to be a composite of "the caring and wished-for mother" and the real father (not his idealized father) whom he loved and trusted. The nurse who suggested his statement that "God may be me in the mirror," indicates Douglas "has a need to be his own God" seems to agree. This, however, is to consider the matter from the side of conventional religion and to dismiss his own rather idiosyncratic religious perspective with a psychiatric judgment. Douglas is clearly seeking—*questing for*—a God who is nonparental, a reflection of the very fact that he *has* accomplished the developmental tasks of adolescence and is therefore, in a very real sense, "his own man." He seeks, therefore, the God in himself who is not based on a defensive self-representation or related to either the internalized mother or father identification.

In *Young Man Luther*, Erikson identifies the "three images" that are "the main religious objects." They are the "maternal matrix" symbolized by "the affirmative face of charity, graciously inclined"; "the paternal voice of guiding conscience, which puts an end to the simple paradise of childhood and provides a sanction for energetic action" while also warning "of the inevitability of guilty entanglement"; and "the pure self itself, the unborn core of creation, the—as it were, preparental—center where God is pure nothing. . . . This pure self is the self no longer sick with a conflict between right and wrong, not dependent on providers, and not dependent on guides to reason and reality" (Erikson 1958, 264). This last image, more primordial than the parental images, beautifully parallels Douglas's own image of the "me" in the mirror. It is not a reflection of defensive grandiosity, nor is it an expression of his vaulting need to be his own God. Rather, it is an image of a self reconciled to itself. I suggest, therefore, that for Douglas O'Duffy, this reconciliation will begin with his bridging of the emotional gulf that separates him from the "skinny, sickly, ungainly, awkward little ferret" he left for dead some thirty years ago. This poor little ferret may not be "the pure self" itself, but he is the way, the opening to it. He holds the key to the door that separates the adult Douglas from the mirror that will reveal the original, healthy, unconflicted, and contented self who lives somewhere inside of him.

If Douglas's melancholic religion has heretofore been based on moral rectitude, his picture of "a God in the mirror" suggests that, at the unconscious level, his religiousness is beginning to take a turn toward the quest. If so, the quest in this regard is one that has taken him back in time (as Rizzuto suggests, his psychic decompensation represents a regression) to the era before he constructed his grandiose, death-defying self-representation. It has also taken him into a previously unexplored interior. Like the ferret who enters the burrow of the prairie dog, he has begun to burrow into a world that is as yet rather foreign to him, but that he means, nonetheless, to inhabit. Significantly enough, access to the God who lives there has required that he, again like the ferret, commit a crime against the religion of moral rectitude.

The Father of Personal Prehistory

If Douglas's God representation was largely based on the God that his mother presented to him in words and actions as an existing being who is "all-powerful and all-merciful, capable of knowing your thoughts," what was its source? As Rizzuto herself shows, it was not based on his representation of his father. In

my view, it was based on "the father of personal prehistory," and thus originated prior to the demolition of the Oedipus complex. This image was subsequently reinforced by his mother's presentation of a God who was similar
to it, and it was not altered by his paternal representation (his own father),
whom he admired and to whom he ascribed the very attributes (infinite perceptivity, available when needed, lovable, etc.) that one would identify in a
God well worth believing in.

Because there is no reference in this case study to Douglas's maternal
grandfather, evidence of this early representation is difficult to find in
Rizzuto's case study. A clue, however, is a statement that Douglas makes about
himself, and that Rizzuto considers relevant to his God representation in that
it reflects his grandiose self-representation: "I used to look at the sun. It hurts.
I did it." I agree, but the connection is not obvious. It needs to be demon-
strated. I realize that the following argument may seem tendentious and
somewhat forced, but it is entirely consistent with the psychoanalytic perspective employed throughout this study.

Of all the counterphobic things that Douglas did to achieve "total mastery" over his body, this act of staring into the sun was surely the most irrational, that is, it served no useful purpose toward his goal of becoming a fine
athlete. We need, therefore, to look for unconscious reasons for this behavior.
I have noted that "total mastery" of his body would include his sexual urges,
especially if he was determined to achieve not only physical but also moral
perfection. I suggest, therefore, that staring into the sun was a counterphobic
action against a long-repressed castration anxiety that had resurfaced at the
beginning of puberty, perhaps as a consequence of compulsive self-masturbatory
behavior. We need to remember that, as a victim of rheumatic fever, he spent
many boring hours in bed; we need also to keep in mind his penchant for spying on priests whom he suspected of sexual misdeeds.

Most children have been warned against staring directly into the sun
because this could cause blindness. Douglas violated this warning. Why?
Because staring into the sun signified his total mastery over his body, and this
included his newly emergent sexual processes. The association of blindness
and castration anxiety has a long history in psychoanalytic thought, a history
that need not be recounted here. Freud, however, viewed Oedipus's blinding
of himself after he realized he had committed incest with his mother as a form
of self-castration. He writes in his essay "The 'Uncanny'" (originally published in 1919):

> We know from psycho-analytic experience . . . that this fear of dam-
> aging or losing one's eyes is a terrible fear of childhood. Many adults
> still retain their apprehensiveness in this respect, and no bodily injury
> is so much dreaded by them as an injury to the eye. . . . A study of

dreams, phantasies and myths has taught us that a morbid anxiety connected with the eyes and with going blind is often enough a sub-stitute for the dread of castration. In blinding himself, Oedipus, that mythical law-breaker, was simply carrying out a mitigated form of the punishment of castration—the only punishment that according to the *lex talionis* was fitted for him. (Freud 1958c, 137)

Freud anticipates objections to his linking of anxiety connected to the eyes and dread of castration, noting that it may seem "very natural that so precious an organ as the eye should be guarded by a proportionate dread; indeed, we might go further and say that the fear of castration itself contains no other significance and no deeper secret than a justifiable dread of this kind" (137). But this view

does not account adequately for the substitute relation between the eye and the male member which is seen to exist in dreams and myths and phantasies; nor can it dispel the impression one gains that it is the threat of being castrated in especial which excites a peculiarly violent and obscure emotion, and that this emotion is what gives the idea of losing other organs its intense coloring. Furthermore, any doubts about this linkage are removed when we get the details of their "castration-complex" from the analyses of neurotic patients, and realize its immense importance in their mental life. (138)

As we have seen, Freud believed that castration anxiety (perhaps related to the trauma of circumcision) is the boy's original anxiety and that repression is therefore a counterphobic measure. We have also seen that Freud associated castration anxiety with the father of personal prehistory, for the way in which this father enforced belief in him was by means of the threat of castration. Circumcision is therefore a symbolic substitute for castration.

If we read Douglas's statements about God from the perspective of this view of the father of personal prehistory as a castrating deity, the fact that many of these statements have little basis in his experience of either his father or mother is easier to explain. This father of personal prehistory is a duplicitous, irrational, and heartless God who is nonetheless deeply etched in his mind. Later Douglas was introduced to church teachings that reinforced this image. In addition, his mother taught him that this Father who, in Douglas's mind, was implicated in the deaths of his brothers, needs to be believed in on the basis of "blind faith." This itself is a form of symbolic and intellectual castration.

By staring into the sun, however, Douglas tried to take matters into his own hands. If there is castrating to be done, he will do it himself. Thus, the defensive grandiose self-representation emerges, and he begins to challenge the father of personal prehistory. If he is able to stare into the sun and suffer no visual damage, this father's castrating power over him will be effectively broken. Moreover, the self-mastery that staring into the sun demanded could be put to use in mastering his sexual urges and, specifically, in curtailing any self-masturbatory behavior. Growing up in a traditional Roman Catholic family in the mid-1940s, he would almost certainly have known the Church's teaching that masturbation is a carnal sin; this could well have been the most shameful sin he would need to disclose to the priest at confession. In *Whatever Became of Sin?* Karl Menninger writes that the

> anguished struggle of religious devotees as pictured in the life of St. Anthony and others, and as experienced by millions of priests and nuns since Augustine, centers largely on masturbation. An incalculable amount of pain could have been spared them, and spared millions of young boys and girls if, in some way, it could have been common knowledge long before 1900 that there is no harm in masturbation, no evil in it, no sinfulness in it, the former religious stipulations notwith-standing. (Menninger 1973, 140)

Douglas may also have been aware of the widely held view that masturbation saps one's physical strength. If he was determined to compete with his brothers athletically, he may have believed he could not do so if he continued to masturbate. The irony then is that the more he developed his grandiose self-representation of the strong, self-reliant young man, the more he actually complied with the moral demands of the father of personal prehistory. In his conscious mind, he was engaging in a program of self-mastery. Yet these very efforts testified to the enormous power of the father of personal prehistory in the shaping of his melancholic religion of moral rectitude. He could reject this father in his conscious mind, but, on an unconscious level, he was this father's obedient son. He was so obedient, in fact, that he spied on the priests who, he suspected, had not succeeded in mastering *their* own sexual urges.

The Limits of a Religion Based on Honor

In *Real Boys*, William Pollack makes a direct association between the emotional separation from their mothers that small boys experience and the development of what he calls "the Boy Code." He cites Deborah David and Robert Brannon's view that this code consists of "four stereotyped male ideals or models of behavior," and notes, "These four imperatives are at the heart of the Boy Code." They include: (1) "The sturdy oak," which implies "that men should be stoic, stable, and independent"; (2) "Give 'em hell," based on "the misconception that boys are biologically wired to act like macho, high-energy, even violent supermen"; (3) "The big wheel," or the "imperative to achieve status, dominance, and power"; and (4) "No sissy stuff," which is "perhaps the most traumatizing and dangerous injunction thrust on boys and men," as it is "the literal straitjacket that prohibits boys from expressing feelings or urges seen (mistakenly) as 'feminine'—dependence, warmth, empathy" (Pollack 1998, 24).

Due to his serious and protracted illness as a small boy, Douglas was unable to act upon this "Boy Code" when he experienced emotional separation from his mother. He was predisposed to it, however, by virtue of the fact that he responded to this separation largely in terms of the desire to be a good boy. Then, in late childhood, around the beginning stages of puberty, he resolved to actualize this "Boy Code." It became the core of his identity as a competitive athlete and then as a state trooper. While he questions its divine legitimation, his actions reflect this religion of honor, based on moral rectitude. However, in the wake of his accident and the failure of the public and his fellow officers to accord him the recognition he sought, the limits of this religion of honor have been driven home to him in a deeply painful way. He has responded to the ultimate failure of this religion with an intense rage and deep bitterness, much of it directed toward others—the public, his fellow officers—but a great deal of it also self-directed: "I must have been a damn fool." At last, his eyes have been opened—truly, not counterphobicly.

Where does he go from here? I have suggested that the way forward is to return to the period of his life before he developed the counterphobic strategy that enabled him to actualize the Boy Code that he had already internalized. His picture of God as the mirror image of the seven-year-old boy he put to death is an expression of his preconscious intuition that herein lies his chance for salvation. Thus, the "regression" to which Rizzuto alludes has been in the service of resurrecting this vulnerable self, and the "recovery" of which she also speaks is one that has begun to demolish the Boy Code and to erect its very opposite in its place. If he has any prior experiences in his life to draw upon for guidance as he makes his way forward, they are the lessons he learned from his very flawed father, who nonetheless presented him a model of "infinite perceptivity" to know when his son needed help or wanted to talk, and who made him feel that even though he "felt sick and rotten that in time I would feel better."

Now that he is able to identify with his fully human father—the one whose career as a state trooper also came to grief—he also knows that his father has given him a chance for salvation, a usable future. Unlike his father, he will not be tempted to engage in illegal activities that sully his otherwise honorable reputation. But perhaps his morality will express itself in a more buoyant, less obsessive-compulsive manner. As Stephen Dunn, who was also raised in a Roman Catholic milieu, acknowledges in his poem "Moralists," he has exhibited a kind of moralism where he knew "the end of my thinking in advance," shutting the door before "it opened wide enough to let in the ill wind, the rude, spectacular visage," and ignoring "the simple truth obstructed in a corner." But he has also known occasions when he could embrace the idea that "there's an advantage even to good behavior," when "what's moral had a new gaiety to it, an exuberence, and I walked through the dull streets like someone ablaze from the inside, as close as I'd ever be, could be, to God" (Dunn 1994, 23).

Perhaps one day Douglas will also be able to embrace the mother who is inside of him, as he was once inside of her. Any man, no matter how melancholic, should be able in time to embrace the preparental mother of his personal prehistory, the mother with whom he—in the form of a pure self—was on intimate terms for the first nine months of his existence. In light of the fact that Douglas was afflicted with rheumatic fever as a child, the previously quoted lines the poet William Stafford wrote to his mother shortly before his death—the moment when the mother of personal prehistory takes her son into her arms and receives him again—are especially appropriate: "All my life I've tapped out our kind of truth. For nine months I studied what your heart was saying." Where melancholia was, let pure mourning be. When the internalized rage has spent itself, the sadness that remains can work its healing ways.

CHAPTER 6

～

Daniel in the Lion's Den
Melancholic Religion as Quest

In the preceding chapter, I used the case of Douglas O'Duffy to illustrate the links between the melancholy self and the religious impulse of moral rectitude, which develops into a religion based on personal honor. In this chapter, I will use Rizzuto's case of Daniel Miller to illustrate the connections between the melancholy self and the religious impulse of searching and questing, which takes the form of a religion based on hope.

However, unlike O'Duffy, who set about to become the very epitome of moral rectitude and a true man of honor, Miller (at least at the time this case study was written) has not thrown himself into a life of questing and searching. Unlike young men who are determined to find compensations for the "lost object" in the external world, and to embark with determination and zeal on a personal quest for affection, admiration, acceptance, and approval, risking disappointment, failure, and despair, Miller seems unable even to entertain the idea that he might search for, let alone find, such compensations. His "questing," if we can call it that, is fitful at best. Just when it seems that he may be in a position, psychologically speaking, to embark on a quest of his own, he loses his nerve, falters, and returns to the relative comfort of his parental home. While we might have wished for a more impressive example of religion as quest, one of a man who went about the quest with considerable zeal, and suffering various setbacks along the way, the case of Daniel Miller enables us to focus on the difficulties that young men experience in severing their emotional dependence on their mothers so that they can in fact embark on this quest for other sources of love, affection, and approval.

Augustine's account in his *Confessions* of how he escaped from his mother's clutches seems to confirm the popular conception of the mother who binds her son to herself and refuses to release him. He tells how he deceived his mother, Monica, so that she could neither stand in the way of his sailing from Carthage to Rome nor make good on her threat to go with him: "I pretended

150

I had a friend I did not want to leave until the wind was right for him to sail. I lied to my mother—to such a mother—and I gave her the slip. . . . That night, I secretly set sail. . . . When morning came, she was crazed with grief, and with recriminations and groans she filled your ears" (Augustine 1992, 81–82). A controlling mother, a son desperate to escape.

But his account continues, and he relates how, when he arrived in Rome, he suffered "the scourge of physical illness," and attributes his recovery to his mother's prayers for his well-being. He thanks God that he "did not allow him to die in this sad condition of both body and soul. If my mother's heart had suffered this wound, she would never have recovered. I cannot speak enough of the love she had for me" (83). Would a son who wants to be free of his mother write this way? Was his physical sickness a psychosomatic reaction to his separation from his mother and the guilt he felt for the manner in which he accomplished it? The emotional tone of this account is hardly that of a young man gloating over the fact that he conned his mother and is now free to enjoy the fruits of his deception. If Augustine is typical of young men struggling with their ambivalent feelings about embarking on their solitary quests, then Daniel Miller's case may be more instructive than that of a young man who sets forth on his quest with nary a look back, facing the future with consummate confidence, and relinquishing his need to believe that his mother cannot bear to see him go.

Miller, twelve years younger than O'Duffy, was more severely disturbed when he came to Rizzuto's attention than was O'Duffy. This is reflected in the fact that he was diagnosed as a "schizoid personality," and thus suffering from a more severe psychological disability than O'Duffy, who was diagnosed as experiencing a "reactive depression" in an "obsessive compulsive personality." Its seriousness is reflected in the fact that, as *DSM-IV* puts it, "Especially in response to stress, individuals with this disorder may experience very brief psychotic episodes (lasting minutes to hours)," and "In some instances, Schizoid Personality Disorder may appear as the premorbid antecedent to Delusional Disorder or Schizophrenia" (*DSM-IV* 1994, 639). While the disruptive effects of obsessive compulsive personality should not be minimized, there is little danger of becoming delusional. As we will see, Miller's behavior certainly bordered on the delusional, as he believed (erroneously) that he was suffering from a fatal illness and also engaged in self-mutilating behaviors.

Interestingly enough, both Obsessive-Compulsive Personality Disorder and Schizoid Personality Disorder appear more often in men than women, which itself suggests that these disorders may be attributed in part to the melancholic condition from which all men, in varying degrees, suffer. (As in my discussion of Rizzuto's case of Douglas O'Duffy, I will forgo citing page numbers, as all quoted material is from her eighth chapter, which comprises pages 130–48 of her book.)

Daniel Miller's Personal Story

Rizzuto describes Daniel Miller as "an appealing, soft-spoken, smiling, friendly man" who, nonetheless, was also a "schizoid personality." She adds, "Having to face adulthood and its tasks at the end of his professional education," he "reacted with massive regression to the childhood period of latency, hoping for his father's help in practical ways and wishing delusionally for identification with him through an organ transplant."

She indicates that he is a "twenty-seven-year-old physician" who "had insisted on being admitted to a hospital for yet another medical examination." His examining physician pressured him into accepting referral to a psychiatric in-patient unit after being repeatedly and carefully examined for evidence of the lethal illness he insisted he had. In light of the fact that he "complained of lower abdominal pain, back pain, and an intense conviction that he was affected by a slow, killing disease," one is somewhat surprised that Rizzuto's statement of his diagnosis did not include hypochondriasis. I will return to this issue of his hypochondriasis in my interpretation of his melancholia.

What seems to have precipitated Daniel's current difficulties is that six months before the onset of these symptoms he had witnessed a medical emergency in which a man his own age with a similar condition narrowly escaped death. Significantly, the first medical doctor whom he consulted about his own symptoms was his father's internist. When this doctor reassured him that his fears were unfounded, he asked for a psychiatric evaluation, and he immediately began weekly psychotherapy with a male psychiatrist. In the course of the next six months he seemed to improve, but then he began to withdraw more and more, and eventually he stopped all his activities and spent a year and a half at his parents' home, doing nothing, though continuing to see a therapist. Four weeks before his admission to the psychiatric in-patient unit, he insisted on having another physical evaluation, despite the fact that he had received several during the two years of psychotherapy. When he was informed that he needed a psychiatric evaluation, he decided not to go back to his therapist. He refused to talk about the motives behind his decision, but since he had been talking with the therapist about homosexual longings, these may have interfered.

Rizzuto provides a detailed biographical account of his life, noting that he was the older of two children (he had a sister) whose "upwardly mobile" parents placed great hope in their children. His father, a self-made man who had left his own home at fourteen, was a representative for a drug company, "thoroughly involved with his work and literally immersed in the medical profession he served." His mother, an elementary school teacher, stopped working to marry. Both parents were in their twenties when they married, and Daniel was born a year later. His parents had wanted a child, but his mother's pregnancy was difficult and she had unpleasant feelings about it. The delivery also was difficult and left his mother unprepared to deal with the needs of a newborn baby. A nurse helped her care for her baby for the first six months. Both parents agreed that he was a "bad" child from the beginning. He was colicky and frequently had eating problems and wet his bed until the age of five. But he was also precocious, walking and talking early and possessed of a remarkable memory. In her pride and joy at having a bright and promising child, his mother would bring him to neighbors so that they could hear him repeat nursery rhymes.

When Daniel was born, the Millers had little money, but his father was determined to build a good economic position for his family, so he worked long hours and often came home late, tired, and irritable. He would readily get into arguments with his wife and child, and frequently had attacks of intense rage, shouting and throwing things. Daniel grew to fear his father and his rages. His father was the one who punished him when his mother reported his bad behavior during the day. Rizzuto notes, "Both parents seemed to take some pride in the fact that he feared his father. There was an unusual gleam in their eyes when, during the hospitalization [of their son], they reported with a smile that Daniel and his sister had hated their father and were still afraid of him." His mother, herself a fearful person, was incapable of handling even minimal emergencies, was totally dependent on her husband, and was terrified of unpredictable events. She worried excessively about her child: "Anything like a crisis would find her helpless, and she would turn to her husband in a frenzy comparable to paralytic panic. Physical illnesses or injuries terrify her." She also had a compulsive symptom of picking at her face, which enraged her husband to the point where he would throw things while he shouted furiously at her. In the context of family life, Daniel became a shy, quiet, lonely child who was even afraid of other children. If his mother invited neighbor children in, he would hide under his bed or refuse to play with them.

Daniel was five years old when his sister was born. During his mother's pregnancy, he was terrified that his mother would abandon him and his father, but he looked forward to a sibling and welcomed her. Soon after, he began kindergarten and suffered from separation anxiety and conscious fear of his teacher and classmates. In first grade, his parents' dreams of a brilliant professional career for their son were dealt a severe blow when his teacher called his mother to discuss the fact that Daniel could not read at grade level. A teacher herself, his mother argued that he was a very bright child, but his teacher disagreed, and his mother's "maternal disappointment was intense and lasting."

He attended Hebrew school as a boy (both parents were Jewish) but "deeply disliked the picture of the Old Testament God whom he felt to be vengeful and lacking in compassion." On the other hand, he liked his bar mitzvah because it enabled him to feel linked with the past and as having gained maturity. The event itself, however, was treated by his parents as a "routine event" because neither of them professed any religious belief or gave any indication of having religious feelings. In fact, "During moments of anger and cynicism his father laughed contemptuously at religious practices and beliefs, saying that religion was superstition." Daniel's mother never gave any direct indication of religious belief, but he attributed belief to her, suspecting that her beliefs were "deep" and that she probably "believes in a benevolent God."

He experienced his first psychosomatic symptoms in his middle teens. He described them as pain "around the area of my heart. I didn't think I was having a heart attack though I was quite concerned about it." The family physician viewed these as merely "growing pains," but Daniel was fearful and "all shook up" about them. The pains lasted for a year and seemed to have some connection with his maternal grandfather, who had had a heart attack about this time but recovered from it.

During this time, his school record remained average, an irritation to his father, who wanted him to go to medical school. His father insisted that he take evaluative and diagnostic tests to assess his intellectual potential, and then demanded that he retake them three times because he was dissatisfied with the results. The tests showed that he was "bright but unmotivated." He had no friends, saw no girls his own age, "and continued to feel awkward, self-conscious, shy, afraid of failure, and fearful of his teachers." The evaluations recommended psychiatric treatment, to which his frustrated father reluctantly agreed in his desperation to fulfill his dream of having a physician son. Two months after Daniel began to see a psychiatrist, however, his father demanded a report. While he never shared with anyone what the doctor said, he was outraged and refused to let his son see the therapist again.

Two years later Daniel entered "a reputable college" and things improved. He lived on campus all four years, made a few friends, and "had some superficial contact with girls of his age for the first time in his life." He viewed these as the best years of his life. He became genuinely interested in his academic subjects and "I enjoyed the freedom of being independent, of making my own decisions." At the end of college, he did not want to apply to medical school but was unable to offer his father any other professional future. He failed to submit applications to medical schools, however, and his father therefore took matters into his own hands, writing out the applications, driving Daniel to interviews, and making him memorize the answers to questions his father knew he would be asked.

Surprisingly, in spite of relatively average college grades, he was admitted to a medical school. It was near his home, so he decided to live in the school dormitory and visit his parents on weekends. Midway through medical school, he left the school dormitory and returned to live in his parents' home, claiming to be more comfortable there. An average student in medical school, he blended in with his less achieving classmates. During his clinical year, he was afraid of his patients' criticism and potential anger, and it was at this time that he witnessed a medical emergency involving a man his own age when he was in charge under supervision. He began to question his ability to practice medicine on his own, apparently because he felt he had not reacted appropriately when confronted with this emergency situation, and he experienced increasing feelings of depression and hopelessness. With graduation approaching, he did not apply for internships and began to dwell on his fear that his father would exercise control over his future private practice. This was when he began to develop psychosomatic symptoms, which included lower abdominal pain, back pain, and burning urination. At this time he dreamed that he was dying of a fatal ailment which could only be controlled if his father donated an organ to him.

Rizzuto does not say what organ this was to be—perhaps the dream itself left this uncertain—but she indicates that "he hoped that the father, through the donation of an organ to his dying son, would make him into a man like himself." This may suggest the donation of his sexual organ, implying a deeply repressed castration anxiety. Rizzuto, however, simply notes that this "quasi-delusional" expectation of an organ donation from his father "had the advantage of keeping Daniel in the passive position without risking his father's rage, while giving the father the occasion to take the initiative to show his love for his son and also to demonstrate that he was willing to give part of himself to his son."

His psychiatrist later reported that the first year of his psychotherapy was filled with tears related to anger at his father: "After some time Daniel worried that a dam of sadness had been opened and he could not control it any longer." One day just before he broke off therapy with his psychiatrist he went to his father's office, and using some medical instruments that he had obtained from the hospital and not knowing exactly what he was doing, he decided to have a sexual experience. He introduced a tube into his urethra and insufflated his bladder to the point of pain. He did this "in a compulsive, driven manner, knowing he had to do it." Subsequent elaborations of this action, which he called "injuring myself," indicated that "one of the fantasies involved was being a woman in face to face intercourse with a man. He was frightened and surprised when he bled from the urethra 'like a woman.'" Rizzuto adds, "It is worth mentioning that the episode happened around the time of his first intercourse, at her urgent insistence, with a woman."

This woman was an acquaintance of his from their adolescent days who had fallen in love with him and was determined to marry him. While able to perform sexually, his response was passive. She, on the other hand, "was loving and passionate and determined to have him," but he "was frightened of her, experiencing with her the inability to get close to people he had known all his life as his most painful trait." Rizzuto adds, "His sexual wishes—at the conscious level mainly heterosexual—and some of his more repressed homosexual longings had awakened during his college days when he saw his friends dating and knew that they had sex with their girl friends but found himself unable to join them. Now he expressed his wish to be able to let people get close and his desire to have 'a girl friend, someone I can confide in, someone I could love.'"

When he was admitted to the psychiatric in-patient unit, he was assigned to a woman psychiatrist. He also made arrangements to work at least two hours a day with a senior physician, helping him with routine tasks no different from those a nurse could do: "He had no courage for more, but harbored the hope that one day he would lose his fear of patients and work in some assigned job to which his father would have no access. He was incapable of even considering the idea of relocating in another state."

Daniel's Parental Relationships and Images

Rizzuto's strategy with all four clinical portraits is to intersperse commentary on the parental images with their God representations, thereby demonstrating the psychodynamic connections between them. In addition, she provides a table of roughly two to three pages in which she juxtaposes the patients' statements about one or both parents with similar statements made about God. Occasionally (as in the case of Douglas O'Duffy) she also juxtaposes a psychiatrist's note and a corresponding comment by the patient concerning God. To simplify matters, I will focus initially on what Rizzuto has to say about Daniel's images of his mother and father, and then comment on his God representations.

In her initial introductory statement of the "propositions" she wants to establish in the ensuing discussion, all but two of these center on Daniel's God representation. The others are the psychiatric diagnosis of Daniel as a "schizoid personality" (already noted) and a proposition regarding his mother. Concerning his mother, Rizzuto proposes that "a cumulative trauma that interfered with [Daniel's] normal development was his mother's inability to provide adult mothering and protection from his father, as well as her failure to sustain a real relationship with the developing child." While she provided for the needs of everyday life, she "failed to provide another adult presence in the house to balance the overwhelming and tyrannical presence of the father." In addition, she submitted to Daniel's father by withdrawing in passive fear, leaving their two children at the mercy of their father. While Rizzuto does not explicitly say this, the case material presented seems to indicate that Daniel was a more direct victim of this failure than his sister because his father (and mother) had very high professional ambitions for him.

In subsequent comments on his mother, Rizzuto highlights her "infantile, schizoid, frightened, inefficient qualities." These made her into "no more than a privileged but submissive child in relation to the father." Daniel felt he loved his mother, and he listed her as the person he loved most in his life at every age except during the latency period (six to twelve), when he felt that he hated both parents because of their open dissatisfaction with his perform-ance at school. While "his mother lost her narcissistic investment" in Daniel after the argument with his first-grade teacher, he "felt his mother's concern for him," as illustrated in his response: "The member of the family whom I loved the most was my mother. I loved her this much because she showed the most concern for my feelings and generally showed affection." But, according to Rizzuto, he also complained about lack of closeness and communication with her, and difficulty relating to her as a person, wishing for a mother who "would treat me more as an adult than as a child." At this point he laughed, saying, "I like the little quirks that she has, I like her disposition." These "lit-tle quirks" were described by the social worker as the traits of a person who is "very passive, very sad, depressed, dependent, and compliant."

Rizzuto notes that Daniel identified with his mother. As he himself explained, "Emotionally I resemble my mother because I tend to be shy and overly sensitive." Citing the social worker's observation that his mother has "some sad feelings about Daniel's situation," Rizzuto suggests that this could also apply to her feelings about her own situation. She concludes her descrip-tion of his mother by suggesting that she served at best as a "sad, sympathetic witness" to his father's mistreatment of Daniel, but "most of the time, possi-bly because of her own fear, she offered up her frightened son to the punish-ment of her husband."

As for his relations with his father, they are "fraught with contradictory feelings. He hates his father, but he also admires him and wants to be like him." Furthermore, while he would like "to be rid of him and get a com-pletely different father," there is "nothing he would like more than to have the love, understanding, and respect of his father. He longs to understand and love him, but he despairs that he ever will." When asked to list chronologi-cally the most hated person in his life, he said that from years one to six and twelve to fifteen it was his father. As indicated, he hated both parents equally from six to twelve. From fifteen to twenty-one he listed himself, and after that he claimed not to hate anyone "because I have more understanding now."

The family member he most admires is his father, because of his self-confidence and concern "with the well-being of his family." He wishes he could be like his father in this respect, but in other ways he dislikes, even despises him because of his bad temper, his failure to consider his son's feelings, and his lack of appreciation for "my likes and dislikes." He guesses that his fear of his father remains to this day and that he has "transferred this fear of him to other people."

Rizzuto notes that Daniel's father "laughs at his son's attempts to be a man and seems to find pleasure in contrasting his own masculine good looks, competence, and seductiveness with his son's total lack of masculinity." This, however, is *his* view of his son. Rizzuto views Daniel not as "effeminate" but as "a frightened boy." The social worker observed that his father described Daniel "as a neuter, sexually, saying that he has never seen any evidence of any kind of a sexual drive in his son—and he laughs about it." Since Daniel was actually involved in his first sexual experience with a woman at the time his father said this, Rizzuto suggests that his father needed to see him as an asexual person.

When asked about his unsatisfied needs, a "good relationship" with his father was at the top of Daniel's list. Asked to indicate what he wished he could have changed at various periods in his life, from ages three to six he would have changed "my father's disposition, to make him a little more affectionate." At age fifteen to twenty-one, it would have been "improved relations" with his father. As for his "ideal father," he would "probably get another father" (see, in this connection, my discussion of "the desire to be another man's son," in Capps 1995, 112–15).

Rizzuto concludes her discussion of Daniel's relations with his father with the observation that because of the impossibility of identifying with his father due to his intense fear and hatred of him, "Daniel remains like his mother, a passive, uncommitted, helpless child, under paternal guidance." This is a defensive position, for while his ideal is to be like his father, he "cannot get himself to compete with such a dangerous being particularly since the father tolerates neither his independence nor his competence nor his sexuality." The "solution" he fashioned for himself was his illness, which appeared when he had no choice but to become "an efficient male." This illness has left him in a "suspended state," like "a small helpless boy who would feel like 'a fish out of water' if he left his childhood." As he put it himself, "It is as though I haven't entered adolescence yet."

Daniel's God Representation

As we saw in the previous chapter, Rizzuto indicates that all the subjects in her study fit into one of four categories in terms of their relation to God. She places Daniel in category three, or among those who are amazed, angered, or quietly surprised to see others deeply invested in a God who does not interest them. Thus, whereas Douglas (category two) wondered whether or not to believe in a God he was not sure exists, Daniel's perspective was that of a man who had little if any emotional resonance with the God in whom others took considerable interest.

Rizzuto offers several propositions regarding Daniel's God representation, including:

1. His God is a well-defined person with a wide range of emotions and characteristics.

2. His God image takes its characteristics exclusively from his father, as seen and experienced by a boy in need of protection by an aggressive adult male who is admired for his own aggressiveness and efficiency.

3. His representation of God has undergone little elaboration or transformation because this would require an emotional encounter and his is only one of intellectual inquiry. The attraction of his God representation is conceptual, and it occurs only at the defensive level. Unconsciously, the God he has avoided dealing with is identical to his father, and this God has not been elaborated upon at all.

4. To avoid an encounter with his God representation, he utilizes isolation of affect, intellectualization, withdrawal into himself, and a general state of passivity and waiting. These defenses protect him from an unwelcome encounter with himself, inadequate and afraid as he experiences himself to be, and an overpowering, critical, destructive God incapable of any consideration for him.

5. He does not "use" his God representation, behaving as though he does not know or feel what God is like. As he puts it, "I do not have any explicit feelings about God. I am not sure I believe in God." Rizzuto suggests that this inability to "use" God is not the result of repression but of avoidance and isolation of affect. She sees a paradox in this, for Daniel doesn't know whether he believes or not but is constantly preoccupied with a God he cannot understand, saying, "I find it difficult to love something I don't know or understand" and "I consider God as an Enigma because I have no clear-cut attitude about God."

6. In relation to official religion, the God offered by his Jewish faith was too similar to his father. As Daniel comments, "The biblical God was a bit too revengeful to suit me" and "I feel that God should have more compassion than he is portrayed in the Bible."

In Rizzuto's view, all of this adds up to a God representation that reflects the latency period of childhood. While derived from earlier parental representations (in this case, paternal), it became fixed, as it were, in the latency period (ages six to twelve), which she describes as involving "careful observations and descriptions of persons . . . based on well-established reality testing" but not "psychological elaboration of motives," the latter being the task of adolescence. This is also the period when the libidinal (or sexual) drive is relatively dormant, being stored up, so to speak, for its powerful reappearance in adolescence. By viewing Daniel's God representation as having been fixed in the latency period, Rizzuto is able to account for the absence of any emotional attachment to it. While his God representation is "a well-defined separated person with a wide range of emotions and characteristics," Daniel relates to this "person" as though he were a "concept," or, at most, an "Enigma," toward whom he has "no clear-cut attitudes."

In her analysis of Daniel's statements about God (plus the picture of God that he was asked to draw), Rizzuto suggests that his "father representation is the only visible source of this God representation." As she has argued, on theoretical grounds, that God representations are comprised of both parental images, this "poses the difficult question of what happened to the maternal representation and its elaborations." Moreover, Daniel's God representation does not include any elements of Daniel's own sense of self. While God, for him, has the characteristics of "a living object," this God is totally absorbed in his own wishes and personal interests. He is as narcissistic as Daniel's father. In her view, these very absences have their own explanatory value.

In the table comparing Daniel's statements about God and his father, there are other direct parallels, such as "If there is a God, then I have dissatisfied him, because I have not made the best use of my abilities," and "My father always insisted I make the best use of my abilities." Other parallels include absence of "closeness" to God, not "resorting" to God, not praying, being "resentful" of "the biblical God" for being "revengeful," and never having expressed "hate" for God but having felt "exasperated at my situation or fate." These comments about God have parallels in comments about his father. The one significant difference in this list of parallels concerns divine punishment. Daniel's father physically abused him. As Daniel himself describes it, "My mother used to tell my father how bad I had been during the day and I used to get hell from my father. He yelled at me, he hit me a number of times on the face with his hand." He doesn't feel, however, that "any punishment comes from God," and, in any case, "I could not believe in a God that punishes."

As noted, Rizzuto accounts for the lack of affect in Daniel's God representation on the grounds that it was fixed in the latency period of development. Thus, his God representation is more conceptual than relational. His lack of affect toward his God representation, however, may also be related to his experience of having suffered his father's physical abuse (and his mother's complicity in it). If his father's most self-evident expression of emotion toward his son (and Daniel's own most self-evident expression of passivity) occurred in these punishment episodes, this would help to explain Daniel's lack of affect toward his God representation. A common response of young children toward parent-inflicted physical abuse is dissociation, a splitting-off of mind from body so that one becomes, in a sense, a detached observer of these physical assaults. In this way, one does not "feel" the pain.

A withdrawal of emotion from the infliction of the pain is therefore integral to this dissociative move. One "submits," knowing that it would be fruitless to avenge oneself against one's abuser, who has an overwhelming physical advantage. It is not inconceivable that Daniel learned this dissociative strategy from his mother, who responded "passively" to her husband's abuse of her. It also appears that she reported her son's misbehaviors to her husband—Daniel claims that he was only "a little bit mischievous"—so that she herself would not be the object of his father's attacks when he, as Daniel says, "came home grouchy." Daniel reports that these punishments occurred when he was between age six and twelve. Given the fact that his misbehaviors occurred while he was at home, there is every reason to believe that they occurred earlier as well, before he went off to kindergarten. Nonetheless, his recollection is consistent with Rizzuto's judgment that his God representation became "fixed" in the latency period, and also with the fact that his mother "lost her narcissistic investment in [Daniel] after the argument with his teacher in the first grade." If she had defended Daniel earlier— though there is no indication that she did—she appears to have lost all interest in doing so in the latency period. The birth of his sister when he was five may also have allowed a transfer of her narcissistic investment from her son to her daughter.

The fact that Daniel "could not believe in a God who punishes" may also help to account for the "paradox" that he has a clear conception of God—modeled on his father—but no actual relationship to this God. If the most powerful emotionality that occurred in his relations with his father was associated with the punishment episodes, then a God who is modeled after his father but *who does not punish* is necessarily one with whom Daniel would not feel any emotional connection. In a sense, the same strategy of dissociation occurs here as well. An emotional relationship with this God would necessarily involve punishment. Thus, the "paradox" reflected in his view of God as "an Enigma" has a certain inevitability: "I don't feel any punishment comes from God. . . . I am not sure of the existence of God. . . . I would not believe in a God that punishes." While these three statements may seem inconsistent, they make perfect psychological sense when viewed in light of his father's physical abuse (and his mother's complicity in its instigation and her emotional passivity in reference to the episodes themselves).

Having presented these parallels between Daniel's statements about God and his father, Rizzuto addresses the absence of any indication that his maternal representation contributed to his God representation. In her view, the explanation lies in his mother's "infantile, schizoid, frightened, inefficient qualities." The social worker described her as "very passive, very sad, depressed, dependent, and compliant." Thus, according to Rizzuto, "the picture emerges clearly of a childish mother who submits totally to her husband and who is incapable of offering any protection to the children against a tyrannical father controlling the domestic universe. I propose that such a mother could not be used to elaborate an image of God because of her submission to an existing superior person." On the other hand, she could be "a partial model for a God one wishes might exist, a God capable of a certain sadness at his own impotence."

Daniel's picture of God (see figure 2) is relevant in this regard. It bears the following explanation: "This represents my image of God—Extremely Wise—but sad at men's inhumanity to man—also patient and sensitive to suffering of mankind." Rizzuto notes in this connection that he saw his mother as "overly sensitive" and that "the social worker wrote that [his mother] has 'some sad feelings about Daniel's situation; perhaps also—I would add—her own.'" Rizzuto also notes that Daniel's portrayal of God in the picture is more that of an "impotent witness" to man's inhumanity to man and human suffering than of a God who intervenes. She suggests that "Daniel, caught between his parents, hoped that his mother was such a witness—and sometimes, indeed, she may have been. But most of the time, possibly because of her own fear, she offered up her frightened son to the punishment of her husband."

Figure 2

This picture of God—one that Daniel, without any clear evidence, believes his mother shares—is, however, "a mere possibility, a consoling hope that helps a desperate man to maintain minimal psychic balance." This God, who "looks very much like the face of Daniel's father (and his own face)" is "unquestionably a male face" and "certainly comes from the paternal representation." In Rizzuto's view, then, God's image bears, as it were, the shadow of his maternal representation. This is reflected, it seems, more in what God is not than in what God is. As we have seen, his mother did not punish Daniel directly, leaving this task to his father. Also, as Rizzuto points out, there were times when she was probably a "sad witness" to the beatings inflicted on her son by her husband.

Later I will argue that, while this picture of God bears the shadow of his maternal representation, this is not because it is directly based on his experience of his mother. Instead, it derives from her "belief in a benevolent God" (a belief Daniel intuits) and his pre-Oedipal identification with the father of his personal prehistory, who is best personified for him in his maternal grandfather. This would explain discrepancies between this image of God and his experience of his mother, such as the fact that she was complicit in his father's punishments of him. As I will argue on the basis of Freud's theory of melancholia, Daniel identifies with his mother's sadness—an important feature of his drawing of God—but he also felt rage toward her for her complicity in his suffering. His picture of God contains no sign of rage, however, even at the fact of God's seeming impotence. This picture, then, is more congruent with that of a maternal grandfather who, himself vulnerable and dependent, observes his grandson being abused by his son-in-law with the tacit support of his own daughter, and sorrows over "men's inhumanity to man."

Rizzuto also believes that Daniel's God representation, while reflective of his father, was also largely supported by the God representation he was offered in Hebrew school. Indeed, Hebrew school directly reinforced it: "The Old Testament God he met in his Hebrew school frightened him as much as his father and offered no alternative to the God representation he had already formed." Rizzuto cites in this connection Daniel's own criticism of "the biblical God" as "a bit too revengeful to suit me," and his view that "God should have more compassion than he is portrayed in the Bible."

Rizzuto's analysis of Daniel's picture of God as he ideally views him—the God he would like to be able to believe in—centers on its relationship to his maternal representation. There are, however, indications that this image bears some resemblance to himself. As Rizzuto suggests: "In his heart he wonders, ponders about this God who 'is a subject for conjecture and deep thought.' Caught between his fear and his wish, he remains in a fog, undecided and fearful, *sadly contemplating* those who, unlike him, seem so committed and involved with a God they claim loves them." As previously indicated, he terminated his psychotherapy when he began to worry that "a dam of sadness had been opened" that "he could not control," and it was at this time that his concerns about his physical health returned and he began to seek medical evaluations instead of continuing in psychotherapy. This is also when he had the dream that he was a dying man desperately in need of his father's donated organ. Since, as Rizzuto points out, the face of God in his picture looks like his own face (as well as that of his father, whom he physically resembles), we have grounds for believing that this image of God was informed by his self-representation. The sadness and impotence that he sees in the face of God is at least partially his own. Rizzuto's view that he identifies with his mother (and that his ideal God image reflects her own shadow) also supports this view.

Daniel's Melancholy Self

As we have seen, Rizzuto does not diagnose Daniel as a melancholic, but as a "schizoid personality." *DSM-IV* indicates that the "essential feature of Schizoid Personality Disorder is a pervasive pattern of detachment from social relationships and a restricted range of expression of emotions in interpersonal settings. This pattern begins by early adulthood and is present in a variety of contexts" (638). An individual may be diagnosed as having this disorder if there are four or more of the following: The person (1) neither desires nor enjoys close relationships, including being part of a family; (2) almost always chooses solitary activities; (3) has little, if any, interest in having sexual experiences with another person; (4) takes pleasure in few, if any, activities; (5) lacks close friends or confidants other than first-degree relatives; (6) appears indifferent to the praise or criticism of others; and (7) shows emotional coldness, detachment, or flattened affectivity (638).

Persons with this disorder may also exhibit these associated features: (1) particular difficulty expressing anger, even in response to direct provocation, which contributes to the impression that they lack emotion; (2) their lives seem directionless, and they may appear to "drift" in their goals; (3) they often react passively to adverse circumstances and have difficulty responding appropriately to important life events; (4) because of their lack of social skills and of desire for sexual experiences, they have few friendships, date infrequently, and often do not marry; (5) occupational functioning may be impaired, particularly if interpersonal involvement is required, but individuals with this disorder may do well when they work under conditions of social isolation; and (6) especially in response to stress, they may experience very brief psychotic episodes (639).

As for the period of onset, it may be first apparent in childhood and adolescence with solitariness, poor peer relationships, and underachievement in school, "which mark these children or adolescents as different and make them subject to teasing" (639). The disorder is diagnosed slightly more often in males and may cause more impairment in them; it may also be more prevalent in the relatives of persons with Schizophrenic or Schizotypal Personality Disorder. It is distinguished from the latter, however, by the absence of cognitive and perceptual distortions. Because persons who are "loners" may display similar personality traits, a diagnosis of Schizoid Personality Disorder is appropriate only when these traits are inflexible and maladaptive and cause significant functional impairment or subjective distress (640).

This summary of the *DSM-IV* account of Schizoid Personality Disorder indicates its clear applicability to Daniel. In fact, the episode of witnessing an urgent and unforeseen medical emergency when he was in charge under supervision may have caused him to begin to think about his ability to practice medicine because it brought frighteningly home to him the fact that he often reacted "passively to adverse circumstances" and had "difficulty responding appropriately to important life events." This awareness of his passive nature may in turn have roots in the defensive strategy of dissociation that he developed as a coping strategy in response to his father's beatings. Because the medical patient in this case was similar to Daniel in age, his dissociation from physical attacks against himself were psychodynamically related to his passive response to the medical emergency.

The view that Daniel suffered from a melancholic condition does not entail a rejection of the psychiatric diagnosis of Schizoid Personality Disorder. Nor, in fact, does it challenge the accuracy of Rizzuto's reconstruction of the psychodynamics involved in Daniel's parental relationships. In fact, it assumes their fundamental accuracy and builds upon this foundation, which is itself derived from psychoanalytic theory. What an interpretation of Daniel as a melancholy self provides, however, is both a name or label for this psychodynamic situation and an explanation for why he is "constantly preoccupied" with a God he cannot understand. The correlations that Rizzuto demonstrates between his statements about God and about his father make a convincing case for her claim that his God representation "takes its characteristics exclusively from the father," but these do not explain why he is preoccupied with God, or why, to put it another way, he is "incurably religious" despite his doubts about the very existence of this God.

Daniel's Hypochondria

An interpretation of Daniel as melancholic may appropriately begin with his hypochondria, which is not included in Rizzuto's own diagnosis in spite of the fact that his admission to the psychiatric in-patient unit was based on his acceptance of his medical doctor's referral after he was repeatedly and carefully examined for evidence of the lethal illness he insisted he had. As previously noted, he had earlier terminated psychotherapy when a "dam of sadness" had been opened up that he feared he could not control, and it was at this time that his concerns about his physical health returned. Thus, his hypochondria was directly related to progress that was occurring in his psychotherapy, which in the first year had centered on his anger at his father and was now, it seems, beginning to focus on feelings associated with his mother, with whom he shared "a dam of sadness." I believe that if he had allowed himself to confront his sadness, he would also have uncovered his repressed rage toward his mother, which was hidden beneath his sadness for her as well as his sadness for himself because she had abandoned him when he needed her. Thus, while their shared sadness was itself a difficult subject to address, his rage toward her was even more so. He terminated therapy, then, just as he was about to uncover the roots of his melancholia.

Although his first psychosomatic symptoms seem to have occurred in his middle teens (with pains he associated with his maternal grandfather's heart attack), his mother, we are informed, was terrified by physical illnesses or injuries. We may assume, then, that she witnessed her husband's beatings of her son with considerable fear, as these could have resulted in serious physical injury. If Daniel's troubles in his *pre*adolescent years did not manifest themselves in hypochondriacal symptoms, this may be because he sensed that his mother was especially terrified by physical illnesses and injuries, and that these symptoms would not have evoked maternal sympathy but a response of excessive worrying, even, perhaps, of panic. In addition, it might have provoked his father's anger and ridicule.

I emphasize the *apparent* absence of psychosomatic symptoms in Daniel's childhood because, as Susan Baur points out in *Hypochondria: Woeful Imaginings*, "Hypochondria among the young is not an unusual condition, though the disorder goes by so many names that its prevalence is not always obvious. 'Psychosomatic problem patient' often means hypochondria, and 'patient with recurrent abdominal pain' can too" (Baur 1988, 50). She notes that "among children the stomach seems to be the most common of all unfounded complaints, with headache and chest pain a distant second and third" (50). In *Phantom Illness* (1996), Carla Cantor notes that hypochondria is often passed down from one generation to the next in families, and Baur points to "vicarious hypochondriacs," or the parent who imagines that her child has a serious illness either because the parent is a hypochondriac and is displacing her symptoms onto the child or because the parent is using a "sick" child as an excuse to ask for personal help. She notes that parents sometimes bring healthy children into the emergency room, almost demanding that the children be admitted for some totally imaginary condition. In many cases, an episode of child abuse follows an unsuccessful effort to have the child hospitalized, indicating that the parent fears that he or she is liable to harm the child. While there is no clear evidence in Rizzuto's case study that Daniel's mother suffered from hypochondria (though her terror of physical illnesses or injuries, bordering on "paralytic panic," is certainly noteworthy), this association of vicarious hypochondria and child abuse, which we know occurred, is quite significant. Daniel's mother both worried about physical illnesses and injuries and, seemingly paradoxically, was complicit in abuse that could very well have been physically injurious to her son.

Studies of hypochondria and ethnicity indicate that the highest levels of hypochondria are found among Jews, followed by Italians (Baur 1988, 65). Cantor cites research by medical anthropologist, Mark Zborowski, who found that whereas Italians were concerned with relieving their immediate pain, Jews "tended to focus on the implications of their symptoms and what they meant for future health and welfare--their own and their families" (Cantor 1996, 178). Hypochondria is also prevalent among medical students (Baur 1988, 61–65), who are prone to make inaccurate self-diagnoses on the basis of their new medical knowledge. Thus, being both Jewish and a medical student, and having a mother who had a mortal fear of physical illness, Daniel was at high risk to become hypochondriacal.

According to *DSM-IV*, the essential feature of hypochondria (or hypochondriasis) is the "preoccupation with fears of having, or the idea that one has, a serious disease based on a misinterpretation of one or more bodily signs or symptoms" (*DSM IV* 1994, 462). This preoccupation also includes other prominent features. It (1) persists despite appropriate medical evaluation and reassurance; (2) causes clinically significant distress or impairment in social, occupational, or other important areas of functioning; and (3) has a duration of at least six months. If this preoccupation reaches delusional intensity, a diagnosis of "Delusional Disorder, Somatic Type" is then indicated. While Rizzuto refers to Daniel's "quasi-delusional" wish for identification with his father through an organ transplant, the fact that the psychiatrist reports this as a dream warrants caution in viewing him as suffering from a delusional disorder. On the other hand, *DSM-IV* recognizes the difficulty of differentiating hypochondria from Delusional Disorder, Somatic Type, the main difference being that the person who suffers from hypochondria holds the fear of having a serious disease with less than delusional intensity (i.e., the individual can at least entertain the *possibility* that the feared disease might not be present).

DSM-IV notes that while hypochondriasis can begin at any age, the most common age of onset is thought to be in early childhood. It tends to be chronic, with waxing and waning symptoms, but complete recovery sometimes occurs. Because of the chronicity, some view it as having prominent "trait-like" characteristics (i.e., a longstanding preoccupation with bodily complaints and focus on bodily symptoms). It may be significant that "psycho-social stressors, in particular the death of someone close to the individual, are thought to precipitate hypochondriasis in some cases" (464). As noted, Daniel's first hypochondriacal episode occurred in his teens, when his grand-father suffered a heart attack. Later he dreamed that his father would donate an organ to him so that he could live. While this dream suggests that his father would provide the cure for his fatal illness, it may also, at a deeper level, contain an unconscious death wish against his father, for the organ donation implies his father's own death, and suggests that Daniel's chance to live depends upon his father's death. This interpretation is consistent with his response when questioned about his ideal father, "I would probably get another father," and the fact that, while he "harbors the hope" of working in some assigned job to which his father would have no access, he cannot even consider the idea of relocating to another state. Given the relative hopeless-ness of freeing himself from his father, his father's physical death would surely have presented itself to his unconscious mind as the solution to his many problems. His dream seems to provide confirmation of this.

Hypochondria and Melancholy

My interpretation of Daniel's melancholic condition began with the subject of his hypochondria because, as Stanley W. Jackson shows, the two disorders have been "closely allied" historically (Jackson 1986, 308). I will not review this history in detail (Jackson devotes a whole chapter to the subject), but I do want to note the centuries'-old tradition of linking melancholia to gas-trointestinal disorders. This is directly relevant to Daniel's lower abdominal pain. A poorly functioning spleen, whose function is to modify the structure of the blood, was considered the major physiological cause of melancholia, but organs associated with the digestive system (liver, stomach, colon, kid-neys, etc.) were also implicated. (Daniel's complaints about back pain would be related, for example, to the belief that his kidneys were diseased.) Thus, whereas the locus of his symptoms was originally, in adolescence, in his blood-vascular system, in young adulthood they had spread, as it were, to his gastrointestinal system as well. If he was also now complaining about burn-ing urination, especially at the very time that he had become somewhat sex-ually active, this would suggest that the "disease" had begun to affect virtually all of his vital organs.

   While several nineteenth-century psychiatrists challenged the association of melancholia and hypochondria, Jackson notes that this association was "still alive" at the turn of the twentieth century. However, as the term *melan-cholia* began to fall into disuse, the issue became whether there is a hypochon-driacal form of depression and whether many instances of hypochondriasis are cases of "masked depression" (309). These discussions, which were current at the time Jackson's book was published, are relevant to the fact that Daniel's hypochondria emerged precisely at the time his psychotherapy had opened up "a dam of sadness" that he feared he could not control. However, on the basis of Freud's argument that internalized rage against the lost object, manifesting itself in the form of self-reproach, is the central dynamic in melancholia, I suggest that melancholia affords a more complete interpretation of Daniel's problems.

A bridge to this interpretation is provided by Carla Cantor's reference to another form of hypochondria, one that occurs chiefly in Southeast Asia. It has relevance both to Daniel's symptomatology and to the psychodynamic aspects of his melancholia, especially as related to his parental relationships. *Koro*, or *suk-yeong*, is the "frightening preoccupation that one's genitals are shriveling and will disappear into the abdomen." The syndrome most frequently involves the penis, and its victims "may use clamps, string, rubber bands, clothespins, anything, to prevent shrinkage." Cantor suggests that this fear reflects "acute castration anxiety with hypochondriacal overtones" (Cantor 1996, 171).

While Daniel's symptom of burning urination may not have precipitated his desire to have a "sexual experience" in his father's office, the same combination of "acute castration anxiety with hypochondriacal overtones" is nonetheless apparent. His intention to injure himself is also related to our earlier discussion of autoeroticism and the popular view (to which William James subscribed) that "self-abuse" is a major cause of melancholia. While this view has since been discredited, there is certainly evidence that a sense of sexual inadequacy looms large in Daniel's melancholic self-reproach.

The Psychodynamic Roots of Daniel's Melancholia

Daniel's Mother as "Lost Object"

I have argued that the melancholic condition in males is primarily due to their emotional separation from their mothers in early childhood. While this means that all men have a predisposition toward melancholia, a particularly traumatic separation from one's mother can lay the grounds for a more severe case of melancholia. I believe this is precisely what occurred in Daniel's case. In accord with the "positive" pole of Freud's Oedipus complex concept, Daniel was faced with a partial relinquishing of his object-choice of his mother so that he might intensify his identification with his father. She remained, of course, his primary object-choice.

His emotional separation from his mother was exacerbated, however, by several factors. One was her tendency to "offer him up" to his punishing father, and her inability to intervene when his father physically abused him. Another was her own "infantile, schizoid, frightened, inefficient qualities," all of which made it difficult for her to respond appropriately to his desire that his love for her be reciprocated. Even as he had to intuit that she believed in God, so he had to assume—on the basis of ambiguous evidence—that she truly cared for him. The final blow came when her argument with his first-grade teacher over Daniel's intelligence concluded in her withdrawal of her investments in him. As Rizzuto puts it, her maternal disappointment was "intense and lasting." The emotional separation was now complete. In a word, she had abandoned him, and the fallacy of his having made his mother his object-choice was now self-evident. His was the problem of unrequited love. No wonder Rizzuto follows this comment on his mother's "maternal dis-appointment" with the observation that "emotionally he remained a 'loner,'" and that Daniel himself indicated that, while he loved his mother the most in his life at every age, the latency period was the exception, for during this period he "hated both parents intensely."

If his object-choice of his mother suffered an unusually severe blow in early childhood, his identification with his mother was actually intensified. This intensification was based on his perception that they were both the vic-tims of his father's abuse. He witnessed her passivity (and adopted it as his own strategy against his father), her ineffectiveness (and became ineffectual himself in personal relationships, in determining his life's goals, and in con-fronting his father's dominance over him), and shared her underlying sadness for what might have been.

Thus far, my interpretation of Daniel's melancholia follows Rizzuto's own analysis of his relations with his mother. What such an interpretation adds, however, is the internalization of his mother as his lost object and the various consequences of this internalization. The consequence most central to the melancholic core of his personality is the fact that his rage against his mother for her failure to justify his object-choice of her becomes self-directed. While he is aware of his hatred toward his mother in the latency period—the very period in which a boy's sexual feelings toward his mother have gone into a temporary hiatus—there is no similar awareness in the other periods in his life. In those periods, she was the person he felt he loved the most. This was possible because any rage he felt toward her for letting him down was self-directed. Given that she was a rather pathetic person, and was already the object of his father's abuse, young Daniel must have felt that any overt expres-sion of rage toward her would be devastating to her. In turn, he would not have been able to endure the guilt and shame he would feel for doing this to her.

This self-directed hatred was expressed in his hypochondriacal belief that he was suffering from a fatal illness. (Carla Cantor refers to hypochondria as a veiled death wish, a kind of living suicide [Cantor 1996, 288–89].) It reached its culmination in the episode in his father's office when he injured himself and bled "like a woman." This event was a self-inflicted attack on the

DANIEL IN THE LION'S DEN   171

"woman," his mother, whom he had internalized. It also occurred at precisely the same time when it had become at least theoretically possible for him to transfer his object-choice of his mother to an external sexual object, the woman who was "determined to love him." This self-directed hatred prohibited him, however, from seriously entertaining such a transfer.

Since Daniel's hatred toward his mother during the latency period sub-sided during adolescence, we may assume that, as Freud argues, his sexual feelings toward his mother returned with even greater force with the onset of puberty. This also means, however, that his self-directed hatred would also have returned, since his hatred for his mother, more clearly focused during latency on her, was now, in adolescence, being directed toward himself. This was the period when he first began experiencing psychosomatic symptoms, indicating that his self-hatred was manifesting itself in the form of physical symptoms. Perhaps it was no coincidence that his symptoms centered around his heart, for, metaphorically, the heart is the symbolic locus of feelings of love. Thus, his concern that he might have a heart attack was symbolically sig-nificant, for, in a psychodynamic sense, he was experiencing emotional pain "around the area of my heart." This pain centered on his object-choice of his mother. How could he consider transferring his object-choice from her to an external sexual object when she was so pathetic and needy? Perhaps, in his more grandiose ("quasi-delusional"?) moments, he may actually have felt that he could be his mother's rescuer from her abusive, tyrannical husband. But he knew, realistically, that he was no match for his father. As the title to this chapter suggests, he was the biblical Daniel in the cage of a lion—his abusive father—who was altogether capable of eating him alive, both physi-cally and psychologically.

It was during this period of adolescence, however, that Daniel's identifica-tion with his mother was also intensified. Like her, and unlike his competent father, he became ineffectual. He was, at best, an average high school student, raising doubts that he would do well enough in college to be admitted into medical school. His inability to transfer his object-choice from his mother to another female sexual-object and his intensified identification with her appears to have engendered feelings, largely unconscious, that Rizzuto identi-fies as "homosexual" in nature. While we do not know what so enraged Daniel's father about the psychiatrist's report two months after Daniel had begun treatment—maybe it was simply critical of his father's dominating behavior toward his son—it is not inconceivable that the report included ref-erence to Daniel's discomfort with relationships with females. Even if this was not the case, we do know that his father subsequently ridiculed his son for "his total lack of masculinity," and took the view that Daniel was "a neuter, sexually." This could also mean that as long as Daniel did not commit him-self to relations with other female sexual-objects, his father experienced him as threatening to his own prerogatives with Daniel's mother, and therefore needed to believe that Daniel was totally lacking in masculinity. This may have been, in other words, the sole leverage that Daniel had with his father, and for this reason, he could not risk relating to young women. This meant, however, that he was also depriving himself of any symbolic blessing his father might bestow on him, for, as we saw earlier, the father's blessing depends on the son's transfer of his object-choice from his mother to another woman. With this transfer, the son is also able to free himself from his father's domination.

Daniel's inability to take the initiative in relationships with young women seems to confirm Freud's view that the adolescent boy who identifies with his mother tends to adopt a "feminine" or "submissive" attitude regarding external sexual objects (Freud 1960a, 27). His one heterosexual relationship at the very moment that he was beginning to disintegrate emotionally was one in which he "responded passively" (in this, he clearly identified with his mother, whose relationships were also marked by passivity). It may not be coincidental that this other woman was "an adolescent acquaintance" of his, suggesting that, despite his age (twenty-seven years old), this relationship was, for him, psychodynamically rooted in his unsuccessful adolescent struggles to separate from his mother. As we have seen, Rizzuto refers to his "repressed homosexual longings," which were awakened during his college days when he saw his friends dating and he knew they were having sex with their girlfriends. Relegated to the role of imaginary observer of these sexual scenes, and perhaps fantasizing himself as the "passive" woman in them, he nonetheless expressed his wish for "a girl friend, someone I can confide in, someone I could love."

This "girl friend," I suggest, is his image of the mother whom he loved *before* the emotional separation he experienced as a small boy, when he (like his "seductive" father), was the playful seducer, given to mischief, and still capable of being passionate toward his love-object. But when his mother turned him over to his father, the emotional separation began, and his playful, mischievous behavior in her company was driven out of him. His melancholy disposition—his inner sadness, his self-directed rage—emerged at this very point in his life. To be able to respond emotionally to the young woman who had passionate feelings for him, he would need somehow to "triumph" over the internalized object, that is, his mother. As Freud indicates in "Mourning and Melancholia," such a triumph occasionally happens, usually in the context of a manic moment when the son's ego finds strength enough to destroy this internalized object. In succumbing to the same kind of schizoid behavior characteristic of his mother, Daniel seems to have taken the very opposite course. His identification with his mother was only further intensified.

Daniel's Surrender to His Father

This brings us to Daniel's relations with his father. As noted, he felt he loved his mother the most in every age except the latency period, when he hated both parents intensely. He could not be expected, however, to remember that he loved his father the most at some point in his pre-Oedipal years; in fact, Rizzuto appears to have asked her subjects only about ages three to six, not the earlier years, on the assumption that they would have had no conscious recollections of anything prior to age three. In any event, there is little overt love for his father in this case report, and his father actually appears to take pleasure in the fact that he is hated by his son. On the other hand, unlike his hatred toward his mother (with the sole exception of the latency period), Daniel's hatred of his father was externalized. His death wishes toward his father, while certainly disguised in his dream of his father's organ donation, were less deeply repressed than similar feelings toward his mother. When asked about his ideal father, he could say that he "would probably get another father." While he says, "If I can change the situation, I would like to make my parents over in some way," there is no similar statement about getting another mother. As we have seen, such a thought would produce enormous feelings of guilt and shame.

On the other hand, he indicates that he desires his father's love. As Rizzuto puts it, "there is nothing he would like more than to have the love, under-standing, and respect of his father. He longs to understand and love him, but he despairs that he ever will." This suggests that there is an unbridgeable emo-tional gulf between the two men, and that his perception that his father does not love him is reciprocated by his feeling that he does not really love his father either.

He does, however, identify with his father. As Rizzuto observes, while he hates his father, "he also admires him and wants to be like him." His father is the member of the family he most admires "because he is confident and con-cerned with the well-being of his family." Daniel can say the latter in spite of the fact that his father is abusive, ridicules him, is domineering, tyrannical, and, of the two parents, "had the least appreciation of my likes and dislikes."

If we view these seemingly contradictory feelings from the perspective of Freud's Oedipus complex concept, we can readily see that Daniel's feelings toward his father are highly ambivalent. No doubt there are vestiges here of his original object-choice of his father, of his desire to have his father as his own. These, however, are countered by his hostility and hatred for his father, and by his genuine desire to identify with him instead. In one sense, his rela-tionship as a small boy with his father has followed the prescription of the demolition of the Oedipus complex. He has relinquished his father as his object-choice, has replaced his love for his father with an ambivalent love/hatred toward him, and has intensified his identification with him.

The problem is that his father has been unable to perceive, much less encourage, this identification. Rizzuto refers to his father's "narcissistic investment" in his son, as reflected, for example, in his involvement in Daniel's homework to the point of actually doing it for him, and later, in the fact that he filled out Daniel's applications to medical school and coached him on how to answer the interviewers' questions. We should probably look for the source of his narcissistic investment in his son in his own unrealized ambitions to be a medical doctor. He seems to have settled for what was for him a lesser career, "a representative for a drug company," which meant, among other things, that he was not as financially successful as he had wanted to be, nor did he enjoy the social status to which he aspired. Daniel's identi- fication with his father paid few dividends, especially when it became clear that his abilities fell far short of his father's expectations of him.

This, of course, raises the question of whether his father's own ambiva- lence toward his son's success required that Daniel *not* live up to his father's ambitions for him. Rizzuto points to his father's need "to see him as an asex- ual being," as if to suggest that there could only be one "man" in the Miller family, and a very "seductive" one at that. Did his father's need to view his son as sexually ineffectual also extend to professional attainments? Did his father subtly sabotage his son's educational, vocational, and professional growth while seemingly doing all that was in his power to assist Daniel in this regard? In fact, did he destroy any inner motivation that Daniel might have had to become professionally competent in whatever vocation Daniel might have chosen for himself by insisting that Daniel enter the very profession to which he had unsuccessfully aspired? Could Daniel have borne the guilt that would have resulted from succeeding where his father had failed? In his own way, Daniel seems to have complied with this hidden message, failing to "become a man" in the two areas of life where the young adult's manhood or mas- culinity is proven: sexual and vocational. From his father's point of view— and his own—he has failed in both respects. Little wonder then that, as the *DSM-IV* description of the schizoid personality indicates, he seemed to "drift" in his goals. Having so identified with his father that he has internal- ized his ambivalence, it was virtually inevitable that he would fail at the very tasks his father ostensibly promoted.

As we have seen, Freud suggests that a son may separate from his father at the end of the adolescent period in one of two ways. If he has been antago- nistic toward his father throughout childhood, he can liberate himself from his father by reconciling with him. If, on the other hand, he has been sub- servient to his father, he can free himself from his father's domination. Both situations have relevance in Daniel's case. Regarding the former, his desire between ages fifteen and twenty-one was that there would be a reconciliation between himself and his father; "I needed a combination of things: closeness to my father, a willingness on both of our parts to come to an understanding, discussing what my problems were and why I reacted the way I did towards him." On the other hand, while Daniel says that he hated his father through out childhood, he was not openly antagonistic toward him. There was no overt rebellion. He did not, for example, refuse to fill out application forms for medical school; he simply didn't get around to it. Also, he apparently complied with his father's suggestions for how to answer the interviewers' questions. While he was conscious of his hatred toward his father, he did not attack him or openly express his anger toward him. Instead, he became subservient to him, trying—to the degree that he could—to satisfy his father and to make him proud of him. As Rizzuto puts it, it was not so much that he was "effeminate" as that he was a "frightened boy." Fear of his father required that he be subservient to him.

The primary developmental task that he faced at the end of adolescence, then, was to free himself from his father's domination—not just socially, but psychologically as well. In this light, it is not surprising that the best period in his life was when he was away at college: "I enjoyed the freedom of being independent." Notably, he took interest in his academic work at this time. But it didn't last. He allowed his father to take his professional future into his own hands when he could not offer (did not dare to offer?) an alternative to his father's desire that he enter medical school. After a year of living in the dormitory (though spending weekends with his parents), he returned to his parents' home, "claiming that he was more comfortable there." Then, as the time to apply for internships arrived, he did not make any applications, thus ambivalently inviting, while also fearing, his father's intervention at this stage of his career. This is when his hypochondriacal symptoms emerged and he stopped working altogether. Clearly, he was unable to free himself from his subservience to his father. Failing in this regard, he eventually ended up in the psychiatric in-patient unit.

I have argued that male melancholia is not directly related to the loss of the object-choice of one's father (though homophobia is). I have also argued that identification and bonding with one's father, as the two expected outcomes of the separation-individuation process in early childhood, are mutually exclusive. These two suggestions apply to Daniel's relationship with his father from childhood through adolescence and into young adulthood. Identification with his father did occur, but emotional bonding—a mutual love for one another—did not. He now finds himself longing for his father's love, but the vicissitudes of his identification with his father preclude this. The implicit blessing that would derive from a successful transfer of his object-choice from his mother to an external sexual object (of either gender) remains elusive, in part because Daniel "knows," at least unconsciously, that his father needs him to be an asexual person. Thus far, his father has not donated the organ that would enable him to claim his manhood, and, unconsciously at least, Daniel knows that he never will.

The Father of Personal Prehistory

One of the most striking aspects of Rizzuto's case study of Daniel Miller is that his God representation and the picture he drew of God are remarkably similar to his father, but the explanation that accompanies the picture is very different. The drawing, he explains, portrays a God who is "extremely wise— but sad at men's inhumanity to man—also patient and sensitive to [the] suffering of mankind." As Rizzuto points out, "He drew a man very similar to his father but attributed to God a wisdom and kindness that are totally foreign to his father." She views this as "defensive intellectual idealization, colored by his wish that God could be that way, although he is totally unaware that this is the case." She adds that "he also assumes that his mother believed in a God who is benevolent," while "in actuality, his mother has never shown any signs of belief in God." Rizzuto concludes that this portrayal of God is part of "his system of defenses," which "is at the service of protecting his schizoid positions of a tremendous wish for closeness and an overwhelming fear of the object of his wishes."

I believe, however, that Freud's idea of "the father of personal prehistory" provides a better explanation for the discrepancy between his God representation and this depiction of God. It makes sense and is consistent with Rizzuto's project of identifying influences in the child's interpersonal environment on the adult's God representation to ask what the experiential source of this picture may be, especially since it is so contrary to his representation of his father. The clue may be in the fact that Daniel assumes, with little factual foundation, that his mother believes in a benevolent God (and may not dare to communicate this belief because she fears her husband would ridicule her for this). I think that Daniel was intuitively correct about this—in William Stafford's phrase, he had "studied her heart"—and perhaps her own empirical basis for believing this was the fact that, as a small girl, she experienced her own father—Daniel's maternal grandfather—as a benevolent man. I realize, of course, that the case report provides no concrete evidence of this, but it is a hypothesis worth considering, as it helps to account for the one difference between his God representation and his paternal representation—that God does not punish—and enables us to identify the ontogenetic source of his pictorial representation of God.

As indicated in chapter 4, Freud believes that "the father of personal prehistory," as phylogenetically transmitted, requires the small boy to relinquish his object-choice of his father and to make his mother his object-choice instead. I also presented the psychoanalytic tradition that the person in the boy's immediate environment who personifies this father of personal prehistory is the maternal grandfather. Rizzuto's single reference to Daniel's maternal grandfather is therefore intriguing. It concerns Daniel's first psychosomatic symptoms in adolescence—the pains around the area of his heart—which "seemed to have some connection with his maternal grandfather, who had had a heart attack and recovered from it."

While this single reference to Daniel's maternal grandfather gives little insight into his relations with the older man, or his feelings toward him, it at least suggests some sort of identification with him, especially one that centers on Daniel's own sense of physical vulnerability and fears for his life, which were rearoused when he had medical responsibility for the life of the young man his own age a decade later. As we have also seen, these psychosomatic symptoms eventually developed into a hypochondriacal belief that he was afflicted with a fatal illness, with its cause located in one of his internal organs.

I believe that his maternal grandfather also figured into his perception of God—not, however, in the verbal God representation dominated by his paternal representation, but in the picture he drew of his image of God. This image portrays a God who is extremely wise—as his father is not—but sad at man's inhumanity to man, and patient and sensitive to human suffering. This image, I believe, is Daniel's "father of personal prehistory," and his maternal grandfather is the one who best personifies this God in his life. Suffering from his own heart problems, his maternal grandfather may have had the very qualities that Daniel ascribes to the pictorial God. Since, as Rizzuto notes, his pictorial image of God resembles both himself and his father, but his descriptive account below the picture bears no resemblance whatever to his own father, the picture may also reflect his identification with his maternal grandfather: With his wisdom, his sadness, his patience, his sensitivity to human suffering, but also with his impotence to do anything about it. Daniel can dare to depict his own image in his pictorial representation of God because there is a personal, if not a physical, likeness between himself and his maternal grandfather.

This conclusion is congruent with the psychoanalytic tradition's view that the most likely personification of the father of personal prehistory is the maternal grandfather, with whom the pre-Oedipal boy identifies, and who ensures the termination of the boy's object-choice of his father. However, it reflects a further development or elaboration of this "father of personal prehistory," one that came about in Daniel's adolescence when he not only witnessed but also identified with—through similar physical symptoms—his grandfather's physical vulnerabilities. Thus, he incorporated into the father of personal prehistory an attribute of vulnerability. This father lacks the strength or power to compel men like Daniel's father to treat their sons with kindness and to accord them the dignity and respect they desire, especially from their own fathers. This elaboration of the father of personal prehistory reflects a theme that Freud himself explored in *Totem and Taboo* and reintroduced in his final book, *Moses and Monotheism*, where he accounts for totemic religion by positing that at some point in human prehistory the sons rose up against their powerful father and killed him, thus proving his vulnerability. This theme is a part of the phylogenetic history of God, and it was in adolescence—a period of religious questioning—that Daniel perceived the vulnerability of the seemingly all-powerful father of personal prehistory. Indeed, he could not be simultaneously all-wise and all-powerful.

Thus, it appears that in adolescence, Daniel identified with his maternal grandfather, sensing that the two of them shared a similar fate. As his grandfather was stricken with a heart attack, Daniel was also emotionally stricken, experiencing pains in the area of his heart. If he indicated in response to Rizzuto's question regarding his "ideal father" that he would "probably get another father; a father who likes children," this "ideal father" could very well have been based on his experience of his maternal grandfather.

The hopeful aspect of this self-identification with his maternal grandfather was that his grandfather recovered from his heart attack. Similarly, the hopeful aspect of his picture of "the father of personal prehistory" is that, while unable to intervene—even as his maternal grandfather seemed helpless to intervene in his grandson and daughter's abuse at the hands of their father and husband—he is neither dead nor uncaring. God may be "an Enigma," but Daniel refuses to declare, once and for all, that God does not exist. In fact, Rizzuto's view that Daniel fits in her category three—that is, persons "who are amazed, angered, or quietly surprised to see others deeply invested in a God who does not interest them"—is itself belied by her own observation that he is "constantly preoccupied with a God he cannot understand."

This interpretation of the maternal grandfather as the source of Daniel's "father of personal prehistory" helps to account for the very tenuousness of his image of God. This image is based on an intuitive sense that his mother believes in a benevolent God, but it is not supported by the instruction Daniel received in Hebrew school of the biblical God who "was a bit too revengeful to suit me" and his view that God "should have more compassion than he is portrayed in the Bible." The God presented to him in Hebrew school resembles his own father, especially in his inability to treat his son with compassion. Such a God is to be feared, perhaps even admired, but is very difficult to love. This, of course, was also true of Daniel's feelings toward his father. If Daniel had been able to endorse this God, however, he may have been able to use him to empower a revolt against his own father. Instead he identified with his vulnerable grandfather, incorporating this vulnerability into his own image of his father's view of him as weak and unmanly. As Freud suggests, the two ways in which an adolescent boy can free himself from his father are to reconcile himself with his father if he has been antagonistic toward him, or to break away from his father's domination if he has lapsed into subservience to him. In Daniel's case, the primary problem was subservience, and, ironically, his awareness of the vulnerability of God, in itself a profound insight, made him less capable of using his religious proclivities as a basis for challenging and breaking free from his father's domination.

Daniel's Melancholic Predicament: Hope, Fate, and the Chance of Salvation

I have suggested that two primary religious impulses emerge in early childhood with the boy's emotional separation from his mother, and that a third such impulse develops over against them. One is the development of a moral sensibility, the determination to be a "good boy" in order to win his mother back. The other is the tendency to search for vestiges of the "lost object" in the external world. While Daniel may have thought at one point in his life that he could win his mother back through good behavior, this is not a prominent feature of their relationship. As we have seen, she apparently needed for him to engage in "bad" behavior so that she could report him to his father and thus protect herself from her husband's abuse. Far more evident is the fact that she is out of reach emotionally because she is depressed, fearful, and anxious. After she begins to doubt that he will live up to her ambitions for him, which could have given her own life a meaning and purpose it otherwise lacked, she seems to have withdrawn her emotional investment in him, leaving him permanently bereft and forsaken. This would create a predisposition to develop a melancholic religion reflective not of moral rectitude designed to regain the original lost object, but of searching and questing for a substitute in the external world.

As we have seen, he went about this search in a decidedly fitful manner. Instead of transferring his object-choice of his mother to another object, he intensified his identification with her. Even so, his view of God as a nonpunishing deity—the one quality that distinguishes his God representation from his image of his father—suggests that a religion of moral rectitude had little interest for him. Instead, a melancholy searching and questing is portrayed in the picture he drew of God ("Enigma"), which, as I have argued, reflects the father of personal prehistory as represented in the form of his maternal grandfather, and in his own self-identification with him.

As Rizzuto suggests, this is the picture of a God who "has no real substance," whose existence is "a mere possibility," but "a consoling hope that helps a desperate person maintain minimal psychic balance." She also observes that his confidence in what he takes to be his mother's belief in God "coincides with his ideal image of God" and "is a way of maintaining hope against hope," thus offering an alternative to his actual world, which "offers no hope, no way out, no rest, no peace." In her view, the fact that he has "never experienced the need to solve the problem of God" is "not simply a developmental lag that affects him" but also "the tragic tension between his longings and his fears," his "hoping against hope that one day his father will come through" and be "the father he longs for," though "he despairs that he ever will." He also "harbored the hope that one day he could lose his fear of patients and work in some assigned job to which his father would have no access."

Thus, in Rizzuto's portrayal of him, he is a young man who wants to hope, though he has at present few grounds for doing so. One reason why his hope is more a "hoping against hope" than a confident hope is his strong sense of fate and his doubts that his fate could possibly change. In one of his statements about God, he notes that he has "never expressed hate for God but has felt exasperated at my situation or fate." When asked about what he would wish had happened between ages three and six, he replied, "*If I can change the situation*, I would like to make my parents over in some way. I probably would change my father's disposition, to make him a little more affectionate" (my emphasis). He views the question, even now, as essentially hypothetical.

This response to how he would change the situation in the years that were so formative for him is specific about how he would have liked to make his father over. He says nothing about how he would make his mother over. I believe that this reflects most men's rather melancholy view of their mothers as simply who they are, and of their own need simply to make the best of it. While they can entertain at least the possibility that their fathers might change, hopefully for the better, and that they themselves might be instrumental in helping their fathers to change, they tend to think more in terms of how they might adapt *themselves* to their mothers' habits and moods. Consequently, they consciously or unconsciously identify their mothers with fate itself (i.e., with that which cannot be changed or altered).

In his essay "Fate," Ralph Waldo Emerson writes, "Men are what their mothers made them" (Emerson 1983, 947). In his essay "Experience," he claims that our temperament "is the iron wire on which the beads are strung," and attributes a man's temperament to how his mother bore and raised him (474). David Leverenz perceives in Emerson's comments about the power of a mother to control and seal her son's fate a "displacement of anxiety about manhood into passive indictments of mothering," and suggests that Emerson's essays typically retreat "from his hopes for manly transformation to a private depressiveness that fitfully snipes at the women he takes for granted" (Leverenz 1989, 70). For Leverenz, Emerson makes mothers a convenient excuse for men's failures to realize their hopes and aspirations, their inability to become the men they envision themselves to be.

But is there an element of truth in this melancholic—Leverenz says "misogynist"—notion that a man's fate is largely determined by his mother, especially in how she bore and raised him? Freud certainly thought so. He concludes his essay "The Theme of the Three Caskets" (originally published in 1913) with the observation that there are "three inevitable relations" that a man has with a woman: "that with the mother who bears him, with the companion of his bed and board, and with the destroyer." Or, put another way, there are "three forms taken on by the figure of the mother as life proceeds: the mother herself, the beloved who is chosen after her pattern, and finally the Mother Earth who receives him again. But it is in vain that the old man yearns after the love of woman as he once had it from his mother; the third of the Fates alone, the silent goddess of Death, will take him into her arms" (Freud 1958b, 75). This suggests that the mother is the very personification of fate, the Delphian oracle in the flesh.

In his analysis of Freud's own dream of "The Three Fates," which Freud presents in his *The Interpretation of Dreams* (originally published in 1900), Erik Erikson suggests that, in the final analysis, the dream reflects Freud's awareness that his mother is identified with fate. After discussing some of the dream's images and themes, Erikson concludes that the dream confirms the dreamer's realization that "If your own mother is made of earth or dirt, or worse, and if your name is like a curse, you cannot trust mother, origin, or fate: you must create your own greatness." Thus, the implied "dream wish" is the fundamental desire to "change your fate" (Erikson 1964, 183). Erikson suggests, therefore, that the dream of the Three Fates "illustrates the way in which the dream life reaches down from the actuality of the day to the earliest stages of life when disappointments and unfulfilled promises were experienced which have remained forever ready to be actualized" (185). In our terms, the melancholic self—as reflected in the case of Daniel Miller—stands poised between fate and hope, and his hope is centered on the question of whether any man can actually change his fate. Can the unfulfilled promises of early childhood be realized in spite of all that has gone wrong in the meantime?

In light of the fact that William James considered himself a melancholy soul, it is noteworthy that James himself believed that the fundamental contribution religion makes in any man's life is that it engenders hope. He concludes *The Varieties of Religious Experience* with the observation that the power of religion is not that it offers "assurance of salvation"—it cannot make good on such an extravagant claim—but that it offers "the *chance* of salvation." And this, he affirms, is enough: "No fact in human nature is more characteristic than its willingness to live on a chance. The existence of the chance makes the difference . . . between a life of which the keynote is resignation and a life of which the keynote is hope" (James 1982, 526–27). Daniel Miller's hope—a hope against hope—comes down, finally, to the question of whether it is possible to change his fate. To the extent that he believes there is even a chance of this happening, he has not lost all hope.

Whether the unrealized promises of "the earliest stages of his life" have any chance of being actualized in the future are, of course, open to question. Daniel himself appears to believe that they depend primarily on his ability to gain freedom from his father's dominance over his life (by finding a way to work in some assigned job to which his father would have no access); and, secondarily, to his father becoming "the father he longs for." These, in effect, reflect the ideal resolution of separation from one's father in adolescence, that is, freedom from one's father's dominance while also realizing a reconciliation between son and father.

This does not, however, address what I consider to be the more powerful—because it is more subterranean—threat to his hopeful future, namely, his failure thus far to transfer his object-choice from his mother to an external sexual object, the other developmental task that is, ideally, accomplished at the end of the adolescent era. This could be facilitated by unearthing his deeply repressed rage toward his mother, which is based, in part, on his intuition as a small child of her ambivalent feelings toward him. This rage has thus far been inaccessible due both to his perception of her as a sad, pathetic person and to his own identification with this aspect of her. To see her in this fuller light may enable him to recognize that she has the capacity to survive without him, that, in fact, his independence of her may release her from an onerous burden, that of the mother who has failed her son. Whether his "adolescent acquaintance" who has fallen in love with him is his "chance for salvation" is not for me to say. But, as Rizzuto puts it, he *did* express "his desire to have a 'girl friend, someone I can confide in, someone I could love.'"

Or perhaps his "chance of salvation" lies in accepting what Rizzuto calls his "more repressed homosexual longings" and searching, therefore, for a male friend as the one he "can confide in, someone I could love." In this case, a more "radical" (i.e., deeply rooted) bid for salvation would be to accept his intensified identification with his mother in his adolescent years as integral to the man he has become, and to overcome his father's domination—and his own subservience to him—by transferring his original (pre-Oedipal) object-choice from his father to another man. By accepting the sad truth that a satisfying emotional bond between himself and his father will remain forever elusive, he may free himself to embark on a search for another man to love and be loved in return. This bid for salvation would, I believe, have the endorsement of the father of personal prehistory portrayed in his drawing. Since the dictionary defines hope as "the expectation that what is wanted will happen," it would be my hope that he would take a chance, for his salvation may just depend on his acceptance of the rather enigmatic—but strangely inspiring—fact that someone in this world actually finds him lovable.

CHAPTER 7

~

Humor—Remedy for Melancholia

I have argued that the two major religious responses that small boys make to their emotional separation from their mothers is the resolution to be a good boy (the basis for a religion of moral rectitude) and the search for substitutions and compensations in the real world to which they have, in effect, been abandoned or exiled (the basis for a religion of questing). Thus, the melancholic condition in which boys find themselves spawns an honorable self and a hopeful self, both of which are reactive to the melancholy self. Neither of these, nor both together, affords a cure for melancholy, but they provide remedies for melancholia and are therefore functionally valuable. In this sense, melancholia may be likened to the common cold. There is no cure, but there are a vast array of remedies, religion being a particularly effective one as long as one does not become addicted to it.

How does one avoid becoming so addicted? I think the answer lies in humor, which has an ambiguous relationship to religion, sometimes viewed as one of its components, but most of the time viewed as unrelated to religion, if not in competition with it for men's very souls. In concluding this study of the melancholy self, I want to make a serious case for the more inclusionary view. For this, I will draw on Freud's essay entitled "Humor" (originally published in 1928).

Humor and the Economy of Affect

In this essay, Freud returns to the subject that inspired his *Jokes and Their Relation to the Unconscious* (originally published in 1905). This book followed his classic text, *The Interpretation of Dreams* (originally published in 1900) and showed that the same "techniques" that dreams employ are also found in jokes. In his much later essay on humor, he says that what he wanted to do in the earlier book was to "discover the source of the pleasure derived from humor," and he claims that he was able to show that this pleasure derives "from a saving in expenditure of affect" (Freud 1963b, 263). To explain what he means by this, he cites this example: A criminal being led to the gallows on a Monday morning observes, "Well, this is a good beginning to the week." This bit of humor may save both himself and those who are witnesses to his execution an expenditure of affect. That is, he may be feeling anger, fear, horror, or despair, or all of these together. But instead of expressing these feelings, he makes a joke. The person watching the scene is likely to expect that the victim will show signs of one or more of these affects, and may be prepared to follow his lead and experience similar emotions. But the victim's joke intervenes and counters this expectation. The satisfaction that the joke affords both victim and viewer is the saving of the expenditure of painful emotions. Thus, humor is a form of psychic economy.

In *Jokes and Their Relation to the Unconscious*, Freud suggests that the affect that would have been expended if humor had not come to the rescue is often anger. He cites Mark Twain's story about how his brother constructed a subterranean dwelling, into which he brought a bed, a table, and a lamp, and which he roofed over with a large piece of sailcloth with a hole in the middle. At night, however, after the hut was finished, a cow that was being driven home fell through the opening of the roof onto the table and put out the lamp. His brother patiently helped to get the beast out and put the establishment to rights again. Next night the same interruption was repeated and his brother behaved as before. And so it was every following night. Repetition makes the story comic, but Twain ends it by reporting that on the forty-sixth night, when the cow fell through again, his brother finally remarked: "The thing's beginning to get monotonous." Freud comments, "At this our humorous pleasure cannot be kept back, for what we had long expected to hear was that this obstinate set of misfortunes would make his brother *angry*. And indeed the small contributions of humor that we produce ourselves are as a rule made at the cost of anger—instead of getting angry" (1960c, 231).

A particularly useful contribution of humor is that it spares us the expenditure of anger at persons who claim superiority or privilege over us. Freud cites another story by Twain, in which he presents the reader with his family tree, which he traces back to one of Columbus's fellow voyagers. He then describes this ancestor's character and how his baggage consisted entirely of a number of pieces of washing each of which had a different laundry mark. Freud comments, "Here we cannot help laughing at the cost of an economy of the feelings of piety into which we were prepared to enter at the beginning of this family history. The mechanism of the humorous pleasure is not interfered with by our knowledge that this pedigree is a fictitious one and that the fiction serves the satirical purpose of exposing the embellishments in similar accounts by other people" (230–31).

Another affect that humor spares us is pity, for others certainly, but also for ourselves. Freud suggests that "an economy of pity is one of the most frequent sources of humorous pleasure," and notes that Twain's humor often works with this mechanism. Thus, in an account of his brother's life, Twain tells us how he was at one time employed on a great road-making enterprise. The premature explosion of a mine blew him up into the air and he came down again far away from the place where he had been working. Freud suggests that we "are bound to have feelings of sympathy for the victim of the accident and would like to ask whether he was injured by it. But when the story goes on to say that his brother had a half-day's wages deducted for being 'absent from his place of employment' we are entirely distracted from our pity and become almost as hard-hearted as the contractor and almost as indifferent to possible damage to the brother's health" (230).

This story, and the preceding one, also has a secondary benefit derived from the fact that Twain's *brother* is the hapless victim. As we saw in the case of Douglas O'Duffy, one brother's resentment over the fact (or perception) that another brother is mother's favorite may be a significant dynamic in the formation of the melancholy self. The Smothers Brothers, a comedy team of the 1960s, made the accusation that "Mom always loved you best" the signature of their routine. In Twain's story, his brother may be employed in a "great road-making enterprise," but in the story itself he is cutting a rather ludicrous figure as he flies through the air and comes crashing down far from the place where he had been working. Thus, Twain's story spares the storyteller and his listeners from the affect of sibling resentment.

In his later essay on humor, Freud notes that, because it spares us the expenditure of affect or emotion, humor has a *liberating* element. In addition, there is "something fine and elevating" about humor, namely, "the ego's victorious assertion of its own invulnerability. It refuses to be hurt by the arrows of reality or to be compelled to suffer. It insists that it is impervious to wounds dealt by the outside world, in fact, that these are merely occasions for affording it pleasure. This last trait is a fundamental characteristic of humor" (265).

Suppose, Freud says, that the criminal being led to execution on a Monday morning had said, "It doesn't worry me. What does it matter, after all, if a fellow like me is hanged? The world won't come to an end." This speech would display "the same magnificent rising superior to the real situation," but there is not a trace of humor in it. In fact, it is based on an appraisal of reality that runs directly counter to that of humor, for humor "is not resigned; it is rebellious." Thus, humor signifies the triumph not only of the ego but also of "the pleasure principle" (which Freud contrasts with "the reality principle"), which "is strong enough to assert itself here in the face of the adverse real circumstances" (265). These last two characteristics—the denial of the claim of reality and the triumph of the pleasure principle—give humor "a dignity which is wholly lacking, for instance, in wit, for the aim of wit is either simply to afford gratification, or, in so doing, to provide an outlet for aggressive tendencies" (265). Thus, wit may be used to put one's opponent in his place, to cut him down to size. Humor doesn't do this. Instead, the humorous attitude is one that refuses to undergo suffering, that asserts the invincibility of one's ego against the real world, victoriously upholding the pleasure principle. Also, in contrast to delusions and intoxication, it does this without abandoning "the ground of mental sanity" (266).

In psychodynamic terms, Freud contends that the superego is the source of humor. We are used to thinking of the superego as the voice of conscience, which often demands from us more than we can reasonably be expected to give (the religion of moral rectitude with its ultimate goal of perfection). Freud suggests, however, that the superego also has a kinder, gentler side. This side of the superego is not unlike an adult who recognizes and smiles at the triviality of the anxieties and worries that loom so large in the mind of the child. Because "genetically the superego inherits the parental function, it often holds the ego in strict subordination, and still critically treats it as the parents (or the father) treated the child in his early years." But what if it uses its superiority over the ego to say to it, "Look here! This is all that this seemingly dangerous world amounts to. Child's play—the very thing to jest about!" In other words, it tells the distressed, frightened, or anxious ego, "There's much *less* here than meets the eye." In this way, the superego, through humor, speaks "kindly words of comfort to the intimidated ego," enabling the ego to gain victory over the sufferings that the world inflicts upon it. And, as Freud emphasizes, it does this in such a way that one need not leave the ground of mental sanity (i.e., via dissociation). Humor, he concludes, is thus "a rare and precious gift" (268).

In light of our concern with the melancholy self throughout this study, Freud's comparison of humor to the alternation that occurs in the mind when melancholia shifts into mania is especially noteworthy. What happens in this case is that "a cruel suppression of the ego by the superego" (in melancholia) leads to "the liberation of the ego" (in mania). He suggests that humor has a similar liberating effect, but it occurs under the agency of the superego itself—not in the overthrowing of the superego—and therefore it is not nearly as reactively violent. In humor, the superego itself forgoes its prerogatives as the stern and cruel taskmaster and takes a kind and protective interest in the beleaguered ego. It decides, as it were, that the real world already inflicts enough pain and suffering on the ego, so nothing useful is gained by its own infliction of gratuitous pain (as reflected, for example, in its demand for moral perfection).

Freud's essay suggests that humor is the primary way in which the superego liberates the ego so that it is able to refuse to be hurt or compelled to suffer by the arrows of reality. Humor is the refusal to be affected. The title of a book by Paul Watzlawick, *The Situation Is Hopeless, But Not Serious* (1983), not only makes Freud's point with beautiful accuracy but also indirectly offers a critique of "the religion of quest" (even as Freud's essay provides a critique of "religion as moral rectitude"). It says to the melancholy self: Questing has its own rewards, so the search for the "lost object" in the various guises in which it will represent itself to you is all to the good. But humor can be a rare and precious gift when the evil day comes, as the author of Ecclesiastes has it, and the quester concludes that all is vanity, a striving after the wind. At this point, only humor can speak a kindly word of comfort: "The situation is hopeless, but not serious" is what it tells the discouraged, intimidated ego who would otherwise despair.

In a similar way, Billy Collins' poem "Another Reason Why I Don't Keep a Gun in the House" (Collins1988, 50), reflects the use of humor to save the expenditure of an emotion he would otherwise feel and perhaps act upon.

Another Reason Why I Don't Keep a Gun in the House

The neighbors' dog will not stop barking.
He is barking the same high, rhythmic bark
that he barks every time they leave the house.
They must switch him on on their way out.

The neighbors' dog will not stop barking.
I close all the windows in the house
and put on a Beethoven symphony full blast
but I can still hear him muffled under the music,
barking, barking, barking.

and now I can see him sitting in the orchestra,
his head raised confidently as if Beethoven
had included a part for barking dog.

When the record finally ends he is still barking,
sitting there in the oboe section barking,
his eyes fixed on the conductor who is
entreating him with his baton
while the other musicians listen in respectful
silence to the famous barking dog solo,
that endless coda that first established
Beethoven as an innovative genius.

As the title clearly indicates, the emotion in this instance is rage. A couple of years ago, I read a newspaper account of a man who had become so frustrated by his neighbor's barking dog that one day, when his neighbor was not at home, he shot and killed the dog. Afterward he expressed remorse for having done this and acknowledged that it was a terrible thing to have done, but he said that it was a blistering hot day, that he had previously complained to his neighbor about his dog, and that he eventually just lost control. The owner of the dog said he wished that he had realized how upset his neighbor was, but he also said that what the man had done was totally inexcusable.

Faced with a similar situation, Collins opts for humor instead. When his effort to drown out the dog's barking by playing a Beethoven symphony full blast proves unsuccessful, he imagines Beethoven including a part for a barking dog. Warming to this obviously ludicrous idea, he develops it further by placing the dog in the oboe section, "his eyes fixed on the conductor," and barking out "the famous barking dog solo" while "the other musicians listen in respectful silence." He caps this idea off by claiming that this solo, an "endless coda to the whole symphony," was responsible for establishing Beethoven as "an innovative genius."

This bit of humor changes nothing in the real world. The dog has succeeded in ruining Collins's evening, and will do so, we assume, again and again and again. But Collins has found a way to avoid the expenditure of an affect—rage leading to possible violence—he would prefer not to allow himself, since it isn't worth it and only hurts himself. His recourse to humor is liberating in this sense; it constitutes the difference between himself and the man who did in fact use the gun to which Collins alludes in the title. There must also have been a certain satisfaction in the fact that a publishable poem came out of this experience. He has the barking dog to thank for this.

Luther's "Soft Spot" for the Sow

Erik Erikson notes in *Young Man Luther* that the Danish psychiatrist Paul J. Reiter, in a major study of Luther published in 1937, diagnosed the Reformer as suffering from "a state of severe melancholia" (Erikson 1958, 33). Erikson objects to Reiter's "textbook" analysis of Luther, but he agrees with Reiter's diagnosis, and traces it to Luther's relationship to his mother in early childhood (120–22). He notes that Luther's mother "bore many children and lost some of them" (72), and links Luther's own melancholia to his "devouring will to live" (121), forcing his mother to give him the physical and emotional nourishment that he needed to stay alive. I have already noted Erikson's view that it was in the Bible that Luther "at last found a mother whom he could acknowledge: he could attribute to the Bible a generosity to which he could open himself, and which he could pass on to others, at last a mother's son"

(208). In effect, he turned to the religion of quest (hope) following his realization of the inadequacies of the religion of moral rectitude (honor), finding a compensation for the loss of his mother in the Bible's maternal presence.

But Erikson shows that Luther was also a man who believed in the liberating effects of humor. An example of his humor immediately precedes Erikson's discussion of Reiter's very serious professional diagnosis of Luther's personality. The humor occurs in the context of "an otherwise hateful pamphlet written in his middle forties" in which Luther is seeking to make clear that there is a prereligious state of mind. He bids his readers to consider in this light the sow who

> lies in the gutter or on the manure as if on the finest feather bed. She rests safely, snores tenderly, and sleeps sweetly, does not fear king nor master, death nor hell, devil or God's wrath, lives without worry, and does not even think where the clover might be. And if the Turkish Caesar arrived in all his might and anger, the sow would be much too proud to move a single whisker in his honor. And if at last the butcher comes upon her, she thinks maybe a piece of wood is pinching her, or a stone. (32)

The sow, in her prereligious state of grace, "has not eaten from the apple, which in paradise has taught us wretched humans the difference between good and bad" (32–33).

Erikson suggests that "in Luther's rich personality there was such a soft spot for the sow so large" that it may be considered "one of Luther's identity elements" (33). When this element became dominant, Luther could be so vulgar that he was "easy game" for Reiter, who quotes "with relish" the following advice from Luther: "Thou shalt not write a book unless you have listened to the fart of an old sow, to which you should open your mouth wide and say 'Thanks to you, pretty nightingale; do I hear a text which is for me?'" To be sure, one could produce many other examples of Luther's vulgarity, but Erikson asks, "What writer, disgusted with himself, has not shared these sentiments—without finding the right wrong words?" (33).

As illustrated here, Luther's humor exemplifies Freud's view that humor saves us the expenditure of painful affects—hurt, fear, horror, possibly even despair—and thereby has a liberating effect without causing us to leave the ground of mental sanity. If the book of Proverbs advises, "Go to the ant, you lazybones; consider its ways, and be wise" (6:6), Luther advises us to consider the sow who is much too proud to move a single whisker in an invading conqueror's honor, and faces her death with equanimity, thinking that the lethal knife the butcher wields is a piece of wood or maybe a stone that is causing her some slight discomfort. She refuses to be hurt by the arrows of reality or to be compelled to suffer. Her attitude—and Luther's identification with her—is comparable to Freud's triumphant prisoner whose humor has a liberating and elevating effect: "Look here! This is all that this seemingly dangerous world amounts to. Child's play—the very thing to jest about!"

I have spoken often in this study about the father of personal prehistory. Erikson suggests that, for Luther, religion has its own prehistory, and this prehistory is reflected in the sow, a mother who, to adopt Heinz Kohut's phrase, provides "a calming structure" (Kohut 1984, 30), one so natural and pervasive that no human mother who knows the difference between good and bad could be expected to provide her own little ones. We could say, of course, that the sow fails to provide her offspring the necessary emotional frustrations that will toughen them to endure the pain and suffering that the real world will inflict upon them. But for Luther, a melancholy man if there ever was one, the sow whom he observes outside his study window saves him from an expenditure of painful affect, that of sadness for and rage against his internalized mother. If, as Erikson suggests, Luther has a "soft spot" for the sow, one large enough to be viewed as one of the identity elements of his rich personality, this is because she is the source—and object—of humor. In her own prereligious state of grace, she is reminiscent of the mother Luther knew before the separation that led to the formation of his melancholy self.

The Gospel of Relaxation

I have suggested throughout this study that the religion of the melancholy self takes two primary forms—the religion of moral rectitude (where a man becomes an honorable self) and the religion of quest (where a man becomes a hopeful self)—and that there is a countervailing form, a third way in which a melancholy self may be religious, namely, the way of humor. In a justly famous passage, the apostle Paul wrote, "And now faith, hope and love abide, these three; and the greatest of these is love" (1 Cor. 13:13). I suggest that the religion of the melancholy self—whose religion cannot but be a rather unconventional, idiosyncratic one—is comprised of honor, hope, and humor, and perhaps the greatest of these is humor.

The desire to be a man of honor is hardly to be disparaged, especially in a world where men act dishonorably with impunity and even a certain nonchalance. But it will not win mother back, nor will it necessarily be rewarded or gain the applause and approval of others. The search for compensations for our original loss of unconditional love often results in human relationships that are deeper, more profoundly satisfying than the original one could ever be (or have been). But the searching itself is strewn with false starts, with missteps along the way, with accrued burdens that impede our progress toward what seems an ever-receding goal. We experience frustrated hopes, elusive dreams, shame, guilt, remorse. Even those who have been lucky enough to find love and happiness cannot ignore the haunting realization that their relationships will inevitably terminate when death comes to claim its victims. When a man begins to succumb to rage over the fact that acting honorably does not guarantee respect and approval, or when he feels a profound sadness over the fact that love does not last forever, in such times as these, the superego suddenly turns kindly, telling the distressed, frightened, or anxious ego that the situation, while neither rewarding nor hopeful, is not exactly serious either. That it has failed in these other respects confirms this liberating truth. In turn, this liberating truth may enable a man to act with honor and entertain hopes with less calculation, less desperation, and greater self-abandon, thus making, as William James puts it, "easy and felicitous what in any case is necessary" (James 1982, 51). If men are incurably religious, perhaps they may live their religion according to what James calls "the gospel of relaxation."

James looks around him and sees men, "intense, convulsive workers," who are on the verge of collapse. The common explanation is that this is due to the nature and amount of work they do, but James thinks otherwise. The cause lies rather "in those absurd feelings of hurry and having no time, in that breathlessness and tension, that anxiety of feature and that solicitude for results, that lack of harmony and ease" that we idealize as "the admirable way of life," but are instead "the overflowers of our measure of wear and tear and fatigue" (James 1992, 833). In contrast, "It is your relaxed and easy worker, who is in no hurry, and thoughtless most of the while of consequences, who is your efficient worker; and tension and anxiety, and present and future, all mixed up together in our mind at once, are the surest drags upon steady progress and hindrances to our success" (833). Somehow "we must change ourselves from a race that admires jerk and snap for their own sakes . . . to one that, on the contrary, has calm for its ideal, and for their own sakes loves harmony, dignity, and ease" (834).

How can we do this? Admitting that overnight change is unlikely, James suggests that one thing we can do is to become "indifferent" to ourselves, to take ourselves much less seriously. The individual who is the most mindful of self is the "melancholic patient" who "is filled through and through with intensely painful emotion about himself. He is threatened, he is guilty, he is doomed, he is annihilated, he is lost" (835). The remedy lies in becoming indifferent about oneself, unconcerned, unworried. "Worry," says James, "means always and invariably inhibition of associations and loss of effective power. Of course, the sovereign cure for worry is religious faith; and this, of course, you also know" (838).

But religious faith of what kind? In his poem "Allegiances" (Stafford 1998, 128–29), William Stafford suggests that there is more to life than heroics and questing, and that it has something to do with embracing the truth that we are, after all, "ordinary beings," and that we are already in possession of the things that we love—a liberating thought, surely, for those of us who feel we still have something to prove to the mother, so close and yet so far, who continues to live inside of us.

Allegiances

It is time for all the heroes to go home
if they have any, time for all of us common ones
to locate ourselves by the real things
we live by.

Far to the north, or indeed in any direction,
strange mountains and creatures have always lurked—
elves, goblins, trolls, and spiders:—we
encounter them in dread and wonder,

But once we have tasted far streams, touched the gold,
found some limit beyond the waterfall,
a season changes, and we come back, changed
but safe, quiet, grateful.

Suppose an insane wind holds all the hills
while strange beliefs whine at the traveler's ears,
we ordinary beings can cling to the earth and love
where we are, sturdy for common things.

References

~

Allport, Gordon W. 1950. *The Individual and His Religion: A Psychological Interpretation*. New York: Macmillan.

———. 1960. "What Units Shall We Employ?" In *Personality and Social Encounter: Selected Essays*. Boston: Beacon Press.

Argyle, Michael, and Benjamin Beit-Hallahmi. 1975. *The Social Psychology of Religion*. London: Routledge & Kegan Paul.

Augustine. 1992. *Confessions*. Trans. Henry Chadwick. Oxford: Oxford University Press.

Bakan, David. 1968. *Disease, Pain, and Sacrifice: Toward a Psychology of Suffering*. Chicago: University of Chicago Press.

Batson, C. Daniel and W. Larry Ventis. 1982. *The Religious Experience: A Social-Psychological Perspective*. New York: Oxford University Press.

Baur, Susan. 1988. *Hypochondria: Woeful Imaginings*. Berkeley: University of California Press.

Beck, Aaron T. 1967. *Depression: Causes and Treatment*. Philadelphia: University of Pennsylvania Press.

———. 1976. *Cognitive Therapy and the Emotional Disorders*. New York: International Universities Press.

Boodin, John Elof. 1996. "William James as I Knew Him." In *William James Remembered*. Ed. Linda Simon. Lincoln: University of Nebraska Press.

Boswell, James. 1980. *Life of Johnson*. Ed. R. W. Chapman. Oxford: Oxford University Press.

Boyd, Stephen B. 1995. *The Men We Long to Be: Beyond Domination to a New Christian Understanding of Manhood*. Cleveland: Pilgrim Press.

Burton, Robert. 1979. *The Anatomy of Melancholia*. Ed. Joan K. Peters. New York: Frederick Ungar.

Cantor, Carla. 1996. *Phantom Illness: Recognizing, Understanding, and Overcoming Hypochondria*. Boston: Houghton Mifflin.

Capps, Donald. 1993. *The Depleted Self: Sin in a Narcissistic Age.* Minneapolis: Fortress Press.

———. 1995. *Agents of Hope: A Pastoral Psychology.* Minneapolis: Fortress Press.

———. 1995. *The Child's Song: The Religious Abuse of Children.* Louisville, Ky.: Westminster John Knox Press.

———. 1997. *Men, Religion, and Melancholia: James, Otto, Jung, and Erikson.* New Haven, Conn.: Yale University Press.

———. 1999. *Social Phobia: Alleviating Anxiety in an Age of Self-Promotion.* St. Louis: Chalice Press.

———. 2000. *Jesus, A Psychological Biography.* St. Louis: Chalice Press.

Carnes, Mark C. 1989. *Secret Ritual and Manhood in Victorian America.* New Haven, Conn.: Yale University Press.

Carroll, Michael P. 1986. *The Cult of the Virgin Mary: Psychological Origins.* Princeton, N.J.: Princeton University Press.

Collins, Billy. 1988. *The Apple That Astonished Paris.* Fayetteville, Ark.: University of Arkansas Press.

Diagnostic and Statistical Manual of Mental Disorders. 1994. 4th ed. Washington, D.C.: American Psychiatric Association.

Dittes, James E. 1967. *The Church in the Way.* New York: Charles Scribner's Sons.

———. 1985. *The Male Predicament: On Being a Man Today.* San Francisco: Harper & Row.

———. 1996. *Driven by Hope: Men and Meaning.* Louisville, Ky.: Westminster John Knox Press.

Douglas, Ann. 1988. *The Feminization of American Culture.* New York: Doubleday Anchor Press.

Emerson, Ralph Waldo. 1983. *Essays and Lectures.* New York: Library of America.

Erikson, Erik H. 1958. *Young Man Luther: A Study in Psychoanalysis and History.* New York: W. W. Norton.

———. 1959. *Identity and the Life Cycle: Selected Papers.* New York: International Universities Press.

———. 1963. *Childhood and Society.* Rev. ed. New York: W. W. Norton.

———. 1964. "The Nature of Clinical Evidence." In *Insight and Responsibility: Lectures on the Ethical Implications of Psychoanalytic Insight.* New York: W. W. Norton.

———. 1964. "Psychological Reality and Historical Actuality." In *Insight and Responsibility: Lectures on Ethical Implications of Psychoanalytic Insight.* New York: W. W. Norton.

———. 1968. *Identity: Youth and Crisis.* New York: W. W. Norton.

————. 1975. "Identity Crisis in Perspective." In *Life History and the Historical Moment*. New York: W. W. Norton.

————. 1977. *Toys and Reasons: Stages in the Ritualization of Experience*. New York: W. W. Norton.

————. 1987a. "Children's Picture Books." In *A Way of Looking at Things: Selected Papers from 1930 to 1980*. Ed. Stephen Schlein. New York: W. W. Norton.

————. 1987b. "The Ontogeny of Ritualization in Man." In *A Way of Looking at Things: Selected Papers from 1930 to 1980*. Ed. Stephen Schlein. New York: W. W. Norton.

————. 1987c. "Psychoanalysis and the Future of Education." In *A Way of Looking at Things: Selected Papers from 1930 to 1980*. Ed. Stephen Schlein. New York: W. W. Norton.

"Facts and Figures." 2000. *The Lutheran*. (June): 8.

Ferguson, Harvie. 1995. *Melancholy and the Critique of Modernity: Soren Kierkegaard's Religious Psychology*. London: Routledge Press.

Freud, Sigmund. 1939. *Moses and Monotheism*. Trans. Katherine Jones. New York: Vintage Books.

————. 1950. *Totem and Taboo: Some Points of Agreement between the Mental Lives of Savages and Neurotics*. Trans. James Strachey. New York: W. W. Norton.

————. 1952). *An Autobiographical Study*. Trans. James Strachey. New York: W. W. Norton.

————. 1958a. "The Occurrence in Dreams of Material from Fairy-Tales." In Sigmund Freud, *On Creativity and the Unconscious*. Ed. Benjamin Nelson. New York: Harper & Row.

————. 1958b. "The Theme of the Three Caskets." In Sigmund Freud, *On Creativity and the Unconscious*. Ed. Benjamin Nelson. New York: Harper & Row.

————. 1958c. "The 'Uncanny.'" In Sigmund Freud, *On Creativity and the Unconscious*. Ed. Benjamin Nelson. New York: Harper & Row.

————. 1959. *Beyond the Pleasure Principle: A Study of the Death Instinct in Human Behavior*. Trans. James Strachey. New York: Bantam Books.

————. 1960a. *The Ego and the Id*. Trans. Joan Riviere. New York: W. W. Norton.

————. 1960b. *Group Psychology and the Analysis of the Ego*. Trans. James Strachey. New York: Bantam Books.

————. 1960c. *Jokes and Their Relation to the Unconscious*. Trans. James Strachey. New York: W. W. Norton.

————. 1961. *Civilization and Its Discontents*. Trans. James Strachey. New York: W. W. Norton.

————. 1963b. "Humor." In Sigmund Freud, *Character and Culture*. Ed. Philip Rieff. New York: Collier Books.

————. 1963c. "Mourning and Melancholia." In Sigmund Freud, *General Psychological Theory: Papers on Metapsychology*. Ed. Philip Rieff. New York: Collier Books.

————. 1963d. "Obsessive Acts and Religious Practices." In Sigmund Freud, *Character and Culture*. Ed. Philip Rieff. New York: Collier Books.

————. 1963a. "The History of an Infantile Neurosis." In Sigmund Freud, *Three Case Histories*. Ed. Philip Rieff. New York: Simon & Schuster.

————. 1964. *A General Introduction to Psychoanalysis*. Trans. Joan Riviere. New York: Washington Square Press.

————. 1965. *The Interpretation of Dreams*. Ed. James Strachey. New York: Avon Books.

————. 1989. *The Psychopathology of Everyday Life*. Trans. James Strachey. New York: W. W. Norton.

Friedman, Lawrence J. 1999. *Identity's Architect: A Biography of Erik H. Erikson*. New York: Scribner.

Frost, Christopher J. 1992. "Melancholy as an Alternative to the Psychological Label of Depression." *International Journal for the Psychology of Religion* 2: 71–85.

Garbarino, James. 1999. *Lost Boys: Why Our Sons Turn Violent and How We Can Save Them*. New York: Free Press.

Gay, Peter. 1988. *Freud: A Life for Our Time*. New York: W. W. Norton.

Gilligan, Carol. 1982. *In a Different Voice: Psychological Theory and Women's Development*. Cambridge: Harvard University Press.

Glück, Louise. 1990. *Ararat*. Hopewell, N.J.: Echo Press.

Hall, Donald. 1990. *Old and New Poems*. New York: Houghton Mifflin.

————. 1998. *Without*. Boston: Houghton Mifflin.

Jackson, Stanley W. 1986. *Melancholia and Depression: From Hippocratic Times to Modern Times*. New Haven, Conn.: Yale University Press.

James, William. 1950. *The Principles of Psychology*. 2 vols. New York: Dover Publications.

————. 1982. *The Varieties of Religious Experience: A Study in Human Nature*. New York: Penguin Books.

————. 1992. "The Gospel of Relaxation." In *William James: Writings 1878–1899*. Ed. Gerald E. Myers. New York: Library of America.

Jung, C. G. 1961. *Memories, Dreams, Reflections*. Trans. Richard and Clara Winston. New York: Random House.

Kohut, Heinz. 1984. *How Does Analysis Cure?* Ed. Arnold Goldberg. Chicago: University of Chicago Press.

Kohut, Heinz, and Ernest S. Wolf. 1986. "The Disorders of the Self and Their Treatment: An Outline." In *Essential Papers on Narcissism*. Ed. Andrew P. Morrison. New York: New York University Press.

Kristeva, Julia. 1987a. *In the Beginning Was Love: Psychoanalysis and Faith.* Trans. Arthur Goldhammer. New York: Columbia University Press.

———. 1987b. *Tales of Love.* Trans. Leon S. Roudiez. New York: Columbia University Press.

———. 1989. *Black Sun: Depression and Melancholia.* Trans. Leon S. Roudiez. New York: Columbia University Press.

———. 1995. *New Maladies of the Soul.* Trans. Ross Guberman. New York: Columbia University Press.

Lane, Christopher. 1999. *The Burdens of Intimacy: Psychoanalysis and Victorian Masculinity.* Chicago: University of Chicago Press.

Lebacqz, Karen, and Ronald G. Barton. 1991. *Sex in the Parish.* Louisville: Westminster John Knox Press.

Leverenz, David. 1989. *Manhood and the American Renaissance.* Ithaca: Cornell University Press.

Levinson, Daniel J. 1978. *The Season's of a Man's Life.* New York: Alfred A. Knopf.

Lewis, R. W. B. 1991. *The Jameses: A Family Narrative.* New York: Farrar, Straus & Giroux.

Menninger, Karl. 1973. *Whatever Became of Sin?* New York: Hawthorn Books.

Miller, Alice. 1990. *The Untouched Key: Tracing Childhood Trauma in Creativity and Destructiveness.* New York: Doubleday.

Moyers, Bill. 1995. *The Language of Life: A Festival of Poets.* New York: Doubleday.

Muecke, D. C. 1970. *Irony.* London: Methuen.

Murray, Henry. 1967. "Henry A. Murray" (autobiography). In *A History of Psychology in Autobiography,* vol. 5. Ed. Ernest G. Boring and Gardner Lindzey. New York: Appleton-Century-Crofts.

Öhman, Arne. 1986. "Face the Beast and Fear the Face: Animal and Social Fears as Prototypes for Evolutionary Analyses of Emotion." *Psychophysiology* 23: 123–45.

Osherson, Samuel. 1986. *Finding Our Fathers: How a Man's Life Is Shaped by His Relationship with His Father.* New York: Fawcett Columbine.

Parker, Rozsika. 1995. *Mother Love/Mother Hate: The Power of Maternal Ambivalence.* New York: Basic Books.

Pipher, Mary. 1994. *Reviving Ophelia: Saving the Selves of Adolescent Girls.* New York: Ballantine.

Pittman, Frank S. 1993. *Man Enough: Fathers, Sons, and the Search for Masculinity.* New York: Perigee Books.

Pollack, William. 1998. *Real Boys: Rescuing Our Sons from the Myths of Boyhood.* New York: Random House.

Professional Guide to Diseases. 1998. 6th ed. Springhouse, Pa.: Springhouse Corporation.

Radden, Jennifer. 2000a. "Love and Loss in Freud's 'Mourning and Melancholia': A Rereading." In *The Analytic Freud: Philosophy and Psychoanalysis*. Ed. Michael P. Levine. London and New York: Routledge Press.

———, ed. 2000b. *The Nature of Melancholy: From Aristotle to Kristeva*. New York: Oxford University Press.

Rank, Otto. 1964. *The Myth of the Birth of the Hero and Other Writings*. Ed. Philip Freund. New York: Random House.

Rapaport, Ernest A. 1958. "The Grandparent Syndrome." *Psychoanalytic Quarterly* 27: 518–538.

Rizzuto, Ana-Marie. 1979. *The Birth of the Living God: A Psychoanalytic Study*. Chicago: University of Chicago Press.

Saroglou, V., and J.-M. Jaspard. 2001. "Does Religion Affect Humour Creation?" *Mental Health, Religion, and Culture* 4: 33–46.

Sophocles. 1959. *Oedipus the King*. Trans. Bernard Knox. New York: Washington Square Press.

Stafford, William. 1998. *The Way It Is: New and Selected Poems*. St. Paul, Minn.: Graywolf Press.

Styron, William. 1990. *Darkness Visible: A Memoir of Madness*. New York: Random House.

Vickers, Joanne F., and Barbara L. Thomas. 1996. *Men on Midlife*. Freedom, Calif.: Crossing Press.

Watzlawick, Paul. 1983. *The Situation Is Hopeless, But Not Serious: The Pursuit of Unhappiness*. New York: W. W. Norton.

Whitaker, John O., Jr. 1998. *National Audubon Society Field Guide to North American Mammals*. Rev. ed. New York: Alfred A. Knopf.

Winnicott, D. W. 1971. "Playing: A Theoretical Statement." In *Playing and Reality*. New York: Penguin Books.

———. 1993. "Hate in the Countertransference." In *In One's Bones: The Clinical Genius of Winnicott*. Ed. Dodi Goldman. Northvale, N.J.: Jason Aronson.

Wulff, David M. 1997. *Psychology of Religion: Classic and Contemporary*. 2nd ed. New York: John Wiley & Sons.

Index

~

and religion of honor, 44–45, 53,
139–41, 186
and self-directed sadism, 43, 52–53
See also superego
counterphobic behavior
in O'Duffy case, 118, 131, 146–47

Demos, John, 59–60
depression
as clinical pathology, 4–5, 25n, 30
and hypochondria, 168–69
and male failure, 32
in O'Duffy case, 110, 129–30
See also sadness
dissociation
in Miller case, 160–61, 165
Dittes, James E.
critique of Freud's Oedipus complex
theory, 64–66
and male predicament, xvi, 78, 107
on religion as quest, 49
on resistance, xiii
Douglas, Ann, 37–39, 101
Dunn, Stephen, 149

Emerson, Ralph Waldo, 180
emotional separation
as acute in boys, 18
enduring consequences of, 27–31
and father relationship, 33
in Miller case, 179
mother's facilitation of, 19–20
in O'Duffy case, 142
and religion of honor, 44–45
and religion of hope, 45–49
Erikson, Erik H.
and children's picture books, 42–44,
52–53
on fate, 180–181
his emotional loss of mother, 21–22
and internalized mother, 40–44
life cycle theory of, 20–21

on Luther, 46–47, 188–90
on maternal grandfather, 94–95
personal quest of, 47
on play, xiv
on primary religious images, 144
on religious melancholia, 55n
on the self, xv

fate
Freud's essay on, 181
and mother, 180–82
father
bonding with, 56, 73
as distant, xi, 57
distorted image of, 58
identification with, 56, 73–77, 95,
99–100
as judgmental, 57, 61
and mortality, 62–63
as provider, 59–61
and sense of betrayal, 58–59
son's object-choice of, 73–77
son's surrender to, 173–76
"father hunger"
as contemporary problem, xii, xiv, 60
its roots in patriarchy, 96–98
father of personal prehistory
and castration anxiety, 92–93, 146
and demolition of Oedipus complex, 95
Freud's concept of, 87
as jealous God, 95, 100
and Judaeo-Christian God, 88–89,
95
and maternal grandfather, 89–96
in Miller case, 163, 176–79
and object-choice of father, 87–88
in O'Duffy case, 144–47
as phylogenetic, 88–89
and superego formation, 109
as vulnerable, 177–79
Ferenczi, Sandor, 89–92